Gender, Sexuality and Global Politics

Series Editors: **Ali Bilgic**, Loughborough University, UK, **Synne L. Dyvik**, University of Sussex, UK, **Gunhild Hoogensen Gjørv**, UiT The Arctic University of Norway, Norway, **Thomas Gregory**, The University of Auckland, New Zealand and **Swati Parashar**, University of Gothenburg, Sweden

Expanding the boundaries of International Relations, this series reflects on politics globally with innovative and transdisciplinary perspectives.

With a focus on feminist, lesbian, gay, bisexual, trans and queer activism, the series critically examines existing hierarchies, practices and power relations, investigating the often violent effects of these on different peoples, geographies and histories.

Also available

Queer Politics in Contemporary Turkey
By **Paul Gordon Kramer**

Queering Conflict Research
New Approaches to the Study of Political Violence
Edited by **Jamie J. Hagen**, **Samuel Ritholtz** and **Andrew Delatolla**

Forthcoming

Boundaries of Queerness
Homonationalism and Racial Politics in Sweden
By **Katharina Kehl**

Black Masculinities and Colonial Legacies
The Global Politics of Jamaican and Diasporic Constructions of Gender
By **Shardia Briscoe-Palmer**

For more information about the series and to find out how to submit a proposal visit
**bristoluniversitypress.co.uk/
gender-sexuality-and-global-politics**

International Editorial Board

Linda Åhäll, University of Gothenburg, Sweden
Terrell Carver, University of Bristol, UK
Shine Choi, Massey University, New Zealand
Bina D'Costa, Australian National University, Australia
Paula Drumond, O Instituto de Relações Internacionais PUC-Rio, Brazil
Cynthia Enloe, Clark University, US
Des Gasper, Erasmus University, Netherlands
Inanna Hamati-Ataya, University of Cambridge, UK
Catarina Kinnvall, Lund University, Sweden
Rauna Kuokkanen, University of Lapland, Finland
Peace Medie, University of Ghana, Ghana
Annie Paul, University of the West Indies, Jamaica
Manuela Picq, Amherst College, US
Vicki Squire, University of Warwick, UK
Cemal Burak Tansel, University of Warwick, UK
Maria Tanyag, Australian National University, Australia
Cai Wilkinson, Deakin University, Australia

For more information about the series and to
find out how to submit a proposal visit
**bristoluniversitypress.co.uk/
gender-sexuality-and-global-politics**

BODILY FLUIDS, FLUID BODIES AND INTERNATIONAL POLITICS

Feminist Technoscience, Biopolitics and Security

Jenn Hobbs

First published in Great Britain in 2026 by

Bristol University Press
University of Bristol
1–9 Old Park Hill
Bristol
BS2 8BB
UK
t: +44 (0)117 374 6645
e: bup-info@bristol.ac.uk

Details of international sales and distribution partners are available at bristoluniversitypress.co.uk

© Bristol University Press 2026

British Library Cataloguing in Publication Data
A catalogue record for this book is available from the British Library

ISBN 978-1-5292-3794-8 hardcover
ISBN 978-1-5292-3795-5 paperback
ISBN 978-1-5292-3796-2 ePub
ISBN 978-1-5292-3797-9 ePdf

The right of Jenn Hobbs to be identified as author of this work has been asserted by her in accordance with the Copyright, Designs and Patents Act 1988.

All rights reserved: no part of this publication may be reproduced, stored in a retrieval system, or transmitted in any form or by any means, electronic, mechanical, photocopying, recording, or otherwise without the prior permission of Bristol University Press.

Every reasonable effort has been made to obtain permission to reproduce copyrighted material. If, however, anyone knows of an oversight, please contact the publisher.

The statements and opinions contained within this publication are solely those of the author and not of the University of Bristol or Bristol University Press. The University of Bristol and Bristol University Press disclaim responsibility for any injury to persons or property resulting from any material published in this publication.

Bristol University Press works to counter discrimination on grounds of gender, race, disability, age and sexuality.

Cover design: Blu Inc
Front cover image: Unsplash/sharonmccutcheon

Bristol University Press' authorised representative in the European Union
is: Easy Access System Europe, Mustamäe tee 50, 10621 Tallinn, Estonia,
Email: gpsr.requests@easproject.com

Contents

About the Author		vi
Acknowledgements		vii
1	Introduction	1
2	Theorizing Assemblages and Feminist Technoscience	14
3	Life-giving, Life-threatening: Plasma Donation at the US–Mexico Border	32
4	Racializing Fluids: Vomit, Airports and the 2013–16 Ebola Pandemic	52
5	Securing Cisheterosexuality: Semen and Genitourinary Injuries	73
6	Finding, Following, Fluids	97
7	Concluding Is the Wrong Verb	113
Notes		124
References		127
Index		157

About the Author

Jenn Hobbs is Lecturer in International Relations at the University of Leicester. Her research focuses on the intersections between health, gender, sexuality, race and security. Her work has previously been published in journals such as *Security Dialogue* and *Review of International Studies*.

Acknowledgements

Writing the acknowledgements is the loveliest part of any project, and it's also the section of a book I never skip, because I'm very nosy. If that's why you're reading this, too – enjoy.

I owe a great debt of gratitude to the Gender & Sexuality series team at Bristol University Press. Thank you to the series editors for their insightful comments and support of this project and its author. A huge thank you to all the reviewers of this book, too, whose comments and considerations have been instrumental for me in doing better. Thanks to Stephen Wenham and Zoe Forbes for their hard work in making this book possible, and for dealing very gracefully with my tendency to use 1,000 words for a title and mysteriously put paragraphs into italics by accident.

I owe much to the support of the University of Manchester who made this research possible, via a PhD studentship. I will also always be most grateful to Manchester for introducing me to Cristina Masters and Laura McLeod. They are the feminist role models that everyone deserves to have in their lives. It is their hard work and gentle care over the years that made this book (and me today) possible. Thank you, both, for everything. Heartfelt thanks to Laura Sjoberg and Aoileann Ní Mhurchú for taking the time to read this when it was a thesis, and for all their patience and kindness in discussing it with me. Thanks to all my former colleagues at Manchester, in particular the members of the Critical Global Politics Cluster, many of whom read drafts of this work in earlier forms; in particular Martin Coward and Maja Zehfuss whose comments on paper drafts for me during this time have improved this work immeasurably. And to Sabrina Villenave, Rachel Massey, Joanna Flavell, Anna Sanders, Anh Le and Franco Galdini for being such a nourishing community of good eggs.

Thank you to my wonderful colleagues at the University of Leicester who have been so encouraging and supportive, and excellent company during the writing away days when I actually finished this book.

To Jess, Em, Alex, Steph, Charlotte, Kat, Jana, Sofia, Elli, Sabrina, Thea, Freya, Chris, Paul and Liam; thanks for bringing me joy during the writing of this book, for reminding me to celebrate, and for looking after me.

This book is dedicated, with love, to Trevor, Clare, Kat, and Mary Louise Hobbs; I'm sorry it's about gross stuff.

1

Introduction

How close does COVID-19 feel to you, now? For some it is likely a distant and half-forgotten fever dream. For some it remains close, intimate; a continuing struggle with long COVID; the grief felt for those who died as a result of the virus; or those who are still being infected, and suffering, and dying around us. In this book, COVID-19 lingers beneath the words on the page, both in terms of the implications of the analysis I offer here, and as the material context for the writing and research itself.

Approximately half of this manuscript has been written with my laptop resting on an ironing board, which is my budget solution to a standing desk. My writing set up might not be particularly noteworthy were it not for the fact that, as I wrote the bulk of this book in the UK, I was working from home not by choice, but as a result of government directive. I was simultaneously very alone and kept company by the rest of the country, where we were all meant to be at home. At the time of writing, this was the case around much of the world. In April 2020, roughly one third of the world's population were subject to some form of restriction in an attempt to slow the spread of COVID-19. In the UK, at that point, residents were told to stay home, leaving only in order to exercise, to buy food or medication, or to travel to work if they cannot work from home (Prime Minister's Office 10 Downing Street & The Rt Hon Boris Johnson MP, 2021). Pubs, restaurants and non-essential shops were closed. People were instructed to keep two metres apart from each other in public. Police had the power to disperse groups of more than two people, and fine others failing to observe these measures (Cabinet Office, 2020, para. 15). My local supermarket had a traffic light system over the door to let you know whether the shop was at capacity or that it was safe to enter. It was a legal requirement to wear face masks on public transport and inside shops. Schools and nurseries were closed (except for the children of key workers) and summer exams were cancelled (Department for Education & Williamson, 2020).

Despite the rhetoric of being 'in it together' as a nation, which the UK has been deluged in, even the early stages of analysis demonstrate that we are not all 'in' the thick of this pandemic in the same way. Mortality outcomes vary widely according to different demographic factors. Our older and/or poorer and/or black and brown neighbours have a much greater chance of dying from COVID-19 than do our younger and/or white and/or wealthy communities (Blundell et al., 2020; Briggs, 2020; Public Health England, 2020; Razai et al., 2021). And the number of those dying because of COVID-19 continued to grow. Now, in September 2021, the death toll in in the UK, one of the richest nations in the world, is at a staggering 160,824 (Public Health England, 2021). By the time you read this, that number will be higher. That's the problem of writing about a pandemic, while you're in a pandemic – the scale of the trauma continues to grow even as you type.

In assembling a range of restrictions to attempt to inhibit the spread of COVID-19, government and health authorities attempted to regulate the spread of bodily fluids. The coronavirus pandemic provides us with a particularly pertinent and grim example of why and how bodily fluids come to matter in international security. COVID-19 is spread through bodily fluids, such as saliva (in the case of coughing, sneezing and spitting) and the water vapour we exhale when we breathe out. The risk of coming into contact with other people's bodily fluids – breathing the same air, touching the same surfaces – rules/ruled public life. COVID-19 has rendered bodily fluids as subjects of intense scrutiny and enhanced security measures around the world, and they were utterly central to the current global pandemic. Fluids rapidly became the focal point of new security practices that have rapidly transformed daily life around the globe. The quarantine measures many countries introduced attempted to control the movements of bodily fluids, by limiting the ability of bodies to exchange them and thus further the transmission chain of the disease. With the potential to rapidly spread disease, generating a pandemic whose effects will be felt for years to come, bodily fluids matter as they have the ability to affect both individual health security as well as national security practices.

Many government responses entailed a set of biopolitical governance practices, whereby the state attempted to regulate and control biological life at a population level, often through the production and management of 'risk' (Dillon & Lobo-Guerrero, 2008; Esposito & Campbell, 2009; Foucault, 2008). All responses to the pandemic therefore pose a set of biopolitical decisions. Who counts as a life in need of protection? Whose life is put at greater risk, how, and for whom? Whose labour and continued heightened risk of exposure is mandated in order to protect the rest of 'us'? And how do the answers to these questions violently coincide with racialized and gendered systems of power?

COVID-19 and the government response to it reminds us, as critical scholars, that security practices are reliant upon measures implemented at the mundane, small level of daily life. These exceptional emergency measures operate through and are reliant upon people altering their daily routines in ways that are both small and significant. Security governance relies upon the grand spectacle of entire nations being confined to their homes, and this sweeping upheaval means that adjustments to daily patterns of living are vital to these forms of governance. The COVID-19 response is reliant upon people changing their grocery shopping patterns; performing caring labour at home (or performing increased caring labour at home); adopting new forms of greeting each other in public, without touch; calling your elderly relatives on the phone or the screen rather than visiting; it is reliant upon the ironing board standing desk to keep people working. As feminists have long reminded us, not only is the personal political, but it is also international (Enloe, 2014, p. 343). The COVID-19 pandemic reminds us to ask how the international biopolitical is also the mundane and personal.

At this point, despite what you might now be expecting, I want to tell you that this is not a book about COVID-19. It's a book about bodily fluids, and queerfeminist thought, and what these two things can teach us about biopolitics. But I wanted to start with a brief consideration of COVID-19 for two reasons. Firstly, COVID-19 illustrates the painful importance of bodily fluids to practices of international security. Secondly, even a brief discussion of COVID-19 illustrates why the relationship between bodily fluids and security matters – because bodily fluids play a profound role in the attempted governance of life and death. While COVID-19 has made us newly sensitive to this fact, this book demonstrates bodily fluids have mattered since well before the advent of this disease.

Critically interrogating the role bodily fluids play in internationals politics, however, is more pressing than ever. As academic attention turns to investigating and exploring the impact of COVID-19 and public health measures, much research continues to be profoundly policy oriented. Early health security work focused largely on the utility of bringing 'health' and 'global health' under the umbrella of security politics (Coker & Ingram, 2007; Elbe, 2005, 2006; Ingram, 2005, 2009). In recent years, scholars have also worked to understand how 'health' is governed at a global level through the work of international institutions and policy (Davies et al., 2015; Harman, 2011; Heymann et al., 2015; Rushton, 2019); and critical scholars have begun to question what a feminist health agenda would look like, and the importance gender plays in global health governance today (Davies et al., 2019; Harman, 2016; Wenham, 2021). Of course, we need policy-focused research that focuses on how public health measures could better heal everyone, and distribute 'health' and 'safety' more equitably among populations. But we also need to take a critical position to explore how the oppression of these groups is produced and recirculated through healthcare governance. The question is not only how and why health interventions fail to heal everyone, but also how health interventions can also actively cause and reproduce various forms of harm and violence.

It is such a project of critical analysis that this book embarks upon, using bodily fluids as a way to critically explore how biological life is regulated and governed; and how the distribution of life in the international arena can only be understood in conjunction with the concurrent distribution of death. To do so, this book offers a series of journeys into security sites. In making these journeys, I draw upon the concepts of biopolitics and life–death in order to investigate how turning our gaze toward the role of bodily fluids yields new knowledge about practices of international security. Taking bodily fluids as our prime focus leads us to see not only new things, but also to see familiar things anew. We can generate new understandings of the relationships between bodies, governance, and violence within these settings, demonstrating that these elements are tangled in a series of complex and contextual relationships.

In focusing on bodily fluids writ large, the research for this book orbits one central question. Answering this question has necessitated a tangled assemblage of plasma, thermometers, feminist technoscience studies, semen, vomit, biopolitics, airplanes and genital surgery. The primary question this book is focused upon, then, is: how are bodily fluids made to matter within the governance of bodies in international politics? In thinking through this question, this book has also spawned and engaged with a further set of related questions: what practices and relationships do bodily fluids make visible in international politics? How do we study bodily fluids?

The rest of this book goes on to argue that bodily fluids are made to matter through the distribution of life–death between bodies. This distribution is affected through mundane, daily encounters between loose groupings of assemblages; bodies, sex, gender, biopolitics, technologies, race, security. Studying international security through bodily fluids allows us to bring various bodily relations uniquely into view; and the organization of these relationships is always specific, always particular to the enmeshed contexts that bodily fluids emerge in relation with. Before we get to this, however, there's some disciplinary business that needs to be attended to, and some clarification of how this book does and doesn't wield various languages. For the remainder of this introduction, I clarify this book's relationship to security studies and the term 'security'. I then lay out the queerfeminist curiosity guiding this book, drawing upon a history of feminist curiosity as a research device, and arguing in favour of coupling it with queer logics of both/and. The introduction ends by mapping the rest of the book and offering a brief aside about my own research method.

The language of security studies

In this book I am intensely engaged with the politics of security in regards to the body. By this, I mean the practices through which bodies and subjects are produced/disassembled and organized hierarchically within international politics. It is vital that we pay attention to the violence and harm inherent in these processes. We must also, to play with Robert Cox's famous caution about International Relations (IR) theory (1981), ask how and why bodies are produced in particular ways, and who benefits from these productions.

Despite engaging with the politics of security, the language often associated with security studies (referent objects, securitizing actors, national security) is absent from this book. The choice not to deploy the linguistic schema of security studies reflects the fact that, despite working within the same spaces and engaging some of the same ideas, the analytical direction of this book diverges from mainstream security studies. Rather than focusing on the ways in which objects are 'secured', the book asks after bodies and the various relations they form in security settings. This differing focus reflects an ontological position eschewing exploration of objects in terms of how they are made 'secure' or 'insecure' (whatever is meant by these terms, often deployed as if their meaning is universal within security studies). Such a traditional approach presumes that objects exist in fixed forms, and that they can be shifted by power relations along an axis that has 'insecurity' at one end and 'security' at the other. These two terms often exist in normative opposition to each other, where 'insecurity' is presumed to be a violent and undesirable state of precarity, and 'security' constitutes a desirable and stable sense of being (Rossdale, 2015).

That the common language of security studies constructs a security terrain featuring bounded objects, where to be secure is 'good' and insecure 'bad', produces a limited and limiting space to begin thinking critically about the politics of securitization. We are, as Judith Butler argues, always already vulnerable, always dependent on our relations with others (2003, 2011). As such, the binary language of security/insecurity often mobilized within security studies sits at odds with an ontological position that sees insecurity as a fundamental condition of being, and one that is not necessarily negative and inherently violent. Rather than seeing the object of study as a thing that can be moved along a binary scale of (in)security, this book approaches objects (primarily the body and bodily fluids) as entities that *are* insecure in so far as they are not fixed, complete or determinate, but rather continually mobile and operating within evolving assemblages. These assemblages are not so much rendered secure/insecure in comparison *to* other objects, but produced through their relationships *with* other objects. As such, this book does not engage with ideas of 'insecurity' and 'security' that presume that one is heavily desirable in comparison to the other. In fact, attempts to produce bodies and subjects as stable and ontologically secure engage their own forms of violence and harm. One can get 'stuck' in stable, secure and violent sets of bodily discourses.

As such, the language of the body and bodily fluids is most helpful to this book. I employ this language of body and bodily fluids as the main terms of debate, rather than security/insecurity. This shift in the language used to think about and express ideas of security has helped me to open new avenues of enquiry. Studying international politics from the points of relation between bodies and bodily fluids provide us with micro-sites through which we can establish the material-discursive relationships between bodies, fluids, practices of governance, gender, race, sexuality and look for the 'wider reverberations' these assemblages have for international politics (Aradau et al., 2014, p. 79).

Queerfeminist curiosity

I do, however, want to be clear that the decision to take bodies and bodily fluids as our terms of debate is not primarily motivated by a desire to pull away from some of the language of security studies. This project is not intended as a rebuke to security studies – instead, it is a love letter to queer and feminist literatures. Rather than framing the terminology here as a move away from 'security', I want to present it as a joyful move towards feminist ways of thinking and speaking. I am propelled here by a queerfeminist curiosity. This is a form of curiosity that requires us to ask questions about the inter-related work that gender, sex, race and sexuality are performing in a setting, and understand any answers through queer logics of both/and. It is profoundly inspired by Enloe's rich and transformative utilization of feminist curiosity as a research principle (Enloe, 2014). By asking questions about where women are in international politics (and how they got there, and what they feel and think about being there) Enloe built a radical, far-reaching project that dragged the gendered underpinnings of international politics into clear focus. In building on this principle of a feminist curiosity, a queerfeminist curiosity should not be understood as just adding LGBT+ subjects onto this list of questions. Rather than conjoining together a 'sexuality variable' with a 'gender variable', a queerfeminist curiosity embraces Enloe's ethos of disruption by reading race/gender/sexuality as mutually constitutive through queer logics of both/and. This section unpacks these double moves of a queerfeminist curiosity in greater depth.

Taking gender/race/sexuality/disability to be entangled and mutually constitutive is a framework heavily informed by the work of black feminists (Bailey & Trudy, 2018; Collins, 2000; Collins & Bilge, 2016; Crenshaw, 1991). Emerging in response to the silence of white feminists on how women of colour experienced the combined effects of racism and misogyny, the term 'intersectionality' was originally coined by Kimberlé Crenshaw to describe the ways in which black women's experiences of intimate partner violence are constituted through 'intersecting patterns of racism and sexism'

(Crenshaw, 1991, p. 1243). From this point, intersectionality has become widely diffused throughout feminist literatures (Collins & Bilge, 2016; Puar, 2012b). Intersectional feminist approaches explore the way in which 'multiple axis of differentiation' work to structure lived experience and social life (Brah & Phoenix, 2004, p. 76). For intersectional theorists, the effects of race, gender, sexuality, disability, and so on cannot be separated out from one another in pure and discrete dimensions of power. Instead they co-mingle, affecting and producing experiences that are not a cumulative addition of multiple power differentials, one on top of the other, but instead mixed fusions (Collins, 2000; Collins & Bilge, 2016; Connell, 1997; Crenshaw, 1991). Intersectionality has given life to its own set of concepts that attempt to capture this more-than-the-sum-of-its-parts affect, such as a misogynoir. Coined by Moya Bailey, and developed in conjunction with Trudy at Gradient Lair, misogynoir refers to the oppression faced by black woman on the basis of their black-woman-ness (Bailey, 2010; Bailey & Trudy, 2018; Trudy, 2013). Misogynoir captures that '[w]hat happens to Black women in public space ... is particular and has to do with the ways that anti-Blackness and misogyny combine to malign Black women' (Bailey & Trudy, 2018, p. 763).

As we can see, intersectional theoretical frameworks argue that forms of bodily differentiation cannot be understood in isolation but instead interact with and inform each other. Intersectional feminist theorizing therefore calls our attention not only to the lived experiences of particular subjects, but also to how the production of bodies and their modalities are constituted through these conjoined relationships. Intersectional feminist work points towards the fact that there is no gendering of bodies without a concurrent racializing of bodies and of gender; no concept of 'race' that exists apart from sex and sexuality; no idea of gender that functions in isolation from discourses of biological sex (for example, see Agathangelou, 2013; Daggett, 2015; Manchanda, 2014; Peterson, 1999, 2014a, 2014b; Puar, 2012a, 2013; Puar & Rai, 2002; Rao, 2014; Richter-Montpetit, 2014, 2018; Shepherd & Sjoberg, 2012; Sjoberg, 2012, 2014; Weber, 2015, 2016; Wilcox, 2017).

Drawing on intersectional feminist approaches, this book mobilizes intersectional ontologies in conjunction with a series of queerfeminist questions and logics. Cynthia Enloe has pioneered the place of curiosity as a research device within feminist international relations. In her groundbreaking work *Bananas, Beaches and Bases: Making Feminist Sense of International Politics*, Enloe is motivated by a commitment to continually asking '[where] are the women? ... How did they get there? ... Who benefits from their being there ... [and] [w]hat do they themselves think about being there?' (2014, p. 355). Pursuing these feminist questions leads Enloe to focus on things, people, and practices that may initially seem far divorced from the stuff of politics and security – dinner parties, garment workers, sex work.

But Enloe's work demonstrates how international politics and the formal arrangements of states and state institutions are fundamentally dependent upon these 'usually unequal ... gendered workings' that are often left out of academic analysis (Enloe, 2014, p. 6). By exploring the teeming worlds that lie beneath the surface of 'international politics', Enloe brought to light the productive and interconnected relationships that link together the everyday lives and doings of women with the sphere of formal high politics. These insights are generated by Enloe's persistent feminist curiosity, and her commitment to continuing to ask after the work of gender and the place of women in international politics.

Taking inspiration from Enloe's curiosity, this book embraces a queerfeminist curiosity in order to conduct an exploration of the body and bodily fluids in international politics that sees race, gender, sex and sexuality as tightly interlocking, not only in the production of embodied experience but for the formation of these bodily markers themselves. A queerfeminist curiosity asks questions not only about women, but also '[w]here is "gender" and what does it matter?'; where is sex, race and sexuality, and 'how do they matter?' (Sjoberg, 2015, p. 435).

Being curious about the ways these bodily markers are produced in and through accordance with each other is a curiosity directed by feminist and womanist work, as we have seen. A queerfeminist curiosity also nudges us towards queer logics and ontologies that acknowledge multiplicity and contradiction. Queer IR theorists have rejected seeing things in terms of either/or, embracing a both/and way of thinking about the world (Richter-Montpetit, 2018; Weber, 2016).[1] Queer IR theory 'deprivileges ... binary opposition', instead working towards an ontology that sees subjects and objects within IR as being able to hold and embody (at least) two contradictory positions at once (Puar, 2005, p. 121). Building from Sedgwick's definition of queer as the excess of sexuality/gender which 'aren't made (or *can't be* made) to signify monolithically', queer theories reject a Western system of binary oppositions as productive of meaning making, instead recognizing that subjects and objects can and do occupy opposing positions at the same moment in time (Sedgwick, 1993, p. 8). Plural queer logics of both/and help explain, for example, how queer subjects within the West can simultaneously function as markers of Western tolerance and inclusivity and retain their position as perverse, unnatural others (Puar, 2006; Weber, 2016).

Taking a note from queer studies also motivates this project's decision to turn towards bodily fluids as a way of thinking about the world. Queer studies are likely to lead us down the garden path when it comes to what constitutes a 'proper' mode of academic study. A disciplinary lineage centred around the LGBTQAI community, their lives, bodies and sexualities, and has a pedigree in seeking out the perverse and the invisible, the constitutive outside of heterosexuality and the lurid underbelly of normativity. As such, queer theory has embraced practices and subjects often left outside the bounds of 'proper' academic study and reads them as powerful, as important, as having something to tell us (Berlant & Warner, 1998; Halberstam, 2011). In the shift of our attention towards the mundane, the not-proper and the perverse, queer theory has pushed us to think about what is risked in turning away from the 'proper stuff' of international politics, and what is enforced by staying there. As such, this book considers several improper bodily fluids and asks what is threatened by turning to these bodily fluids? What is revealed as unstable, and fragile? What is endangered when we leave the (allegedly) proper path of academia, and what might we find in doing so?

Pursuing a queerfeminist curiosity in this way has the potential to lead us towards new understandings of, and relationships with, international politics. Queer theory's turning away from, and refusal of, a 'clearly bounded referent object' makes it possible for us to destabilize understandings of normality in international politics, showing how these regimes are profoundly political (Richter-Montpetit, 2018, pp. 222–224). IR has arguably taken several decades to pay attention to queer theory and queer international theorists. In the meantime queer international approaches have been hard at work unpacking the sexual logics of the state in a variety of domains (Amar, 2013; Crane-Seeber, 2016; Peterson, 1992, 1999, 2014b; Puar & Rai, 2002). Plenty of queer IR works have revolved around objects and themes that might be considered 'classical' within IR, such as states, terrorists, soldiers, security, and so on. However, queer theory does not merely contribute the 'sexuality variable' into our research; rather, it generates new and destabilizing ways of engaging in these objects, contributing a mode of political critique that rejects binary thinking within international politics (Weber, 2015).

A queerfeminist curiosity then encompasses both an intersectional approach to the body along with queer logics that recognize the inherent contradictions that are continuous within international politics. Importantly, queer theory should not (and must not) forget that these lessons have developed from the experiences of LGBT people.[2] David Halperin warns that, in the normalization of queer theory, we risk 'despecify[ing] the lesbian, gay, bisexual, transgender or transgressive content of queerness', and turning it into simple a 'more trendy version of "liberal"' (2003, p. 341). It is in the life worlds and experiences of queer people, with their perverse desires and non-normative lifestyles (defined as such, of course, against the right and proper heterosexual) that the gleeful embrace and exploration of what it means to live outside and beneath proper society, what possibilities are held within that, that queer theory takes it lifeblood from. We should not forget that these ways of being and knowing stem from queer bodies who have made their way inside academia, through becoming researchers or as research subjects. It is these bodies who give queer theory 'its capacity to startle, to surprise, to help us think what has not yet been thought' (Halperin, 2003).

We should also be careful not to vaunt 'queerness' and queer studies as a panacea for oppressive power relations. Numerous scholars have drawn our attention to the ways in which 'queerness' can and does work to uphold understandings of whiteness and racialized hierarchies in international politics (Puar, 2013, 2017b). All too often queers themselves organize, and are organized into, racialized and imperial bodily hierarchies of queerness and sexuality that affords some queers greater protection while ensuring greater violences against 'others' (Haritaworn, 2015; Haritaworn et al., 2014). In drawing on an understanding of queer logics, however, this book forms part of an ongoing attempt to draw from a queer theory that does not abdicate the bodies it was built from and by. Instead, the book unpacks multiple constitutive entanglements of sexuality, race, gender and sex in an attempt to uncover the material-discursive assemblages and relations that work to disenfranchise, impoverish, and murder bodies and lives that fall outside the rigid confines of white, abled-bodied heteropatriarchy.

TLDR; the book map

Chapter 2 of this book details the theoretical ground this book situates itself within, focusing on the concept of assemblage and exploring in greater depth how this book makes use of, and understands, 'the body'. I introduce feminist technoscience studies (FTS) as a framework for engaging ideas about the body as an assemblage. I argue that it is through feminist technoscience that our queerfeminist curiosity can be made concrete, and show how FTS provides us with the tools necessary to engage biopolitics in a detailed and nuanced way, by beginning from a problematization of the body as an object with unclear and incomplete boundaries.

Chapter 3 introduces the first case study: paid plasma donation along the US–Mexico border. The increase in donation centres situated close to the American side of the border has raised fear and concern not only over the ethics of plasma donation in these sites, but also over the safety of the plasma (Daily Mail, 2011; Murray, 2011; Wellington, 2014). Focusing on Mexican plasma donors donating in US-based centres, I argue that these donation practices thus work to produce racialized relationships of life–death along the border, where the life of Mexicana/o donors is valued in relation to white American modes of living. I show that following plasma generates a consideration of the ambivalent relationships through which Mexican bodies are produced in America, as both a threatening source of racial contamination and a vital medical product.

Chapter 4 explores the role of vomit in air travel within the context of the 2013–16 Ebola outbreak in West Africa. As a key vector of Ebola transmission, during the outbreak vomit within the space of the airport and the airplane came to be understood as a security threat. I show that Ebola vomit was produced as a racialized threat, through airport health screening processes that I read as a gendered and colonial form of security gaze. I argue that critical attention needs to be paid to health security practices; as these racialized productions of bodily fluids, bodily matter and disease can produce international responses that focus on containment and quarantine.

Chapter 5 follows semen through medical treatments for US soldiers and veterans that have suffered genitourinary injuries (GUIs). Increasing rates of GUIs in US soldiers following the wars in Iraq and Afghanistan have led to the development of new treatments, both surgical and medical. I show that all available treatment options revolve around facilitating the flow of soldiers' semen in proper, masculine and heterosexual directions. Queer and trans possibilities, and queer and trans lives, are rendered invisible in the curation of meaningful forms of life/bodies in these treatments. At the same time as American soldiers are produced as natural and rightful possessors of masculine seminal capacity, the injured and wounded bodies of Iraqi and Afghani men are produced as available for such forms of injury. The chapter shows that the sexed/sexualized distributions of life–death at 'home' is bound up in racialized/sexualized distributions of life–death elsewhere.

Chapter 6 discusses the underlying methodology of this book at length. I end on methodology in the spirit of Baaz and Stern, who illustrate beautifully how methodologies are often best understood as a research 'finding', something that emerges from the messy process of doing research (Baaz & Stern, 2016, p. 129). The chapter offers a story of this book's methodological development. I unpack the importance of telling a research story that begins with failures, and of a queerfeminist 'gut' in setting a research direction. I then unpack this book's use of 'following the fluid' as a methodological device, one that draws attention to the continued motion and flux of assemblages in international security.

Chapter 7, the final chapter of this book, considers the unique contributions FTS offers us for thinking about biopolitics; namely, that biopolitical governance is at work in everyday and mundane spaces; and, finally, by reminding us that 'bios' is always already racialized/sexed/gendered. I then consider the significance of bodily fluids for the study of future emergent health issues, illustrating this through a sketch of how fluids can help illuminate the burgeoning work on COVID-19 and other such infectious diseases.

Notes on method

As outlined previously, this book thus brings a queerfeminist curiosity to bear upon international politics in order to discover how bodily fluids are made to matter in the governance of bodies. Chapter 1 introduces several key ideas (such as life–death and capacity) and the literature (FTS) that the analysis hinges upon. Following this, you can read the three case studies in any order you choose; while each explores the distribution of life–death in security practices, they offer an analysis of this process that is particular to each given empirical context, and is not intended to be sequential. Each case study 'follows' a bodily fluid into a governance assemblage, a tangle of securitized practices and procedures that attempt to corral a fluid in a particular direction.

I have a lot to say about methodology in relation to this book; you can find a fuller and more detailed unpacking of questions of method and methodology in Chapter 6. The reason methods feature at the end of this project rather than beginning is because the methods/methodology used here did not precede the research; instead, it emerged through the process of attempting to grapple with and make meaning of the world through the lens of bodily fluids. It is as much a product of this project as the arguments themselves are. I do, however, want to offer at this point the bare bones needed to understand how each of the following case studies was built.

Each empirical chapter draws upon a disparate and varied wealth of documentation, which varied in source according to the case study in question. Researching plasma entailed reading a variety of media reporting and media interviews with donors and industry figures. This was a starting point to mapping the various public discourses built around plasma donation; as well a way to see how some of those involved understand the industry and their (and others) participation in it; and what they think and feel about this. In addition to a range of reporting I also utilized trade publications, primarily *The Source*, a quarterly magazine published by industry body the Plasma Proteins Therapeutic Association to see how the industry presents its work and donors to itself, and to others. I drew upon the annual company reports, as well as public-facing material from the websites, of key companies in the field, namely Grifols, CSL and Octapharma. Finally, I also sought out various relevant filings from the Federal Trade Commission to understand the legal and financial state of the industry in the US, and the significance of Mexicana/o plasma donors to supply chains.

When researching vomit, I drew on a variety of policy guidance documents primarily from the World Health Organization and the US Centers for Disease Control and Prevention. Both entities were significant, as is discussed in Chapter 4, in the development of best practice guidelines and policies for the management of the 2013–16 Ebola pandemic in West Africa. This understanding of policy framings and frameworks was expanded through the study of pop-cultural representations of the specific pandemic and of historical Ebola outbreaks through the incorporation of novels, films and news media reporting of the disease, in particular Richard Preston's seminal novel *The Hot Zone* (2014).

Finally, for the chapter on semen, I made use of media articles and interviews on penis transplantation surgeries, particularly those that interviewed injured service personnel and their medical providers. These allowed me to start dissecting how these injuries are framed by those experiencing them, and how they are represented and framed by others. In addition to media reporting, I drew upon policy guidelines, reports and meeting records from the web of agencies and entities involved in the provision of military healthcare; the Department of Defense, the Veterans Association, the Defense Health Agency, and specifically TRICARE. Research produced by the Trauma Outcomes and UroGenital Health in OEF/OIF (TOUGH) programme, and minutes from the Recovering Warrior Task Force, were particularly insightful and helpful here.

For a fuller discussion of the methodology involved – how I attempted to make sense of and read this information – Chapter 6 is the place to go.

2

Theorizing Assemblages and Feminist Technoscience

We all have some instinctive reaction to what is meant by 'the body', usually taking it to be the biological organism that breathes, reads, thinks, moves, touches and is touched, among the many other functions we perform in our daily lives (Vandenberghe, 2008). But when we question what the body is a little further – particularly when we push to assess whether there is a distinction between body and subject – such simple answers quickly become problematic. The experiences of women, for example, suggest that bodies are simultaneously us and not-us, both an object and a subject at the same time (Young, 2005, p. 44). As women are distanced from their bodies by their continual objectification, they are simultaneously imprisoned within it, as patriarchal structures refuse to allow them to transcend their markers of sexual difference from men – they are 'not allowed *not* to have a body' (Haraway, 1988, p. 575; emphasis in the original). The body's ambiguous subject/object status is only complicated further when we question where the limits of the body lie (Grosz, 1994; Haraway, 1991; Puar, 2012b). As Donna Haraway famously asked, do bodies end at the skin (Haraway, 1990, p. 220)? Or can we see them stretching further and beyond?

These questions demonstrate to us that any gesture towards a definition of 'the body' requires serious thought. In this chapter I unpack how this book approaches both bodies and bodily fluids, outlining the key concepts this book employs to conceptualize both. This chapter begins by briefly outlining feminist technoscience studies (FTS) as a loose categorization of feminist literature. I then introduce the notion of the body as an assemblage, outlining assemblage as it appears in Deleuze and Guattari's work. I then return to FTS theory to show that FTS has built a sophisticated understanding of the idea of assemblage, but has often been excluded from traditional International Relations (IR) work on assemblage in favour of non-feminist authors. I show that that an FTS approach makes visible the importance of situating body-assemblages within particular political contexts, and questioning where the boundaries of the body-assemblage lie. The second section of this chapter then unpacks the importance of bodily fluids to assemblages of bodies and international politics. I argue that bodily fluids constitute both/and substances in relation to life and death, and that their governance is vital in attempts to secure relationships of life–death between bodies.

What is feminist technoscience studies?

FTS is a sprawling and transdisciplinary field of research, difficult to define partly because FTS acts as a point that 'famous innovators of feminist theorizing' cross through and build from; as such FTS scholars tend to be portrayed as theoretical innovators in their own light, overshadowing the common empirical and conceptual terrain they share with others (Åsberg & Lykke, 2010). Broadly speaking, FTS is a body of literature that explores the relationship between science, technology, power, bodies/subjectivities, gender and race (Franklin, 2006; Grosz, 1994; Haraway, 1991, 1997; Harding, 1991; Johar Schueller, 2005; Owens, 2017; Plumwood, 1993; Puar, 2005, 2009; Schiebinger, 2004; Shildrick, 2015; Stern, 2005; Washington, 2008).

FTS can trace its lineage back to early feminist critiques of science, which challenged Western science's claims to objectivity and detachment, arguing that these were masculinized (and unattainable) ideals (Fox Keller, 1982, 1992; Franklin, 1995; Hammonds & Subramaniam, 2003; Hawkesworth, 1989). More commonly referred to as feminist science studies, these early criticisms of science were largely focused on biology (Hammonds & Subramaniam, 2003). The shift to feminist technoscience studies reflects not only an engagement with the rest of the 'hard' sciences but also a concern with the 'practices and interventions' prompted by science, reflecting a move towards a Foucauldian-inspired definition of 'technology' as modes of governance (Åsberg & Lykke, 2010). FTS comprises a broad range of theoretical positions and methodologies and is often an intensely cross-disciplinary body of work, drawing authors from across the 'social' and 'hard' sciences and the humanities more broadly. In addition to the philosophical arguments contributed by FTS that have reverberated across numerous different disciplines, FTS has contributed much in the field of medical anthropology and the sociology of health. FTS perspectives have offered an appraisal of a range of topics, ranging from the sexualized, gendered and racialized construction of communities during and through the AIDS epidemic (Epstein, 1996; Flint & Hewitt, 2015; Hammonds, 1997; Patton, 1985); to the relationship between gender and medicalization (Riska, 2010); the surveillance of body fat in medical research, and its potential to undermine sex and gender binaries (Jonvallen, 2010) the queer history of autism science (Gibson & Douglas, 2018); and the economization of menstrual tracking (Fox & Spektor, 2021).

Understanding bodies: assemblages

Assemblage theory is often accredited to Deleuze and Guattari's development of a social ontology based on relationality, a worldview that explores how complex relationships of and between various multiplicities are drawn together to become a loose and shifting *thing* (1980). Discussions of assemblage that draw upon Deleuze and Guattari's work understand objects/subjects as 'living, throbbing confederations' of diverse elements, all of which are embroiled in a series of mobile relationships (Bennett, 2010, p. 24). The concept of assemblage challenges the stability of the world around us, asking us to consider how everything is formed through its position in a webbed series of relationships. Looking around myself in light of assemblage theory gives me a world that is looser, more open, less certain. Take this book, for example. It emerges as a book because I have fashioned it in the shape that a book is expected to be – thousands of words, organized into chapters with introductions, conclusions, and neat subheadings. It is typed and formatted, physically and electronically bound together into a collection of numbered pages. It is a book because the reader (hopefully) takes it to be one, and these expectations of what an 'academic monograph' is owes a debt to the university as an institution, publishers as an academic and commercial business, and decades of academic convention. The words of this book itself are given meaning in relation to each other, and given form by a computer, which becomes a computer because of the relationships between its wires and circuit boards, its connection to a power socket, the national grid, coal and gas and the wind, and because I treat it as a computer and not as a doorstop. It is the relationship between these different elements (and many more) that make 'the book'.

What does it mean for us here to think of the body as an assemblage, then? Taking the body as an assemblage requires us to think about bodies in terms of their relations and connections to others. The body-as-assemblage challenges previous fixed notions of bodies as bounded spaces, individual sealed containers that house the subject. It unpins the edges of traditional conceptions of the body. Through assemblage theory, the traditional contours of 'the body' are blurred, and instead we understand the body as something that is not only engaged with, but fundamentally produced through, a host of human and nonhuman elements. Drawing an example from this book allows us to illustrate how the body-as-assemblage involves a deterritorialization of the body. Imagine the bodies involved in Chapter 3 of this book – the bodies of Mexican plasma donors. Utilizing traditional understandings of the body, we may have some ethical concerns about the effects of plasma donation on donor bodies: whether they are paid fairly, whether their health remains intact, and so on. But donor bodies are bodies that come and go within this equation, crossing the border and moving into the donation centre and then following the same path away. Understanding the body-as-assemblage, however, explodes this neat line of entry/exit of the body into border spaces. Instead, we are able to see how the body is produced by and productive of these border spaces. It is not the case here that the body enters and exits as a pre-ordained and complete entity. Rather, assemblage theory shows how the body is composed *by* and *of* the border, the process of plasma extraction, the various people and technologies involved. The 'space' of the body encompasses these processes and actors who, through their varied relations, are vital in producing the donor body as these things. The donor's relation to/with border security is vital in producing it as Mexican, as not-American. The relations to/with plasma extraction produce the body as a plasma donor, a biological shape that can be punctured with a needle to create extractable liquids. The body's relation to/with testing procedures, and with white-American bodies both present and past (who are also, similarly and simultaneously, being produced through this juxtaposition) produce the donor body as a bundle of risky potentialities with regard to infectious disease. Assemblage theory makes visible how these elements do not just act upon a pre-existing body, but are fundamentally productive of it. The body does not just engage in relations with these other elements, but it comes into being through them.

In focusing on the body's relationality, assemblage theory produces an account of the body as something that is being continually worked and reworked. Assemblage theory sees the shifting web of relations involved in the body as the flow of 'interwoven forces that merge and dissipate time, space, and body against linearity, coherency and permanency' (Puar, 2017a, p. 212). Put another way, assemblage pays attention to the contextual and specific assemblages that make up the body while recognizing that the body is not a singular and linear object. The body contains multitudes and contradictory relations and that is always in the process of changing. Subject, body, a demarcation between them, and their intersection (embodiment) is destabilized in assemblage theory, which sees both as being continually reworked and engaged in an endless process of transformation through relations of difference. This constitutes a challenge to the way in which we theorize the relationship between identity, the subject, and the body. This emphasis on instability, change and flux is written throughout assemblage theory, which argues that 'assemblages are in constant variation, are themselves constantly subject to transformation' (Deleuze & Guattari, 1980, p. 95). Assemblage theory asks how the appearance of stillness and permanency is produced, and how the unravelling that assemblage theory seems to precipitate can also move just as quickly towards resolidification (Lawlor, 2008).

But we started this discussion about assemblage by thinking about FTS in particular. And to this general understanding of assemblage theory, I argue, feminist technoscience scholars have made numerous important contributions. It is for this reason that this book's understanding of assemblage owes far more to feminist scholars than it does to non-feminist scholars who have worked with this term. In order to unpack what FTS specifically adds to this conversation, it is necessary to briefly discuss here some of the feminist problems with a classical, Deleuzian-and-Guattarian concept of assemblage. This is important for two reasons. Firstly, understanding the problems with previous iterations of assemblage throws into sharp relief FTS's contributions and precisely why they are so valuable. Secondly, this helps us to see that not only can we draw upon feminist theory to understand assemblage theory, but that there are compelling political reasons we must.

Assemblage: feminist critiques

Crucial to understanding the relationship between the body-assemblage and subjectivity/identity in Deleuze and Guattari's work is understanding their work on becoming(s). As assemblage theory is rooted in an ontology that sees the world as continually undergoing (re)configuration, for Deleuze and Guattari both the body and the subject constitute assemblages in a process of perpetual becoming (Deleuze & Guattari, 1980, p. 95). As they are continuously immersed in shifting and multiple relations, the assemblage never fully arrives. Neither the body nor the subject is ever complete or final, an idea that is captured in Deleuze and Guattari's elaboration of the concept of becoming(s). Becoming(s) refers to the processes through which assemblages are continually reworking and reconfiguring themselves. Importantly becoming(s) are not about arriving at a fixed state, nor are they a cyclical process (Lawlor, 2008, p. 171). Becoming does not lead to ending. Instead for Deleuze and Guattari becoming(s) reflect their attempts to move beyond fixed ontologies, and to build a theory that rejects the notion of identity or unity and instead attempts to build ways of thinking that focus on 'the movements of linkage and connection' between parts (Currier, 2003, p. 325). In doing so, Deleuze and Guattari's work destabilizes the human subject by rejecting the assumption that subjects and bodies are unitary, stabled and fixed, instead working to destabilize the primacy of the subject through the continual return to the point of difference (May, 2003, p. 150). Embodied subjects are instead immersed in a continual process of becoming-Other, undoing themselves and negotiating transformative relations of difference.

For Deleuze and Guattari, then, the body does not encapsulate a fixed and stable subject. Rather subjects and bodies are continually changing, shifting through endless variations in a process of becoming-Other, whereby stable identities are undermined by the constant movement and entanglement of different elements in an assemblage (Fox, 2002, p. 356). The capacity of the heterogeneous elements of assemblage to form relations between themselves means that both the body and the subject are continually being reworked. The body never corresponds to a fixed identity, because identities can never be fixed. Both body and subject are continually changing, metamorphosing through the relations of difference bodies/subjects form and rupture with others. For Deleuze and Guattari, it is of utmost importance that bodies and subjects are able to continue to become, to continue to form and explore new connections, relations and sensations, constantly pushing at their own dissolution and reformation (Deleuze & Guattari, 1980, p. 187). Becoming(s) are celebrated within their writing as a step towards a true transformation and dissolution of the human subject. Becoming(s) open up new possibilities for subjectivity and embodiment, and new ways to live and think in the world.

Subject, body, a demarcation between them, and their intersection (embodiment) is destabilized in Deleuze and Guattari's work on assemblage, which sees both as being continually reworked and engaged in an endless process of change and transformation through relations of difference. This constitutes a challenge to the way in which we theorize the relationship between identity, the subject, and the body. Stable and fixed identities are not treated favourably by Deleuze and Guattari. Such 'molar' subjects are, for them, 'emptied and dreary' bodies who have diminished or rejected their own capacity for forming new connections and assemblages (Lawlor, 2008, p. 176; Deleuze & Guattari, 1980, p. 187).[1] Feminism's attempts to do anything other or less than actively dissolve gendered subjectivity is effectively dismissed by Deleuze and Guattari as perpetuating sexual hierarchies.[2] The idea of *being* a Woman, existing in and inhabiting that site, seems to be problematic for Deleuze and Guattari. Such a stable identity that is not working to dissolve itself would easily be placed among the stuck, stunted bodies that have already attracted their negative attention, and Deleuze and Guattari provide no reason to believe otherwise.

This attempt to move beyond (the desire for) stable human subjectivity is problematic given its neglect of gendered and racialized subjects that are already excluded from definitions of 'the human'. As Sylvia Wynter argues, such posthumanist attempts to 'move beyond' the human subject remain grounded within Enlightenment thinking that continues to over-represent the white, Western, rational man as if 'it were the human itself', and thus the ultimate human subject in need of dissolution (see Wynter, 2003, p. 260). Deleuze and Guattari's exhortation to feminists to reject gendered subjectivity entirely is arguably thus still confined within a framework that privileges white masculinity in the very definition of the human that they seek to reject (see also Chen, 2012; Rhee, 2018). As Wynter points out, the fact that white Man has been over-represented in the definition of 'the human' means that 'the project of a radical humanism has yet to be begun, must less left behind' (Puar, 2017b, p. 29). In practice, therefore, Deleuze and Guattari's directive to abandon 'woman' and 'the human' in favour of pastures new constitutes a reassertion of white male privilege that is blind to the fact that '[i]n order to announce the death of the subject, one must first have gained the right to speak as one' (Braidotti, 2003, p. 51). Racialized and gendered subjects that have long been deemed to fall outside the bounds of this (white, male) humanism are, arguably, still struggling toward this right.

The lack of consideration Deleuze and Guattari give to embodied sexual and gender differentiation presents serious drawbacks when it comes to considering questions of power and difference in regards to body-assemblages in international politics. These drawbacks become most clear when we examine Deleuze and Guattari's discussion of Little Hans (1980, pp. 298–299). Deleuze and Guattari here discuss the question of whether girls have, in Hans' vocabulary, a 'peepee-maker', which the authors say, of course, a girl does – she too urinates (1980, p. 298). They acknowledge that a girl's body, while performing the same functions as a boy's, does so in a different way, utilizing 'different connections, different relations … different assemblages' (1980, p. 298). And yet, despite this recognition of material difference between bodies, for Deleuze and Guattari this question of difference is collapsed into the function of the assemblage. These differences within and of assemblages are then made invisible, and Deleuze and Guattari argue that, for example, we can say that a whole variety of assemblages possess urinary assemblages – that even locomotives, such as trains, possess urinary assemblages (Deleuze & Guattari, 1980, p. 298). While Deleuze and Guattari's efforts to decentre the human through an emphasis on the function of the assemblage are evident, their efforts to say that trains possess urinary assemblages entirely misses the point of the vital and often violent politics attached to the ways these assemblages are configured differently. Juxtaposing their assemblage of the urinating train with trans bodies and subjects illuminates this. Yes, both these assemblages entail urinary assemblages. But trains do not need to use public restrooms, while trans subjects do. Trains are not attacked, subject to physical and sexual violence and often death, because they are perceived to be in the 'wrong' bathroom. Trans subjects are, routinely. Trains do not struggle to complete their educations because lawmakers have ruled that birth certificates determine that some bathrooms at their schools are off limits to them. Trans subjects do. While parts of different assemblages might perform the same functions, the differences in the way that function is achieved and configured matter. It matters because assemblages, while performing the same functions, are positioned differently to each other in ways that are often gendered/gendering, sexed/sexing, raced/racializing. And the ways in which these differences are produced and structured often lead to profoundly unequal and violent consequences.

Deleuze and Guattari's focus on function in relation to assemblage therefore makes it difficult to even see, let alone engage, the ways in which body assemblages are produced as profoundly different to each other, often through violent means. This leads us to a theory of assemblage that often turns a blind eye to the differences between and within assemblages, leading to a contradictory account of becoming that simultaneously purports to be a process based on difference, while simultaneously collapsing sexual difference and rendering it invisible. As such, Grosz argues that Deleuze and Guattari 'obliterate the very real bodily difference and experiences' of different sexes through a sexually unspecific account of becoming (1994, p. 173). As the previous example demonstrates, the relations of difference that produce women and men are often painful relations for women and those who do not fit into the sexual binary. Becoming(s) are riven with power differences, with a politics of juxtaposition that wounds and injures bodies and subjects, that makes various connections between assemblages easier or harder depending on the body-assemblages interpellation with race, gender and sex. Failure to acknowledge that these relations of difference are ones that not only give life, but often take it, is a failure to challenge these relations.

Feminist technoscience studies lesson 1: the body-assemblage is particular

So, assemblage theory: radical potential, some less than radical elements and implications when we consider the non-feminist variations of this theory. As such, I propose turning to FTS in order to understand assemblage, and this book's understanding and use of the term is grounded in a specifically feminist tradition. This leads us to the first important contribution of FTS to understandings of assemblage; rather than ignoring questions of difference in assemblages, FTS demonstrates that body-assemblages are particular. By this, I mean that understanding assemblages means understanding that they are located within a variety of specific positions in international politics. This allows us to put our queerfeminist curiosity into practice. Through assemblage theory, we are able to pursue a curiosity about what the body *is*. Starting our conversation with FTS and assemblage, however, better equips us to ask how particular body-assemblages are constructed, enhanced and curtailed in different ways according to their location in matrixes of sexuality, race, gender, and so on. What any given body is only makes sense in relation to the other bodies it is not.

Taking body-assemblages as particular requires we locate the body in relation to other assemblages, including other bodily assemblages. Using assemblage to understand the body necessitates we look at the particular and individual relationships between body-assemblages and international politics that work to locate these bodies within corporeal hierarchies of difference. While the notion of the Other occupies a significant place within Deleuze and Guattari's work, as we have seen, their work does not address the ways in which 'Others' are structured hierarchically through assemblages of international politics, because their construction of assemblage theory largely rejects thinking about identity in favour of focusing on linkage and connection (Currier, 2003). However, focusing on linkage and connection at the expense of a consideration of identity and difference renders invisible the ways in which different bodies come to be 'identified', and on that basis are able to access (or not access) linkages and connections according to the body's positioning in international politics. Not all body-assemblages have equal access to processes of change and transformation. Not all body-assemblages can 'become-Other' so easily, and recognizing these differences is important in understanding the way in which power reverberates around and through assemblages. Within queer communities, for example, trans people of colour face much higher rates of violence than their white counterparts, demonstrating how the racializing of bodies impacts the ability body-assemblages have to change, to transform, to become. This book uses assemblage theory to explore how body-assemblages are made to matter differentially in international politics, how they are arranged into hierarchies of worth, and how life and death are distributed by the state on this basis. This thus requires us to ignore Deleuze and Guattari's focus on moving past identity, and instead use assemblage theory to think how body-assemblages are in relation with identities in assembling practices of international politics.

The work of both Elizabeth Grosz and Jasbir Puar is instructive in bringing our attention to difference and identity within assemblages. Grosz brings a focus on culturally and socially powerful forms of bodily differentiation to assemblages, reading assemblage together with a feminist investment in bodies as always 'culturally, sexually, [and] racially specific bodies' (Grosz, 1994, p. xi). This feminist vision of assemblage calls attention to the way in which there 'are always only specific types of body' rather than a generic body-assemblage (Grosz, 1994, p. 19). This is echoed in Puar's joining of assemblage theory with queer and intersectional theories, exploring the ways in which particular bodies come into relation with each other to effect corporeal hierarchies of difference (Puar, 2005, 2012b, 2017a). For Puar, body assemblages are formed and differentiated through their relations with others, and these forms of differentiation are crucial to understand how body assemblages both unravel and restabilize in relation to differentiated others (Puar, 2009). Understanding how body assemblages are produced as different, are made to be different, and how these differences are invested with power, is crucial to interrogating '*which* bodies ... interpenetrate, swirl together, and transmit affects to each other' (Puar, 2005, p. 122, emphasis my own).

This emphasis on how body-assemblages come into being through relations of difference between them is crucial to developing an analysis of assemblage that incorporates questions of power. For FTS scholars such as Puar and Grosz, body-assemblages should not be understood as one and the same.

There is no one body-assemblage. Instead, there are bodies-assemblages, plural; bodies that are specifically positioned and located within the world, and located in relation to other bodies. Paying attention to the specificity of bodies makes visible the racialized and sexualized power relations that govern body-assemblages, not only in their very articulation but also in the relations and connections body-assemblages can form. Jennifer Nash's work, for example, looks at how the conditions in which black women form sexual relations with their bodies/other body-assemblages bodies are profoundly conditioned by racist discourses of black sexuality that figure black sexuality as deviant (2017). Nash shows how various types of relations are made (im)possible according to the racialization of body-assemblages, demonstrating how the particularity of given body-assemblages matter in understanding how assemblages are enabled and circumscribed in different ways according to where, how and who body-assemblages are. Seeing body-assemblages as coming into being through the ways they are differentiated therefore requires us to look at power, and account for the ways power is involved in the (re)production of body-assemblages.

We shall return to these arguments later on in this chapter, when we introduce 'bios' into the mix too. For now, the important point is that FTS scholars work to put together an understanding of assemblage with a specific focus on the ways in which bodily assemblages become through processes of corporeal differentiation. As such, this book draws inspiration from the ways in which FTS scholars have put assemblage to work to investigate and question the violent, hierarchical arrangement of bodies in international politics, which prioritizes the lives of some body-assemblages at the expense of others. Shifting towards an FTS uptake of assemblage theory, I argue in favour of combining the idea of assemblage with a strong feminist focus on the particularities of bodies, and the ways in which they are produced. Rather than looking at how bodily-assemblages become through a process of transformation into the (fantasied, diametrically opposed) Other, this book looks at how bodily-assemblages become through relations *with* others (body-assemblages they exist alongside with, in relation with). This requires us to focus on how body-assemblages are produced through a differentiation with alternate body-assemblages. We must swap a singular focus on becoming-Other to an investigation of how bodily assemblages become-with-others. For this book, the important questions to ask in relation to body-assemblages and international politics are *which* bodies are doing and being done unto in international politics, and *how* these bodies are produced and differentiated.

As such, I take body-assemblages as a diverse and infinite set of relational groupings that are brought into being through particular gendered, raced and sexed relations with other bodies and objects. There is no universal body-assemblage that passes through a series of generic becomings in its journey, and the form and content of body-assemblages cannot be understood in isolation from race, gender and sex. For example, Chapter 4 of this book explores body-assemblages and vomit within airport security assemblages during the Ebola outbreak. The relationships that comprise body-assemblages in these spaces are different depending on whether bodies are read as black-African or white-European. The airport security assemblage is profoundly racializing, selecting black African subjects in these spaces for enhanced screening. The relationships that their body-assemblage therefore comes to form with surveillance technologies and other bodies is dependent on where these bodies are located within a hierarchical ordering of 'raced' bodies (Browne, 2015). As such, I take body-assemblages as located in particular and specific positions in the world, and that this is important for understanding the connections that bodies are able (or unable) to form with others.

Accounting for the differences between body-assemblages matters, because understanding the role power plays in (re)producing body assemblages allows us to understand the often-violent consequences these reproductions have for bodies and people. For example, Jasbir Puar's work shows how the production of sexuality and race is used to normatively differentiate between good queer bodies and bad queer bodies, and how a politics of discipline and governance is then practised based upon these particular visions of body-assemblages (Puar, 2017a). Haraway highlights how gendered interpretations of the animal body-assemblage are used to naturalize and solidify men's and women's body-assemblages and the relationships between these two (Haraway, 1991). Elizabeth Grosz critically interrogates assemblage theory itself, and how the figuring of women's body-assemblages as 'flows' in comparison to men's corporeal solidity works to establish the dominance of masculine bodies and of masculinized metaphysics within philosophy (Grosz, 1994). FTS understands bodily assemblages as never generically human, but as always already occupying particular positions, already invested with/in particular forms of racializing and gendering assemblages (Harding, 1991).

In recognizing the specificity of assemblages, then, the racialized and sexualized politics of assemblages are brought into sharp focus by FTS scholars who interrogate the ways in which specific assemblages effect specific politics of corporeal governance(s). FTS contributes an understanding of body-assemblages not only as particular, but draws our attention to the ways these particularities are political and are generated through/work to reinforce particular modes of politics and governance. This book attends to these same questions, questioning how Mexican bodies are produced as dangerous through their plasma-derived relations with white American bodies; how surveillance technologies at the airport (re)affirm colonial-scientific modes of bodily governance; and how genitourinary injuries connect the bodies of cisgender soldiers with trans bodies through relations that work to (re)affirm binary sex and gender. Within these three contexts I engage body-assemblages by looking at how these assemblages are produced through their relationships with each other; and how modes of life and patterns of governance emerge through these relationships.

Feminist technoscience studies lesson 2: body-assemblages are uncertain

In addition to taking bodily assemblages as specific (and the production of these specificities as political) FTS contributes an intervention into bodily assemblages by taking them as porous assemblages, whose boundaries are continually being reworked in a variety of sites and at a variety of levels. Again, FTS proffers theoretical resources to move upon our queerfeminist curiosity, helping us to question where the boundaries of the body-assemblage lie, and how they are continuously reworked in multiple spaces and relationships.

This is achieved partly through FTS focus on breaking down the body-assemblage even further, into its smaller component assemblages. FTS does not stay at the level of the body-assemblage, simply exploring the relationships these assemblages can form, but works to detail how these assemblages themselves are continually being reworked and generated. This is often investigated by FTS scholars through the body's enmeshment with various forms of technology (Wajcman, 2007). Studying the body-assemblage through the relations it forms with technology allows us to break the body down into a series of smaller assemblages. Seeing the body as a microcosm of assemblages, a trail of interactions that coalesce together into something larger, is vital in understanding the ways in which bio-medical technologies are increasingly being used to produce and govern bodies. Advances in technology in recent decades have meant the body is more open than ever, on a minute and biological basis, to technological intervention. As this book demonstrates, from manufacturing plasma products, surveilling and imaging the interior 'health' of bodies at the airport, and to the development of genital transplant surgeries, biomedical technology increasingly operates on a mechanical understanding of the body as a series of 'bodily fragments' that can be isolated and manipulated individually (Waldby, 2002b, p. 308; see also 2002a). That the body is managed and produced at a cellular level requires us to attend to the politics of the body at this scale, and an FTS focus on technology in conjunction with the body draws our gaze to how technology is used to govern body-assemblages on the biological micro-level.

Understanding the body in this way allows us to recognize the multiple and contradictory engagements bodies are bound up in, forcing us to problematize our assumptions about 'the natural body as fixed' in location, form or meaning (Åsberg, 2010). FTS shows us that we cannot depend on bodies to be neat flesh shapes encapsulated by a hard and fast skin boundary. Instead, FTS engages the body as a porous assemblage, one that is continually reworking its relationships with other elements and thus with its 'own' borders. This is an important contribution to studies of the body, as it presents a profound challenges to masculinized ideals of corporeality, which often valorize an image of the body as having hard, definite lines drawn around it, in order to neatly enclose and seal off the subject from the corrupting touches of otherness (see, for example, Linke, 1997). In classic Western philosophy the body is often positioned as the territory of the self: and ideally this is a territory that has 'defendable personal boundaries', that can be sealed off from others (Waskul & van der Riet, 2002, p. 493). Tracing back to the Ancient Greeks, men and men's bodies have been idealized through synonymity with 'dryness, solidity, firmness and containment' (Linstead, 2000, p. 31). The ideal human (male) has firm bodily boundaries, one that seal off an individual, thereby guaranteeing their self-contained rationality (Grosz, 1994; Longhurst, 2001; Shildrick, 1997).

As the 'dominant cultural ideal' of masculine bodies was to be 'rigidly self-contained and hermetically sealed', FTS presents a profound challenge to dominant depictions of the body through an unsettling of the idea of the body as a firm and bounded space (Stephens, 2008, p. 428). By focusing on the micro-biological relationships that are used to construct and manage body-assemblages, FTS challenges our ideas about the body's boundaries. FTS scholars show how bodies are continually transgressing their imagined boundaries and forming intimate relations across body-assemblages, shifting into and across each other (Franklin, 1995; Haraway, 1989, 1997; Martin, 1992; Shildrick, 1997). FTS pushes us to think about the body not as 'objects with inherent boundaries', but instead as shifting and changing spaces that do not necessarily coincide with the borders of our skin (Barad, 2003, p. 823). Catherine Waldby, for instance, explores how biomedical discourses and practices in regards to the HIV/AIDS epidemic produce certain bodies as risky 'fluid transmission points' (Waldby, 1996, p. 15). Waldby's analysis demonstrates how the firmly bordered heterosexual male body functions as 'the intact body of the nation' (Waldby, 1996, p. 15). During the HIV/AIDS epidemic, these borders were suddenly rendered insecure as HIV positive bodies (represented as queer, deviant others) expanded into and across phallic bodies, through technologies of sex, needle sharing, blood transfusion, and so on (Waldby, 1996). The human immunodeficiency virus and the biomedical practices marshalled to corral it provide Waldby with a way to challenge masculinized body boundaries, as the spread of viral disease reveals the permeability of bodies, even those that function as the hard and solid masculine ideal. Waldby's work serves as an example of the ways in which FTS scholars challenge the body-as-fortress as an impossible and undesirable ideal, a 'chilling fantasy' of separateness and invulnerability that can never be achieved (Haraway, 1991, p. 224). As such, this book also follows in the footsteps of FTS scholars to understand them as 'precarious' and unstable objects (Grosz, 1994, p. 43).

Seeing body-assemblages in terms of their precarity, and focusing on the instability of the boundaries of these assemblages, is important as it demonstrates the ways in which the bodies' precise location is continually in flux and changing. This matters for international politics and the politics of security more broadly as it makes visible the ways in which the production and governance of the body occurs simultaneously across multiple dispersed sites. The making of bodies occurs not only in the space immediately of and surrounding the fleshy matter of the body, but also in faraway spaces and through a variety of human-technoscience assemblages. Through applying an FTS approach to the body-assemblage, this book shows how the bodies of Mexican plasma donors are not only produced through plasma donation at the border, but how these bodies are continually produced and reproduced through the manufacture and treatment of dis/embodied bags of plasma. We can see how black African bodies are produced through surveillance mechanisms at airports, and that these surveillance systems protrude into the body and attempt to visualize race at a biological level. The bodies of soldiers are produced and governed through their enmeshment with other bodies, through their sexual and reproductive lives after their service and the ways this collides them with absented queer and trans bodies. These myriad relations and spaces in which bodies come into being and are governed are made visible by building upon the FTS premise that bodies do not begin and end at the skin; and that they encompass a variety of human and nonhuman relationships.

As we can see, FTS contributes an understanding of the body-assemblage as both a particular (occupying a specific political position that is raced, gendered and sexed), and uncertainly bordered assemblage that is able to stretch well beyond traditional masculine understandings of 'the body'. In this way, FTS works to enact a queerfeminist curiosity, continually asking questions about where the body is constituted and how this is done through a series of relationships. Taking a perspective on the body as produced through a series of relationships that pass through and across the body further muddies attempts by us as scholars to pin or fix a clear border around the body. As the next section of this chapter argues, this conceptualization of the body is vital for understanding governance in international politics. Having addressed how FTS approaches the body, I now turn to explore how this understanding of the body draws us towards studying bodily fluids in international politics, arguing that approaching bodily fluids from an FTS perspective allows us to engage the politics of life and death in more nuanced ways.

Bodily fluids and international politics: assemblages-in-relation

Having thought about how we can understand bodies, I now want to think about the other central elements of this project: bodily fluids. I want to introduce bodily fluids into the conversation at this point not because I see them as the medium that connects bodies and international politics; as this chapter has argued, they are already connected. Talking about bodily-assemblages is to always already be talking about international politics, because body-assemblages are constituted through their relations with international politics. It is these webbed relationships that locate bodily-assemblages, that form them through particular racializing, sexualizing and gendering connections. And the body-assemblage forms assemblages of international politics through these connections, too. The useful work that bodily fluids can help us do, then, is not to join the dots between the two. Rather bodily fluids can help us understand *how* the relationships between body-assemblages and assemblages of international politics are being continually dis/ordered. It is the quality of these relationships, not their existence, that bodily fluids can help us to map.

As we have seen, FTS puts our queerfeminist curiosity into practice by continually asking after how raced, gendered and sexed bodies are constituted in international politics, and where the boundaries of these bodies lie. The following section of this chapter picks up the other component of queerfeminist curiosity, studying bodily fluids through queer logics of and/or. I begin by laying out how bodily fluids can complicate our understanding of life and death in international politics, through their capacity to generate life–death for bodies. Secondly, I lay out why this book uses FTS to frame its approach to biopolitics, rather than some more canonical and non-feminist biopolitical authors (for example, see Agamben, 1998; Esposito & Campbell, 2009; Foucault, 2008). I outline the two key reasons I use FTS to frame this book's analysis of biopolitics. Firstly, FTS contributes a feminist focus on the mundane, showing us that the grand politics of life and death are often played out in small degrees and in a variety of everyday spaces. Secondly, FTS pushes us towards a recognition that the 'bios' of biopolitics does not (cannot, should not) be used to reference a generic and unmarked form of life.

Fluids as and/or life–death

Bodily fluids are substances produced within and by the body, but can come to traverse the body boundary. They are non-solid objects of a variety of textures (for example, I would include faeces and vomit under the broad umbrella of 'bodily fluids', although their textures may be more solid than the aqueous clear liquid of tears). What unites these substances – semen, blood, pus, urine, vaginal fluid, tears, saliva, mucus, bile, breast milk, and so on – is their ability to move beyond and between bodies, to go from the inside of you to the inside of me. Bodily fluids, despite being deeply personal and interior substances that are intimately tied to the corporeal matter of the subject, can also flow and move across and between subjects and bodies. This renders them 'potentially dangerous substance[s]', because they challenge masculinized ideals of bodies and subjects as impermeable, instead revealing the ways in which the borders of the body (and the subject) are uncertain and cannot be made solid (Linstead, 2000, p. 32). It is the ability of bodily fluids to create relationships of potential between different body-assemblages that makes their governance crucial, as they 'confuse body boundaries' through their intermingling flows (Cavanagh, 2013, p. 433). In doing so, bodily fluids deeply unsettle the distinctions made between bodies, challenging our ideas of the separateness and distinctness of differentiated corporealities.

This ability to form relationships between bodies is important in international politics, because of the biopolitical nature of the relationships bodily fluids can affect between us: relationships of life and death. As biopolitical literatures have argued, power in the twenty-first century nation-state has increasingly come to be exercised through the governance and regulation of species-life, the ability not only to regulate and control dying but through the ability to make live, and to make live in particular ways (Dillon, 2007; Esposito & Campbell, 2009; Foucault, 2008; Giroux, 2006; Lemke, 2001; Macey, 2009; Mbembé, 2015). Biopower revolves around the governance of 'both the individual human body and the welfare of the population' at large, intervening upon one in order to manage the life of the other (Athanasiou, 2005, p. 144). Biopolitics refers to modes of political governance in which 'life is distributed, weighed and valued' across populations (Dillon & Lobo-Guerrero, 2008, p. 268). Such scholars largely focus their gaze at the level of the population, studying how embodiment, subjectivity and autonomy are produced through biopolitical governance (Blencowe, 2012, p. 12). In this measuring and distribution of life, particular technologies are deployed by the sovereign in order to intervene upon 'man's biological existence', to regulate species-life at the level of the population (Elbe, 2005, p. 405). These technologies can include public health measures, the collection of demographic information and statistics about the population, and town planning (Braun, 2007, p. 8). Critical security scholars have added to this list, analysing airport screening programmes, development programmes, and torture as biopolitical technologies (Adey, 2009; Duffield, 2005; Wilcox, 2015).

As this book has already argued, queer logics of and/or register the ways in which objects can occupy multiple different (and even contradictory) positions at the same time (Richter-Montpetit, 2018; Weber, 2016). Bodily fluids are able to matter on both sides of these slashes, harbouring the ability to give and extend life and/or death. Through their relationships with human-technoscience assemblages, bodily fluids can make live and make die in a variety of ways. The biological life of an organism can be extended or diminished through forming a relationship with a bodily fluid (lifesaving blood transfusion, contact with viral laced vomit), as can the life and death of idealized subject positions and bodies. For white supremacists, for example, whiteness is endangered by fluid intermingling with bodies of colour, such as through sexual intercourse – a fear formalized in various miscegenation laws. Bodily fluids prompt us to ask not only how biopolitical governance organizes continued cellular existence, but also attempts to control and situate populations within different modes of living and dying.

Crucially, bodily fluids reveal the ways in which bodies are connected through biopolitical governance in ways that are far richer and more nuanced than a simple binary of life/death. Figuring the importance of biopolitical governance in terms only of life and death eclipses the wealth of embodied, meaningful relationships that exist between two imagined poles of 'life' at one end of a discrete spectrum, and 'death' at the other. Both Lauren Berlant and Jasbir Puar's work are particularly instructive in complicating this relationship. Berlant's work on 'slow death' pushes the concept of death beyond a life–death dichotomy, arguing that biopower is also at work in forcing particular populations to live within 'temporal environments' of dying (Berlant, 2007, p. 759). Here dying is figured not as a singular cessation of life (as an end), but as a degraded and restricted mode of being that exists within 'the domain of living on' (Berlant, 2007, p. 759). Berlant's writing demonstrates how death exists alongside and within life, challenging the idea of a binary relationship between the two terms.

Jasbir Puar's work continues with Berlant's writings to argue that biopolitics operates not only in the governance of making live and letting die, but 'through the finessing of gradation of populations' (Puar, 2017b, p. 25). In *The Right to Maim: Debility, Capacity, Disability* Puar argues that biopolitical governance is premised upon the management of 'degree[s]', and that biopolitical governance operates through the production and management of bodies not as alive or dead but as living or dying (or something in between) in *particular ways* (Puar, 2017b, p. 25). Biopolitics, therefore, operates as a 'capacitation' machine, seeking to produce capacity as a property of some bodies through the debilitation of others (Puar, 2017b, p. xviii). Puar's use of debility/capacity to frame her analysis demonstrates that FTS enables us to add some much-needed colour and texture to the relationships biopolitical governance sets up between bodies. The focus of Puar's writing is not simply who lives and who dies, but how people's lives are enriched, stymied, furthered and curtailed in particular ways for the benefit and disadvantage of others. As such, Puar's analysis does not primarily aim to make the case that relationships between bodies are needed for biopolitical governance to operate; but instead, that we need to try to capture the nuance and complexity of these relationships.

Puar demonstrates that FTS scholars have shifted the debate around biopolitics beyond simple binaries of life and death as concrete, diametrically opposed states that are doled out to populations in international politics. *The*

Right to Maim uses capacity/debility to think about the shapes relationships between body assemblages take, with a specific focus on how sexuality and neoliberalism shape and are shaped by understandings of disability. Within this book, I draw from Puar's understanding of biopolitics as a capacitation regime, but my focus here is not specifically upon disability; instead, this book investigates how biopolitical modes of governance operate through/with bodily fluids in order to organize particular modes of living and dying between bodies. As such, while Puar takes capacity and debility as the main terms of her analysis, I employ the concept of life–death to capture the 'degrees' or gradations of biopolitics (Puar, 2017b, p. 25). Life–death refers to the range of relationships between body-assemblages that exist with a kaleidoscope of living and dying. By conjoining these two terms, I attempt to work with an understanding of biopolitics as revolving not around the manufacture of two dichotomous practices – making live and letting die – but instead as a process of governance that attempts to organize and arrange ways of being in the world through ordering relations between bodies, bodily fluids, and security assemblages. Life–death refers to the ways in which we live/die *for* and *through* the lives/deaths of others.

Conclusion

As this chapter has demonstrated, within this book the body is understood through the lens of assemblage theory as a complex series of webbed relations and connections that is continually undergoing change. My use of assemblage theory is profoundly influenced by feminist technoscience studies, which points the ways in which body-assemblages are always highly particular in relation to race, sex, and gender. This focus on how body-assemblages are differentiated allows FTS to develop an analysis of body-assemblages in conjunction with feminist questions about power. FTS also pays close attention to the borders and boundaries of body-assemblages, revealing how common body ideals are highly masculinized and working to challenge these notions of the body. Building from an FTS perspective, the rest of this book uses bodily fluids to explore the connections between body-assemblages and international security assemblages. This chapter has shown how these connections engage bodily fluids through a politics of life–death, arguing in favour of using an FTS frame to understand biopolitical modes of governance. Chapter 3 marks the beginning of the trio of case studies of this book, looking at how these relationships play out through the governance of bodily fluids in relation to plasma donation along the US–Mexico border.

3

Life-giving, Life-threatening: Plasma Donation at the US–Mexico Border*

Both 'the border' between the US and Mexico and the spaces and communities that live alongside it are a common site of study in international politics. Much work has been produced in relation to bodies, governance and biopolitics within the space of 'the border' (Ackleson, 2005; Aldama, 2003; Anzaldúa, 2012; Doty, 1996, 2011; Latham, 2014; Lugo, 2008; Squire, 2014; Sundberg, 2008). To explore how life/death is distributed in these border exchanges, this chapter takes a hitherto invisible substance in this literature – plasma – and follows it from donor body to the border, through the technological whirling of the plasmapheresis process, and then to the recipient. Along the way, I look to see how ideas of race impact upon these technologically mediated bodily exchanges. Following plasma shows us how Mexicana/o donors are desubjectified through plasma donation, as well as the ways in which relations of 'bios' are produced by, and productive of, race. I focus on plasma donation practices in relation to the four major companies involved in plasma collection and fractionation in the US, as identified by the Federal Trade Commission (FTC): CSL, Baxter, Grifols and Octapharma (Federal Trade Commission, 2009, para. 24).[1] While there are smaller companies involved in collecting plasma along the border, I focus on these companies in particular; their dominance over the market is so secure that the FTC has accused them of working as a 'tight oligopoly' to restrict supply and drive up prices (Federal Trade Commission, 2009, p. 2).

---

* An earlier, abridged version of this chapter originally appeared in print as 'Plasma donation at the border: Feminist technoscience, bodies and race' in the journal *Security Dialogue* (Hobbs, 2021). Reprinted here with permission.

To explore plasma donation assemblages, we must first recognize the ways in which they are nestled within the wider assemblage of the US–Mexico border. The US–Mexico border is at once a specific point and location, and simultaneously a diffuse and mobile set of relationships that stretches well beyond the southernmost US and northernmost Mexican states (Aldama, 2003, p. 23). The border assemblage does in part revolve around a line. It is produced through a variety of material entities and landscapes; an assemblage of fences and empty water bottles, customs and border control agents, deserts and beaches, razor wine, bustling highways and bridges. But scholars have also pointed us towards ways in which 'the border' is not only a material barrier but also a sprawling set of relations. These relations rear their heads throughout the US in the form of racism against Latinx folk, and white supremacist discourses that define belonging in terms of whiteness (Anzaldúa, 2012; Calderon & Saldívar, 1991; Moraga, 1981; Saldívar, 1997; Vila, 2000). Drawing from such border studies literatures I take the assemblage of the US–Mexico border as a borderland, a thick and entangled set of relationships of living where, in Gloria Anzaldúa's words, 'the Third World grates against the first and bleeds ... the lifeblood of two worlds merging to form a third country' (Anzaldúa, 2012, p. 25). The borderland is thus a series of entangled ways of living, as well as a physical space. Reading the border as a borderland allows us to recognize the ways in which the US–Mexico border assemblage is not only a space of boundary marking and differentiation, but is also comprised of relations of merger, exchange and connection. The border produces and marks not just separateness, but togetherness, entanglement and inter-dependence.

Taking the borderlands as a complex web of assembled relations makes visible the ways in which the US–Mexico border can produce both racial differentiation and patterns of connection. The borderlands produce racialized differentiation through security practices at the same time as they are simultaneously 'crisscrossed by ... flows of goods ... [and] capital' (Coleman, 2005, p. 186). In addition to goods and capital, bodies have also played a part in relations of exchange, connection and division in the borderlands. Mexican bodies have a series of complex and multiple histories within this space. On the one hand, Mexican bodies and labour have often been highly desirable to US capital and industry. The maintenance of the US economy, both at a local and national level, has relied upon the travel and migration of Mexicanas/os and cross-border trade flows (Coleman, 2005; Gilbert, 2007; Lugo, 2008; Molina, 2011). Yet, on the other hand, Mexicanas/os have also long been subject to colonial and racist violences at border sites, violences that continue today in contemporary American border policy and practice (Aldama, 2003; Anzaldúa, 2012; de León, 1983; Doty, 2007). Mexicanas/os have historically been forced to occupy a set of ambiguous political positions at border sites, where their bodies are produced as both sites of merger and connection as well as racialized differentiation.

This chapter begins by offering some empirical context on plasma donation in the US–Mexico borderlands. I then turn to exploring industry and media representations of plasma donation and Mexicana/o plasma donors, in order to interrogate how life–death are produced and distributed within donation assemblages. Firstly, I analyse how Mexicana/o donors are desubjectified through the production of their bodies as sources of 'life' that others can benefit from. These representations rely upon, and reproduce, racialized hierarchies of life and value. Secondly, I look at how Mexicana/o donors are simultaneously produced as sources of threat, through discourses of Mexicana/o donors as likely to carry infectious diseases. These discourses draw upon colonial histories to racialize donors as 'Mexican', and imbue this identity with racist understandings of the Mexican body. I end with some reflections on how plasma donation challenges binaries of life and death, and instead draws our attention to the distribution of racialized modes of living.

Empirical context

Considered an essential medicine by the World Health Organization (WHO), plasma is widely used in the treatment of burns and shock (World Health Organization, 2017). Individual protein chains within it can be further isolated through fractionation to produce treatments for a wide variety of illnesses, including many forms of immunodeficiency disorders (World Health Organization, 2017, pp. 33–34). This makes plasma both an important and lucrative medicine. The global plasma market was estimated to be worth around US$33 billion in 2021, with estimates projecting it to be worth between US$45 and US$54 billion by 2030 (BCC Publishing, 2023; Polaris Market Research, 2022). The global market is reliant on donations made in the US, 'the OPEC of plasma', which is estimated to contribute roughly 50 per cent of the global plasma supply (Pollack, 2009, para. 18). Unlike in many European countries, in the US donors are commonly financially compensated for their donations and are able to donate up to twice a week (Slonim et al., 2014, p. 183). The payments donors receive vary. Compensation fees are often based on the volume of plasma that can be donated (this is mediated by factors such as age and weight), and donor centres may offer various 'bonuses' for new donors, donation milestones, or for referring others as donors to the centre (CSL Plasma, n.d.-b; Grifols, n.d.-b, paras. 10–14; Octapharma, n.d.-b).

This vital and valuable US plasma donor population and thus the global plasma market is sustained, in part, through Mexican plasma donors. Plasma companies have invested great resources in growing their borderland donation centres over the years. In 2007, there were ten collection centres located in

Texas along the Mexican border (Bult, 2007). At the time of writing, the 'find a centre' pages of Octapharma, CSL and Grifols place 29 donation centres in close proximity to the Texas/Mexico border (CSL Plasma, n.d.-a; Grifols, n.d.-a; Octapharma, n.d.-a).[2] Across the four southernmost US states, the big four operate 40 donation centres within approximately 35 miles of border crossing points (CSL Plasma, n.d.-a; Grifols, n.d.-a; Octapharma, n.d.-a).

The true scale of donations obtained from Mexican citizens was revealed as a result of a legal dispute between CSL Plasma Inc., Grifols, and the US Customs and Border Protection Agency (CBP). For many years, cross-border donation practices took place in a legal 'gray area'; most Mexican citizens donating plasma in the US were entering the country using B-1/B-2 visas, a common temporary non-immigrant visa that allows people to enter the US for a combination of business and tourism (Lind, 2019, paras. 10–11). This visa does not permit the holder to work in the US. Plasma companies had, for many years, been careful to emphasize that the financial recompense donors received was not payment for their plasma and/or labour, but 'compensation' for their 'time and commitment' (donatingplasma.org, n.d., para. 1; see also Grifols, n.d.-d; PPTA, 2016). However, on 15 June 2021, the CBP announced that donating plasma would be considered 'labor for hire', meaning it would be illegal under a B1 visa (Lind & Dodt, 2021). In return, CSL and Grifols sued the CBP; were denied; and won their appeal challenging this decision. At the time of writing, the plaintiffs are therefore clear to file a formal injunction challenging the ban. In the court opinion filed by Circuit Judge Rao upholding the right of plasma companies to file a challenge, she notes that CSL and Grifols had argued that Mexican donors contributed between 'five to ten percent of all plasma collected nationwide' (*CSL Plasma Inc v. US Customs and Border Protection*, 2022, p. 3). This means a substantial minority of the US total volume of plasma collected each year is donated by Mexican citizens who cross the border to donate. Following the change of policy by the CBP, a survey conducted by industry body the Plasma Protein Therapeutics Association (PPTA) of 12 of their members' largest border donation centres noted an average 78 per cent decline in donations at these centres, suggesting Mexican nationals are responsible for the vast majority of donations at borderland centres (Lilburn, 2022, p. 22). While the legal future of Mexican plasma donors at the time of writing remains undecided, after Judge Rao's ruling donation centres have already on social media begun to encourage Mexican donors to return (Talecris plasma-En español, 2022).

Plotting the donation centre locations of the five big players in the border states is a revealing exercise; the Mexican city of Cuidad Juarez stands out in particular, with a total of 11 donation centres owned collectively by the big five clustered close to the America side of the border (and a further two up the road in Las Cruces).[3] That companies are increasingly choosing to situate sites along the border follows a long-running trend in the industry, notable throughout the 1980s and 1990s, where 'source plasma clinics were disproportionately overrepresented in areas characterized by socioeconomic disadvantage' (James & Mustard, 2004, p. 1227). Setting up shop next to the US–Mexico border is in keeping with this trend. Borderland communities are thickly interrelated spaces. These spaces are produced by and productive of racialized forms of poverty. El Paso, Texas, and its neighbouring city of Cuidad Juárez, exemplify this pattern of interrelation and racialized differentiation. At the time of writing, the core companies this chapter focuses on operate seven donation centres in El Paso, the highest concentration in any US border city (CSL Plasma, n.d.-a; Grifols, n.d.-a). In El Paso country, 83 per cent of residents identify themselves as either Latino or Hispanic, with a quarter of the population being born outside the US (United States Census Bureau, 2018). In El Paso County 21.7 per cent of residents live below the poverty line (United States Census Bureau, n.d., fig. 11). Of those living below the poverty line, 22 per cent are Hispanic or Latina/o; this is close to double the proportion of white residents living below the poverty line (11.8 per cent) (United States Census Bureau, 2017).[4] These are the donor communities among which plasma donation centres are increasingly setting up shop, opening their doors and offering money for plasma in spaces where the poorest residents are highly likely to be Hispanic and/or Latina/o, including residents who identify as Mexicana/o.

On the other side of the border, Mexicanas/os resident in Ciudad Juárez are also able to donate plasma in these centres as long as they can produce the necessary paperwork. It is estimated that around 40 per cent of residents in Cuidad Juárez live in poverty, a number that has risen drastically in recent years due to a downturn in manufacturing and recent periods of intense violence spurred by the cross-border drugs trade (Fuentes et al., 2018, p. 12). The Comité Fronterizo de Obrer@s (CFO), an organization that promotes the rights of maquiladora workers, has suggested that for donors resident in Mexico the practice of cross-border plasma donation has been directly prompted by the impact of the North American Free Trade Agreement (NAFTA) and resultant economic hardship. In an open letter to Felipe Calderón in 2009, CFO argued that the devaluation of workers' wages following NAFTA had led many to seek alternative sources of income, resulting in '[m]any … [who] cross over every week to the US border towns to sell their blood plasma' (Comité Fronterizo de Obrer@s, n.d., para. 8). This analysis is echoed in many of the interviews Mexican citizens donating in the US have given to media organizations. Araceli Duran, for example, told reporters that she regularly journeys from Ciudad Juárez to El Paso to donate, due to the fact that in the Mexican borderlands 'the economy is really bad … one job is not enough to feed a family' (Murray, 2011, para. 5). Such stories are not unusual in media representations of Mexican plasma donation. Donors regularly draw attention to the fact that the income they earn from plasma donation is crucial to supporting themselves/their families/ their studies in the economic context of a lack of employment, falling wages and rising expenses in borderland communities (Kocherga, 2016; Murray, 2011; Pollack, 2009; Woodhouse, 2015). As we can see, conditions of poverty in Cuidad Juárez and across the US–Mexico borderlands are heavily related to flows of goods and services between Mexico and the US.

Neither borderland exchanges between bodies and economies nor the racism and hostility that Mexicanas/os face on American territory are new features of international politics. Following plasma through borderland donation assemblages can, however, draw our attention to the ways in which bodily fluids are mobilized by, and bound up in, these relationships. Having provided some empirical context for practices of plasma donation, this chapter now turns to explore how plasma is at work in the structuring and (re)production of life–death within borderland assemblages.

Extracting life

How are much-legislated-against Mexican plasma donors represented within the industry itself? And how is their blood plasma discussed? It is a queerfeminist curiosity that brings me to ask how bodily fluids, racialized fluids, and borders produce each other here, and to wonder whether these relationships suture together neatly, or whether they hold the potential for rupture too. Answering these questions is key to understanding how differently racialized bodies, and bodily matter, are produced within relationships of plasma donation – and what dynamics they become tangled with. In what follows, I show that plasma is represented within industry literatures as 'bios', a quantifiable materialization of life itself. Through technological intervention, the 'bios' of plasma is produced as a substance that can be extracted from Mexicana/o bodies, and redistributed among others. This set of representational practices desubjectifies Mexicana/o donors, as the value of their life is reduced to the bios that can be extracted from them and redistributed to others.

Objectification and raw materials

The application of technological processes is vital in achieving the objectification of plasma. Technoscientific language and processes work to sterilize the bloodied interaction of body and machine and produce plasma as a neatly bagged and sealed product. Plasmapheresis, the process by which plasma is separated from the remainder of 'blood', plays a vital role in attempting this separation between donor body and plasma product. Plasmapheresis became fully automated in the 1980s, meaning that it effectively became a closed 'circuit between the donor and the automated device' (Baker, 2014, p. 30; Penrod and Gustafson, 2009, p. 18). This emphasis on circuitry and technology in representations of plasmapheresis is not unusual. Claims about the safety of plasma are often linked to an image of plasmapheresis as a 'sterile, self-contained, automated process' (PPTA, 2016). Plasma emerges from this process as a 'therapeutic tool', as it is incorporated into 'part of the technology' assembled around the body in the donation process (Hogle, 1999). A single plasma donation becomes a 'unit', the process an 'extraction' and, most poetically, the blood held within the machine is 'extracorporeal volume' (Penrod and Gustafson, 2009, p. 10; Schreiber, 2014, p. 19; Wellington, 2014, para. 18).

These sterile and technological languages are commonplace in industry literatures. They work to objectify plasma and produce it as a disembodied product that is free from the messy traces of particular subjects. The plasmapheresis process, orchestrated and structured by technoscientific practice, functions to render plasma a generic object that originates from clean and hygienic machines rather than any particular human body. The interwoven assemblage of biomedicine, technoscience, and plasmapheresis machine itself physically intervenes upon the donor's body to isolate and separate plasma from a donor's body. Plasma becomes a 'circulating commodit[y]' that is divorced from the donor subject (Lock, 2001, p. 65). These technoscientific processes and tools attempt to 'keep the categories of person and thing separate', simultaneously creating a conceptual and material space between the body and the plasma (Hogle, 1999). Plasma is transformed from a vital part of an individual's body into a commercially valuable 'biologically-derived product' (Farrugia et al., 2009, p. 11).

(Re)presenting plasma as a commodity that can be extracted from bodies is a profoundly desubjectifying process, one that transforms the plasma donor into little more than a site from which value can be extracted. Rather than being figured as the locus of embodied subjects, donor bodies instead become sites of 'raw material', points of 'supply' for the plasma industry (Baker, 2014, p. 28). The bodies of plasma donors are places where the 'precious natural resource' of plasma can be found and extracted (Baker, 2014, p. 31). Repeated references to plasma as a 'source material', or 'raw material', produce the bodies of donors through biological (specifically geological) languages, that summon imaginaries of oil and metal buried below the surface of the earth (Bult, 2007, p. 4; Octapharma, 2017, para. 1). Donors become terrain that can be mined to obtain precious and valuable plasma. Working the geological metaphor to its fullest, donor bodies are sites where plasma ore, the raw material for producing more complex and expensive technoscientific products, can be obtained. The embodied subjects themselves are beside the point in this formulation of worth. It is only through plasmapheresis, through their integration into the technoscientific assemblages that extract plasma, that donors' bodies acquire value. This value is not innate, but a product of the goods that can be extracted and produced from them, from the 'raw material' of their bodily matter. Donor bodies are thus 'biovaluable' within industry literatures, acquiring value only in so far as they 'yield surpluses of both profit and health' in the form of plasma (Mitchell & Waldby, 2010, p. 334).

The production of donor bodies as biovaluable through their desubjectification as inert land mass is heightened by the language used to represent the act of obtaining plasma from the donor. 'Obtain' here is not a neutral word choice. While 'donate' is a common verb employed in industry descriptions of the donation process, 'obtain' and 'collect' are also commonly used (Penrod, 2010; Penrod & Gustafson, 2009; PPTA, 2016). While 'donate' does imply a level of agency and donation as an active process, 'collect' and 'obtain' (which are deployed so frequently as to be commonplace) do not conjure up images of agential subjects. Instead, the prime agent, the locus of action and energy within these sites, is not the donor body but the technology of extraction. Western technoscience performs the role of the do-er, and the bodies of plasma donors become objects that are acted upon, land to be mined in the quest to obtain plasma.

The entrenchment of power relations that invest the bodies of Mexican donors with biovalue cannot be isolated from the racist history of Western scientific practice. Colonized subjects and racial others have often been exploited and objectified through Western science, materialized as fleshy terrain from which value (be that money, matter, labour, or knowledge) can be extracted (Bashford, 2000; Stern, 1999; Tapper, 1995; Washington, 2008). Within contemporary biomedical discourses, bodies are often treated 'like the "virgin" land of the new world', ripe for white masculine technoscientific colonization (Patton, 1985, p. 51). The language of raw materials evokes these familiar Western and colonial discourses of Mexicana/o bodies as valuable terrain that can be mined for the benefits of the West. Under these colonial logics, Mexicana/o bodies are valuable not in and of themselves as embodied modes of life, but are valuable in so far as sites of extractable, transferrable bios.

The gift of life

Donor bodies thus come to be sites where the 'raw material' of plasma can be produced (Baker, 2014, p. 28). In this section I wish to interrogate the substance/effect of this raw material in greater detail. It is my contention that plasma is produced as the medium of life itself, as matter that is able to imbue health and vitality into the bodies of others. In light of manufacturing processes that fractionate and distil plasma into its various components (and finally into branded medical treatments with 'high-tech' names, such as CSL's

Biostate or Octapharma's Octaplex) the notion that plasma is life/bios is often emphasized in industry materials. I use 'bios' here to refer to the ways in which plasma is conceptualized as a materialization of biological life, the raw power of living made manifest in light yellow liquid.

Plasma donation is often depicted by the industry as an act of giving, where 'the gift of life' is transferred between bodies. The PPTA has produced a promotional video with precisely this title (PPTA, n.d.). Companies bill plasma consistently and regularly as 'a source of life' (Grifols, no date b, para. 1; see BioLife Plasma, n.d.) and 'lifesaving' (Octapharma, 2017, para. 2). This refrain is common enough as to be ubiquitous. In the repetition of plasma as a part of a class of 'life-saving pharmaceuticals' (Octapharma, 2017, para. 2), plasma emerges as a source of life, of bios. Industry representations of plasma very literally position it as a materialization of life-force itself. Through the medium of plasma bios is materialized in object form as something that can be given, taken and transferred between bodies. Following plasma through assemblages of donation at the border therefore immediately calls our attention to the politics of this distribution of life, to the ways in which bodies are understood as being able to make others live through technologically mediated relationships.

If bios can be moved between bodies through plasma exchanges, donor bodies are therefore formulated as being composed (at least partially) of detachable elements. Bits of these bodies can be separated from the donors, and parsed out among others. This fragmentation of donor bodies is important to us in questioning the power dynamics of donation when it comes to Mexicana/o plasma donors. Scholars have long pointed to the ways in which new technologies open the body to 'ever increasing atomization' (Sharp, 2000, p. 298; see also Joralemon, 1995; Lock, 2001; Mitchell and Waldby, 2010; Waldby and Mitchell, 2006). In response to these technologies, Lesley Sharp argues that we need to enquire 'how the body is fragmented, and for what purpose, and by whom' (Sharp, 2000, p. 290). Following plasma through donation assemblages requires us to ask these questions, but also to specify *which* bodies are fragmented and put into relation with each other. While all subjects that donate plasma are arguably subject to some of the same general broad dynamics of fragmentation, these relations play out in particular and specific ways when it comes to particular and specific groups of plasma donors.

In focusing on the politics of which bodies are being fragmented and in relation to whom, Cohen's concept of bioavailability is useful. For Cohen, 'to be bioavailable … is to be available for the selective disaggregation of one's cells or tissues and their reincorporation into another body (or machine)' (2005, p. 83). All plasma donors are produced as bioavailable through their engagement with donation technologies. The processes of becoming bioavailable, being available for disaggregation, are different for different donors. This is because plasma donors do not show up to the donation process as plain, unmarked bodies. They arrive as bodies that are always already entangled in particular locations and histories. These histories matter when it comes to understanding how Mexicana/o donors specifically come to be produced as bioavailable, and desubjectified as bodies/natural resources that are open to redistribution. For Mexicana/o donors donating within the US borderlands, the bioavailability of their bodies is informed and made possible through racialized histories of exploitation. These histories are continually being written through the ongoing and violently racist policing of the borderlands, whereby bodies read as Chicana/o, Mexicana/o, and Latina/o by white gazes are presumed not to belong, not to be 'American'. The central exploitative irony of processes of plasma collection from Mexicana/o donors is that while their bios is valuable – precisely because it can extracted and transferred to other bodies – the value of their particular and qualified modes of living in these spaces are frequently (and violently) disputed by white supremacist border discourses (Aldama, 2003; Doty, 2007). As such, the production of Mexicana/o donors as bioavailable are contingent upon wider racist borderland assemblages. These assemblages value the output of Mexicana/o bodies in the borderlands, while remaining frequently hostile to the presence of Mexicana/o modes of living in these spaces.

White American plasma donors are not donating in a geopolitical context that is dubious about their right to exist within the US borders by virtue of their whiteness. For Mexicana/o donors, however, they donate plasma within borderland spaces that often (re)articulate discourses that Mexicanas/os are 'unwanted as human beings' on US soil (Doty, 2011, p. 600). As an illustrative example, the British news agency *The Daily Mail* ran a story about Mexicana/o plasma donors encapsulating the central tensions that Mexicana/o donors are subject to. The article's title, 'Mexican "blood smugglers" cross border twice a month to sell their plasma for $260', makes use of the (entirely unexplained and inaccurate) language of 'smuggling' to draw upon racist discourses that frame Mexicanas/os crossing the US–Mexico border as inherently illegitimate and thus criminal (Daily Mail, 2011). One comment left beneath the online article by 'That's So Wrong' from 'Anytown USA' sums up plenty of racist, anti-Mexican sentiment along the US–Mexico border with 'Great. Another reason to secure the border' (Daily Mail, 2011, para. 22). The framing of the article and the comments attached to it demonstrate the prevalence of racism in popular understandings of Mexicana/o plasma donors, and in understanding the US borderlands as places already thick and sodden with white supremacist discourses.

The politics of making people bioavailable is a profoundly racialized form of politics that is contingent upon donor embodiment. Following plasma through donation assemblages requires us to understand the racist discourses and histories within the borderlands that plasma donation is situated within.

As I have shown, Mexicana/o donors are produced as valuable within industry literatures only in so far as discrete amounts of life (materialized in the form of plasma) can be extracted from their bodies and redistributed to others. Their lives as qualified and particular modes of living are often policed within the borderlands, both by government agencies as well as racialized and racist discourses. But their plasma, their life, is certainly welcomed by plasma companies operating on American soil. Mexican donors are valuable to the US plasma industry as a source of life and vitality; they provide 'important' quantities of this raw material (Bult, 2007, p. 5). The central point of exploitation and contention in the business of border plasma donation is that, while Mexican plasma is valuable in the US, Mexican embodiment is often profoundly less welcome.

Race, disease, plasma

Media and industry productions of Mexicana/o plasma donors are, however, more complex than a singular desubjectifying narrative of Mexicanas/os as sources of bios. A queerfeminist curiosity compels us to think about logics of both/and; how Mexicana/o donors, or perhaps more accurately their bodies, are figured as having the potential to both save and harm the non-Mexicana/o other. Both these stories, contradictory though they are, circulate simultaneously, and often through similar veins and spaces within the plasma industry. Working with queer logics of both/and allow us to recognize and acknowledge these two divergent narrative flows, and see what is made possible through this multiplicity. I now explore the ways in which Mexicana/o donors are simultaneously produced as sources of danger and threat, through the (re)production of racialized discourses of disease. While Mexicana/o plasma donors are positioned as a source of extractable life, they are simultaneously produced within media narratives as a source of threat to the health of American and international populations. This threat is produced through representations of Mexicana/o donors as particularly likely to introduce novel pathogens into the international plasma supply.

There is generally little mention of border donation centres and Mexican plasma donors within industry literatures. It is notable, however, that on the few occasions these bodies and spaces are made visible, it is always in relation to infectious disease. In 2007, industry magazine *The Source* featured two articles that discussed borderland donation centres in depth. The first, a report by the president of the PPTA, begins with a discussion of safety measures in the collection process (Bult, 2007). The report then turns toward a discussion of borderland centres, an issue, which the PPTA board of directors felt was 'necessary' to make a statement upon following 'some discussion about centres located along the United States border with Mexico' (Bult, 2007,

p. 5). The article notes that the primary concerns about these centres is that 'poor Mexican nationals in a poor health condition' may cross the border in order to donate (Bult, 2007, p. 5). The second article, following closely behind the PPTA president's closing words that borderland donation centres are 'centers that the industry can be proud of!', is therefore a glowing profile of a centre manager of a Talecris borderland donation centre in Eagle Pass, Texas (Bult, 2007, p. 6; Noyes, 2007).

Despite praising the 'circle of life and hope' that permeates the aforementioned Talecris donation centre, the prior article clearly demonstrates the prevalence of anxieties within the industry about the health status of Mexicana/o donors. The perceived threat Mexicana/o donors may pose to the safety of the plasma supply is implicit in the PPTA's reactive statement, which highlights safety standards and low viral marker rates (Noyes, 2007, p. 7; Bult, 2007). Mexicana/o plasma donors are materialized in these internal industry discussions as unhealthy and impoverished. The spectre of infectious disease was raised even more explicitly at the PPTA stakeholder meeting of the same year (PPTA, 2010). The 'most anticipated report of the day' was a comparison of viral marker rates in border donation centres with donation centres in the rest of the US (PPTA, 2010, p. 23).[5] That this report was highly anticipated is testament to the industry's level of anxiety around disease and Mexicana/o donors. The repeated emphasis on disease in connection with Mexicana/o plasma donors – indeed, this is the only context in which Mexicana/o donors are made visible in industry literatures – establishes Mexican bodies' infectious safety risks. Questions about viral marker rates in borderland donation centres immediately position donor bodies within these spaces as dangerous, through their location within the US–Mexico borderlands and their proximity to Mexico and Mexican bodies. Closeness to Mexico and Mexicanas/os is produced as a proxy for increased risk of contagion.

These productions are repeated not only in industry literatures but also within popular media discourses of plasma donation in the borderlands. Here, 'the health of the donor population' in relation to specifically borderland donation centres and 'the safe supply of plasma' is produced as a 'concern ... raised by some experts and activists' (Roston, 2009, para. 6). Following the establishment of Mexicana/o plasma donation as a potential problem, the same article then cites literatures that support the idea that the 'diverse' nature of communities in the US–Mexico borderlands is responsible for high rates of communicable diseases in these spaces (Roston, 2009, para. 7).[6] Here, intimacy and proximity between differently racialized bodies in the borderlands is the catalyst for disease. This notion of racial mingling as a catalyst for disease draws upon racist discourses of immunology that equate ethnic and racial 'singularity with health and internal cleanliness, and contagion with ... a merging of one with another' (Waldby, 1996, p. 107).

These discourses are legitimized through appeals to scientific expertise, for example the reiteration that it is 'immunologists' who have expressed 'safety concerns' about borderland donation practices and Mexicana/o donors (Woodhouse, 2015, para. 14). While the nature of these concerns may go undetailed, the invocation of immunology as a relevant field of expertise establishes communicable disease and Mexicana/o donors as the source of concern. These discourses are often produced implicitly in media coverage. For example, the establishment of the presence of borderland donation centres before immediately offering reassurance that 'safety for the donors and the plasma' are 'top concerns' and that plasma collected there will undergo 'rigorous testing to insure it's safety [sic]' (Daily Mail, 2011, paras. 12–14). The placing of Mexicana/o donation practices immediately prior to discussion of safety practices establishes a tension between these two ideas, introducing linkages between Mexicana/o donors and threats to the safety of the plasma supply. Sometimes this discourse is more explicit, for example through the expression of fears that 'novel pathogens that perhaps are found in Mexico but not in the United States' may enter the plasma supply through Mexicana/o donation in the borderlands (Pollack, 2009, paras. 42–43); as one commenter puts it, 'thinking of what unknowns the blood is not tested for ... terrifies me' (Daily Mail, 2011, para. 23).

The next section of this chapter returns to this fear of novel pathogens in greater detail but, before doing so, it is important to pull out the ways in which these discourses of disease are simultaneously desubjectifying and profoundly racializing of Mexicana/o donors. In materializing Mexicana/o bodies as infectious by virtue of being Mexicana/o, Mexicana/o bodies are profoundly homogenized. Any possibility of more individualized subjects is overshadowed by the production of Mexicanas/os as infectious. Being Mexican is not only treated as a reliable indicator of risk in relation to blood-borne diseases, but emerges as a totalizing and singular corporeal signifier. All Mexican bodies, in these discourses, carry the same risk of infecting the global plasma supply. There is no recognition that a person's likelihood of carrying blood-borne viral disease depends on a diverse and enormous group of conditions that varies depending on *which* blood-borne viral disease we focus upon. Instead, Mexicana/o donors are produced as an undifferentiated mass of bodies that are all equally likely, by virtue of being Mexican, to cause problems for the safety of the global plasma supply.

In this articulation of Mexicana/o bodies, race does not exist independently and prior to these discourses. Rather these productions of Mexicana/o bodies are racializing, which is to say that 'Mexican' is produced as a racial category through these discourses of disease and risk. The idea of a 'Mexican' body is (re)produced and invested with meaning through these narratives of plasma, disease and borderland centres/donors.[7] This particular production of the Mexicana/o body is situated within colonial histories of representation, as the next section unpacks in further detail. It is worth noting that through the production of the Mexicana/o body as diseased, plasma also becomes racialized through its relationship to the donor body. Plasma from Mexicana/o donors is risky, and plasma from not-Mexicana/o donors is therefore implicitly safer. It is the circulation of Mexicana/o plasma that is the locus of the disease threat, and plasma is racialized as 'Mexican' plasma long after technological processes have separated it physically from any particular body, demonstrating the potency of race to capture both bodies, subjects and bodily matter.

This articulation of Mexicana/o plasma and bodies is co-produced alongside an imagined idealization of the American body/plasma as not-contagious, as biologically benevolent. As Mexicana/o donors are produced as universally threatening to the plasma supply because they are Mexican, donor bodies that are not-Mexican are constructed as safe. While there are media representations of impoverished American donors as vulnerable to infectious diseases and thus threatening to plasma safety, such representations generally allow for greater differentiation between American bodies to explain levels of disease, often invoking poverty to explain the susceptibility of American donors to disease risks (Edin & Schaefer, 2015; Wellington, 2014). Being an American citizen, or 'Americanness' as an imagined quality, does not emerge within this particular configuration as a risk factor that needs to be accounted for.[8] This is in sharp contrast to productions of Mexicana/o donor bodies, where further explanation is rarely given. The only distinguishing features allotted to these bodies is being Mexican. These discourses of disease are therefore racializing discourses of donor bodies, which produce donor bodies as 'American' and 'Mexican' bodies by making different sense of each in relation to each other and to viral disease.

Novel pathogens and colonial histories

Mexican donors emerge in these discourses of viral disease as particular and exceptional threats to the safety of the plasma supply. Mexicana/o donors are produced, to put it simply, as more likely to be infectious than other donors. This is achieved through the continued articulation of Mexicana/o donation practices in conjunction with mention of the threat of viral disease and safety standards. Within these racializing discourses, not only does 'Mexicanness' itself raise the risk of viral disease, but Mexicana/o bodies are also produced as being likely to carry novel pathogens.

In order to shed light on the hidden discursive links that make these representations of Mexicana/o donors possible, we have to pay attention to colonial histories of representation. These form the landscape in which contemporary fears of Mexican donors and novel diseases are rooted. Stereotypes of Mexico as an unhygienic and diseased space date back to

American colonization. Discourses of disease and hygiene have 'long been an important source of boundary marking in the USA–Mexico borderlands' (Sundberg, 2008, p. 877). The denigration of indigenous peoples' hygiene and practices of 'bodily comportment' were essential in legitimizing white European dominance during colonization (Mitchell, 2005, p. 20). White supremacist fears about 'racial mixing' during this time were frequently expressed in terms of 'pollution', and Mexican peoples in particular were produced as threatening to white supremacy through the (in the eyes of white colonizers) 'mixed blood nature of Tejanos' (de León, 1983, pp. 11–18). For a budding white American nation 'consumed by ideals of racial purity and racial denial', Mexicanas/os and the spaces they occupied were produced as dirty and diseased in comparison to fantasies of 'whiteness' as orderly and hygienic (Haraway, 1997, p. 214). These racist stereotypes of Mexican bodies effected and legitimized practices of violent governance and surveillance of Mexican bodies. During the early twentieth century, hygiene practices were instituted in the US borderlands for Mexicanas/os wishing to enter US territory (Markel & Stern, 1999; Sundberg, 2008).[9] Mexican labourers were required to be frequently 'sterilized' when they crossed the border, a humiliating process that involved being stripped naked, doused with kerosene, examined and potentially vaccinated (Markel & Stern, 1999, pp. 1324–1325). These degrading and invasive 'sterilizing' practices racialized Mexican bodies as Mexican, through the performance of Mexicanas/os as dirty and diseased in comparison to the (imagined as) pure and healthy white American body (Stern, 1999, p. 73).

Such racist stereotypes of Mexican bodies 'run deep in US culture, especially in border-states' today (Sundberg, 2008, p. 877). Anxieties around the circulation of racialized bodily matter in the US surface in contemporary discourses of plasma donation, where novel pathogens that might threaten US plasma supplies are imagined to be lurking within Mexico. Novel pathogens are not imagined within these narratives as emerging from within the US itself, but are a property of Mexicana/o bodies only. It is the 'biologically polluted native' that is imagined to be the source of danger and infection within discourses of plasma donation, and anxieties around unknown infectious diseases are projected onto Mexicana/o bodies as cultural and racial others (Lynch, 1998, p. 235).

The legacy of the HIV/AIDS epidemic lingers in contemporary articulations of racialized anxieties about novel diseases hitching a ride across the border through the bodies of racially 'other' donors. During the HIV/AIDS crisis, there was a reluctance to accept that HIV/AIDS may be a blood-borne disease as this would disrupt comforting racist and heterosexist presumptions that only queers, Haitian and African folk were vulnerable to the disease (Starr, 1999, p. 268). The resultant ban on queer men donating blood and plasma products is testament to the persistent assumption that 'others' are responsible for novel pathogens.[10] Interestingly, some actors within the plasma industry initially resisted bans on queer men donating out of a fear that (in the words of an employee of Cutter Biologic in 1983) it may lead to 'further pressure to exclude plasma collected from the Mexican border' (Starr, 1999, p. 272).

Representations of Mexicana/o bodies and Mexico as riddled with previously unknown and dangerous diseases have their own particular histories. Yet we can see how following plasma within these assemblages leads us to connect the dots between discourses that make use of disease to produce 'others', and legitimize discrimination against them. Mexicana/o bodies and exclusionary tropes of novel pathogens and disease risk can thus be located within wider, historical discourses that scapegoat 'others' for disease in order to assert the American self as pure and healthy. This perpetuates a violent othering of Mexican bodies, a politics of circulation that invokes racist colonial tropes of Mexican bodies in order to legitimize their exclusion, materially and politically, from the body politic. By following plasma through these assemblages, we are able to see how Mexico and Mexicana/o bodies are materialized as a dangerous threat to the US body politic through the circulation of racialized bodily matter.

Relations of living

Through these discourses of race and disease, Mexican bodies are constructed as a threat to the health security of the plasma supply, and thus the recipients of plasma products. The concern over the health of Mexican plasma is not because they are 'infect*ed*, but because [they are] ... infect*ing*' (Waldby, 1996). Even if we were to believe that Mexican donors are more likely to be carriers of viral disease than American donors, the concern is for the safety of the plasma supply and resulting plasma products, rather than the potentially ill donors themselves. I argue that this points to the ways in which the relations of life and living established through plasma donation are not reciprocal relationships. When it comes to questions of disease and sickness, it is the recipients of plasma products whose lives and quality of life matter, rather than those of Mexicana/o donors. This might seem an obvious point to make in relation to practices of Mexicana/o plasma donation. A critical reader will likely need little convincing that the companies that benefit from multi-million-dollar trade flows care little for the migrant labourers whose legal right of presence within the very space of the donation centre, and thus their access to payment, is highly precarious. But when we follow plasma into and through these spaces, we are able to see how there is more to say about this relationship between Mexicana/o donor body and plasma donation than solely inequality. Following plasma allows us to link not only the donor body and corporation in an exploitative relationship, but also allows us to directly connect the donor body and the recipient body in order to understand how relations of bios are differentially structured in this exchange.

As postcolonial FTS scholars have worked to remind us, 'biological engagements with the body are deeply biopolitical projects' (Pollock & Subramaniam, 2016, p. 954). Through the medium of plasma, donor bodies and recipient bodies are directly connected to each other through a relation of bios, of the transfer of life from one body to another. Importantly, plasma and plasma-derived medicines not only simply extend lives but also have the potential to enrich them. Rather than seeing these relationships of bios in quantitative terms – how much life is subtracted from one and added to the other – it is important to identify the modes of bios that are transferred in these relationships. It is not only the quantity but the quality of life that exchanges of plasma can affect. The transference and exchange of bios within plasma donation does not equate to a simple matter of addition and subtraction, where Mexicana/o donors are dying in order to prolong the lives of others. Recognizing that there is a differential transfer in the way in which bios is experienced and felt matters in order to recognize the fullness of the effects of plasma donation.

For example, the most common physical side-effect of plasma donation relates to the use of sodium citrate during donation. Sodium citrate is an anti-coagulant used during donation to prevent blood and plasma from clotting during extraction and production. As a result of raised levels of sodium citrate in the parts of blood that are returned to the donor during plasmapheresis, up to 80 per cent of donors may experience 'mild' physical symptoms such as fatigue, nausea, chest tightness, and tingling or burning sensations in the skin (Amrein et al., 2012, p. 35; Winters, 2006). Donors may also experience (though they may not be aware of this) reduced blood levels of proteins and key antibodies, which could potentially render them vulnerable to an increased risk of infection and illness (Villagran & Dodt, 2019). In addition, some donors have reported feeling lightheaded after donating if they have not eaten enough prior (Pollack, 2009, para. 46). Others report feeling drowsy, or generally 'down' (Woodhouse, 2015, para. 25).

Noting that Mexicana/o plasma donors may feel tingling or burning sensations, or tired and nauseous after donating may seem difficult to connect to the politics of security and international politics more broadly. But knowing this matters in order to understand how life–death is distributed in international politics. Taking our case study of Mexicana/o plasma donation in the US borderlands and following how plasma connects donor and recipient bodies through these practices allows us to cut a window into the ways in which relations of bios produce a hierarchy between bodies. We see the solidification of a global power dynamic in which the lives of particular bodies are enriched by the bios of others. For recipients of plasma-derived medicines, embodied modes of living can be rendered longer, more comfortable, less painful and fraught in myriad ways. This is achieved at the expense of the lives of Mexicana/o plasma donors. Plasma donation is, after all, a one-sided relationship in terms of bios. While donors receive financial compensation that may enrich their lives in certain ways (putting food on the table, textbooks in bags, money into the rent) at the level of bios, donors do not have similar levels of access to the 'anatomical power of the other' in order to nourish their own bodies and modes of living (Scheper-Hughes, 2001, p. 4).

Studying these relationships in plasma donation, therefore, makes more complex our understanding of the politics of life–death in two key ways. Firstly, it challenges binary understandings of the relationship between these terms. In following plasma, we are able to see that this is not a case in which death must occur in order for life to flourish. As I have argued, the maths is more complicated than purely subtraction and addition. The extraction of plasma, of bios, from Mexicana/o donors does not kill them. But it does have the potential to affect the modes in which they live, in which their lives are embodied. Recognizing painful burning dermal sensations and nausea matter in order to acknowledge how life is governed and extended not simply through the death of the other, but through the enactment of particular forms of living by the other. It is particular and qualified forms of life that are produced in relation to each other. The tingles and the fatigue and the reduced protein count donors may experience matter, not because they clearly and directly lead to death (they do not), but because they constitute a slow form of violence that is played out not in the ending of life but in the embodied mode in which it is lived (Berlant, 2007). Rather than being killed, Mexicana/o bodies are debilitated in order for the capacity of other bodies to be enriched. Mexicana/o donors are maintained in a position of health precarity that ensures they remain 'available' as resources for other bodies to consume (Puar, 2017b, p. xvii). Following plasma thus allows us to see that biopolitics is organized through relationships that do not necessarily reproduce a strict life/death binary, but instead play out through slow modes of life–death. Plasma shows us that biopolitical logics operate not only through letting die, but through the production and maintenance of a debilitated population in order to enable 'capacious' lives for others (Puar, 2017b, p. 13).

The politics of life–death are thus not only conducted through a binary relationship, a zero-sum game of extraction and addition, but of modes of life lived by bodies thousands of miles apart but in conjunction with each other. Both are living, both are continuing, and both forms of lives are being governed through the production of the other. The Mexicana/o who donates plasma lives in this mode of donor by virtue of the sickness and suffering of someone in need of treatment; and the plasma recipient lives a nourished and enriched life by virtue of the discomfort of a Mexicana/o donor in the US borderlands. These modes of living are made possible through a complex assemblage of bodies, technology, history and violence. The relationships of life–death that are produced here are global, made so by the international manufacturing and distribution of plasma-derived medicines. The governance of Mexicana/o plasma donor bodies are part of a complex global web of bios. Practices of Mexicana/o plasma donation ripple across this international assemblage, enabling and making possible thousands of different lives.

The second thing that following plasma through donation assemblages reveals to us about life–death is that the 'bios' of biopolitics is always already becoming racialized. Despite the extensive testing and treatment procedures that plasma undergoes, all of which are designed to inactivate viruses, the association of Mexican bodies and plasma with disease persists. This demonstrates how attempts to objectify the plasma of Mexican donors counterintuitively reproduces the racialization of plasma. Technological assemblages of donation produce 'Mexican' plasma as a dangerous entity, while 'American' plasma is produced as safe. Rather than emerging as an anonymous and passive object from these assemblages, plasma from Mexican donors is not fully disembodied. Violent productions of the Mexican body as a harbinger of disease are continually being reiterated, producing and reproducing the racialization of plasma as 'Mexican' (dangerous) and not-Mexican (safer). The imagined Mexican-ness and American-ness of plasma is constantly produced through repetition of discourses of disease, leaving us unable to separate ideas of plasma from wider discourses of race and identity.

When it comes to critically examining plasma donation, following plasma in these ways allows us to see how race and matter are co-constitutive. Matter in plasma donation is subject to continuous and ongoing processes of racialization. Understanding biopolitics and relationships of life–death cannot be complete without attending to the ways in which 'bios' is always already bound up in processes of racialization. This brings us back to reflect on Donna Haraway's appeal to the particular and situated nature of knowledge, and particularly body politics. While Mexican plasma donors are produced as bodies available for disassembly in order to enrich the lives of others, within processes of plasma donation within the borderlands they are simultaneously 'not allowed *not* to have a [racialized] body' (Haraway, 1991, para. 183: insertion my own). The plasma of Mexicana/o donors can leave their bodies, travel thousands of miles and be incorporated into another person's. At the same time, donation assemblages continue to reproduce the imagined 'Mexican-ness' of their plasma throughout these processes. Bios is not allowed to be disembodied within this assemblage. Instead, race and matter are continually produced as profoundly intertwined.

Conclusion

Technologies of paid plasma donation along the US/Mexico border produce Mexican bodies as simultaneously a desirable source of surplus health and a dangerous reservoir of disease. Through the application of plasmapheresis and technoscientific discourses, the US plasma industry attempts to divorce plasma from the body of the donor. This objectification of plasma is an effort to render it as universal and generic bios that can be redistributed among bodies. Mexicana/o donors are desubjectified under these logics. They are produced as valuable only in so far as their bios can be extracted, and therefore only as valuable through their capacity to make others live. Pursuing a queerfeminist curiosity, however, with its emphasis on mutual constitution and queer logics of both/and, helps us to recognize how Mexicana/o donors are simultaneously produced as a source of danger and threat. Racist anxieties about Mexicana/o bodies produce persistent discourses within both industry and media representations of plasma that position Mexicana/o donors as being at high risk of infectious disease. As such, Mexicana/o bodies are both desubjectified and racialized as a homogenous mass of bodies, inscribed with the potential for harbouring novel pathogens.

Following plasma through assemblages of borderland plasma donation demonstrates to us that there are important and political differences in how lives are produced as different. When analysing relations of life–death, this leads us to not only ask who dies for whom but who *lives* for whom, and *how* they are made to live for others. Chapter 4 of this book takes up these questions in relation to a different bodily fluid – that of vomit in airport security assemblages during the 2013–16 Ebola outbreak in West Africa.

4

Racializing Fluids: Vomit, Airports and the 2013–16 Ebola Pandemic

As we shift our attention from plasma to vomit, it is important to remember at the outset that there is no overarching grand narrative of 'fluids'. Different fluids operate and affect international politics and security differently. In this chapter, I follow vomit through airport exit-screening assemblages during the 2013–16 Ebola outbreak in West Africa in order to determine how and why vomit is constructed as a security threat in these practices, and what forms of politics follow from this production of vomit. While the movement of plasma in the US–Mexico borderlands is facilitated by donation assemblages, a politics of racialized containment was mobilized around vomit during the 2013–16 Ebola outbreak. This chapter focuses on exit-screening practices deployed in Liberia, Sierra Leone and Guinea, along with Western European and North American narratives of/responses to the pandemic.[1]

By following vomit, this chapter asks what is 'brought up' when we pay attention to Ebola vomit (Henderson, 2014). Do bodies, race, gender, and life–death surface in airport security assemblages? And if they do, how? Vomit's journey from undigested food stuff to national security threat prompts us to ask a series of questions about how the airport attempts to open up the interior of bodies through surveillance practices. Critical attention has already focused upon airports as a site of security practice: exploring the ways in which bodies are produced and rendered legible through biometric technologies (Beauchamp, 2009; Epstein, 2007; Wilcox, 2015, 2017); how surveillance and biometrics produce and regulate mobilities (Adey, 2003, 2004; Amoore, 2006; Amoore & de Goede, 2005; Sheller & Urry, 2006); and the subjects and assemblages airport surveillance depends upon and is productive of (Lippert & O'Connor, 2003; Salter, 2007). Following vomit through airport assemblages allows us to explore how surveillance technologies increasingly attempt to produce and govern bodies based on their fluid capabilities. Following vomit in airport security assemblages makes visible the ways in which security practices produce and govern risk in relation to bodily fluids, and demonstrates how these practices are interlaced with (re)productions of race and gender.

This chapter draws on a variety of documents from the World Health Organization (WHO) and the US Centers for Disease Control and Prevention (CDC) that detail screening procedures, as well as pop cultural representations of the pandemic, such as novels, films and news media. The chapter begins by offering some empirical context to the 2013–16 Ebola outbreak, and an overview and analysis of screening practices during this period as constituting a form of security 'gaze'. I then paint in the historical context of how Ebola and Ebola vomit have been racialized in Western representations, showing how this context influences contemporary anxieties about Ebola vomit. I show how security gazes attempt to penetrate and regulate bodies in gendered and racialized ways. Finally, I look at the ramifications the governance of Ebola vomit has for relationships of life–death. I show that attempts to govern vomit in these settings attempted to secure racialized modes of living, through the (violent) surveillance and quarantining of West African bodies.

Empirical context

Technological advances mean it is now feasible for people to move between distant countries in a matter of hours, thanks to commercial air travel. With this increased mobility has come an increased fear of the threat infectious diseases pose to national security (Ingram, 2005; McInnes & Lee, 2006; Voelkner, 2011). Newly emergent and re-emergent infectious diseases have aroused security attention for their ability to impact upon regional stability, state sovereignty, and (inter-)national economies (Ingram, 2005). As health threats gain increasing attention from the security sector, it becomes more crucial than ever to focus critical attention upon the bodies and substances at the centre of these fears. It is vital to enquire after the power dynamics structuring both these anxieties, and the responses to them.

The 2013–16 Ebola outbreak is emblematic of these dynamics and their consequences. Ebola virus disease (EVD) is a filoviridae virus, a group of viruses responsible for haemorrhagic fevers. Haemorrhagic fevers destroy blood capillaries within the body, leading to the internal leaking of fluids and plasma; this can lead to shock, deoxygenation, and potentially critical organ failure (Weldon, 2001a, p. 285). Due to the weakening of blood capillaries, haemorrhagic fevers and EVD feature the '[h]allmark' characteristics of bleeding symptoms, such as a redness of the eyes, bruising, nose bleeds and the presence of clots in vomit and/or stools (Goeijenbier et al., 2014, p. 445). Contrary to pop culture representations of the disease, however, bleeding symptoms are estimated to be present in fewer than half of patients, and blood loss is not the primary cause of death in patients (Feldmann & Geisbert, 2011,

p. 851; Rougeron et al., 2015, p. 115). There are currently two approved vaccines for the Zaire species of EVD, and the WHO now recommends two specific antibody treatments for EVD patients (World Health Organization, 2022). However, for the 2013–16 outbreak, these vaccines and treatments had either not yet been developed, or were still undergoing testing and, as such, none were standard responses during this outbreak.[2] In the absence of specific therapies, clinical responses focus on delivering 'basic supportive therapy' (Rougeron et al., 2015, p. 117; Vetter & Kaiser, 2020). Transmission of the disease is reliant upon direct or indirect contact with the bodily fluids of a symptomatic patient (Shears & O'Dempsey, 2015, p. 1).

The 2013–16 outbreak recorded its first cases in Guinea in December 2013, and remains the largest outbreak since the virus was discovered in 1976 (Shears & O'Dempsey, 2015, p. 5). The outbreak was largely centred in Guinea and neighbouring Sierra Leone and Liberia, although small numbers of cases were also reported in seven other countries: Nigeria, Mali, Senegal, Italy, Spain, the US and the UK (Shultz et al., 2016).[3] Within the three primary West African countries, the disease was responsible for the deaths of 11,310 people, and a further 28,616 cases (World Health Organization, 2016). Mortality rates varied between countries. Guinea witnessed the highest case fatality rate at 66.7 per cent; the average fatality rate across these three countries was 39.5 per cent (Shultz et al., 2016, p. 85). The outbreak was declared a public health emergency of international concern (PHEIC) by the WHO in August 2014 (World Health Organization, 2014b). The WHO have since been criticized for the time it took the organization to declare the outbreak a PHEIC; some have suggested that the declaration was initially resisted by senior figures in the WHO due to various political pressures (Kamradt-Scott, 2016; Wenham, 2017).

In August 2014, the WHO recommended that all states with Ebola transmission should conduct exit screenings of all travellers, which, at a minimum, should entail 'a questionnaire, a temperature measurement and, if there is a fever, an assessment of the risk that the fever is caused by EVD' (World Health Organization, 2014d, p. 5). Travellers wishing to fly from international airports in Guinea, Liberia and Sierra Leone had to undergo numerous checks aimed at assessing their likelihood of contaminating other passengers. The checks comprised a primary phase of temperature checks, visual observation, and a health questionnaire (Centers for Disease Control and Prevention, 2014, p. 12). If passengers passed these criteria, they were cleared to travel. If not, they were referred to secondary screening, where public health or medical professionals conducted another questionnaire, temperature check, and a 'brief focused medical exam' (Centers for Disease Control and Prevention, 2014, p. 12). Depending on the outcome of this second round of screening, travellers could be either cleared to travel or refused boarding. If presenting with symptoms of EVD, they could also be referred onwards to a hospital or Ebola treatment centre for medical care where this was possible (Centers for Disease Control and Prevention, 2014, p. 12). In Guinea, Liberia and Sierra Leone, 'anyone who [was] sick [was] not even allowed on the premises', and questionnaires were required to be completed prior to check-in (Robert Koch Institut, n.d., para. 3). These procedures were designed by the WHO in conjunction with the CDC, the International Civil Aviation Organization, and International Air Transport Association (World Health Organization, 2014c). In particular, the CDC worked to provide 'technical assistance' in developing these screening measures and travel restrictions, as well as procuring supplies, developing training, and '[a]ssessing the capacity' of Liberia, Sierra Leone and Guinea to conduct these screening measures (White House Office of the Press Secretary, 2014, paras. 13–44). As such, the US CDC played an important role in developing and implementing exit-screening practices. In order to understand the particular histories and forms of identity politics that are at play in airport screening assemblages, tracing which countries and organizations did what is important. Western agencies, and institutions that relied on their guidance, played a vital role in the development of exit-screening practices in practice at international airports in West Africa.

Several Western European, North American and Asian countries also implemented entrance-screening measures for flights travelling from either Sierra Leone, Guinea or Liberia (BBC News, 2014; Harris et al., 2014). Despite the outbreak beginning in December 2013 in Guinea, it was only in late 2014 that the pandemic began to gain widespread news coverage in the Western world (Abeysinghe, 2016). This followed two high profile cases. The first was that of Kent Brantly, a white American doctor who contracted the disease while in Liberia, and who was flown back to the US for treatment in August 2014 (Monson, 2017). The second was the death of Thomas Duncan, a black Liberian citizen returning to the US from Liberia, who was subsequently diagnosed with EVD and became the first person to die from EVD on American soil (Monson, 2017). Duncan died in early October, two weeks prior to the Department of Homeland Security's order that all flights from one of the three affected West African countries must land at one of five specified airports, to enable the use of 'enhanced' screening practices for travellers (Brown et al., 2014, para. 10).

Seeing disease

So, how does vomit enter the picture here? The health screening measures at airports during the outbreak were designed to identify and filter out passengers who have the potential to infect others. As EVD is transmitted via contact with infectious bodily fluids, airport security assemblages aim to measure the probability of a body producing fluids such as vomit. Screening technologies functioned to quantify the risk of bodies producing infectious fluids such as vomit. The exact purpose of screening technologies is an important point to clarify, as airport screening measures do not attempt to determine whether travellers definitively *have* EVD (this can only be confirmed via a blood test). Instead, they attempt to measure the body's potential likelihood for infecting *others*. By doing so, airport assemblages use screening technologies to try to minimize the risk that a potentially infectious event (such as vomiting) occurs.

There were three key elements of screening technology in place: temperature checks, questionnaires, and visual assessments. Temperature checks may well be the first piece of screening technology that travellers come into contact with. At Lungi airport in Sierra Leone, for example, travellers were required to pass a temperature check at the entrance, prior to even entering the physical space of the airport (Robert Koch Institut, n.d., para. 8). Temperature checks are a vital component of both primary and secondary screening procedures, and in countries with active transmission of EVD, travellers' temperatures were monitored throughout their airport journey with up to as many as four separate temperature checks (Robert Koch Institut, n.d., para. 10). This was common throughout West African countries affected by the disease, with a final temperature reading taken directly prior to boarding the aircraft (World Health Organization, 2014a, para. 2). These temperature checks attempt to translate the likelihood of infectiousness into something quantifiable, a discrete number that indicates either safety or danger.

The questionnaire attempts to measure the body's infectivity through the application of a series of questions. Travellers must answer a series of yes/no questions (Centers for Disease Control and Prevention, 2014, p. 13). Questions include whether travellers have had symptoms such as fever, headache, pain, vomiting, diarrhoea or unexplained bleeding or bruising in the past 48 hours; they must then complete a set of questions related to risk factors for contracting EVD, such as their exposure to bodily fluids of a person with EVD, whether they have provided direct care to or lived with an EVD patient, whether they have handled dead bodies, etc. (Centers for Disease Control and Prevention, 2014, p. 13). The visual assessment attempts to 'read' bodily appearance as a cipher for interior infectivity, and thus the likelihood of producing infectious vomit. Bodies are observed by staff to see if they visually present 'the symptoms and signs of disease that are consistent with Ebola' (Centers for Disease Control and Prevention, 2014, p. 4). In the absence of a strict list of criteria, we can assume staff are looking for anyone who 'looks sick' – perhaps sweating, visible bruising, retching, grimacing, appearing dazed, looking colourless – the potential visible risk factors stretch on.[4]

There are, of course, multiple body fluids that could act as infectious material here. However, I focus on vomit in particular as, out of all possible fluids, vomit is given the most explicit attention in these screening technologies, particularly in the questionnaire. Travellers must answer whether they themselves have vomited recently, or whether they have been 'splashed' or 'exposed' to the fluids of someone with EVD (Centers for Disease Control and Prevention, 2014, p. 13). We can locate the risk or threat here very specifically in the materialization of vomit. A body with EVD can quite literally project infectious disease into public space, threatening to contaminate other bodies with the virus. In order to prevent the spread of EVD, temperature checks, questionnaires and visual assessments attempt to 'see' inside the body, in order to ascertain and measure a body's potential for vomit. Vomit, therefore, comes to function within airport screening assemblages as a cipher for risk of infection.

In order to affect this governance, screening practices must produce vomit as something that *can* be seen, known, and contained, even prior to its materialization outside the body. These screening practices all engage in an attempt to visualized vomit; to bring forth that which is wrapped up within the body, to allow the eye to register its presence and 'see' the likelihood that it will emerge. As Cristina Masters argues, we live in an age where 'the eye dominates', and this particular security assemblage works to cement a relationship between 'vision and knowledge', and between vision and security (Masters, 2015, p. 220). In health screening practices, the techno-security gaze of screening assemblages aims to look within the body to assess its infectivity. Vomit stands in as a measure of this risk. Questionnaires, temperature checks and visual assessments are all ways in which the eye of the security agent (augmented by various technological 'eyes') attempts to *look at* vomit. In this moment of looking, this direction of visuality, there is also a particular relationship established with knowledge. To see the inside of the body, to visualize vomit and its potentiality, is simultaneously to be able to *know* the level of risk. Airport screening technologies function as the necessary 'condition[s]' for a visual 'apperception of the status of the [interior] ... body' (Brinkema, 2011, p. 65). Screening procedures therefore focus on identifying the potentiality of Ebola vomit, as their primary goal is to 'identify persons with possible symptoms of or risk of exposure to Ebola ... and to prevent them from further travel' (Centers for Disease Control and Prevention, 2014, p. 3). These screening procedures therefore enact a series of travel restrictions that aim to 'prevent the exportation' of Ebola, 'protect travellers and air crew', and 'foster [the] compliance' of 'exposed or symptomatic persons' (Centers for Disease Control and Prevention, 2014, p. 3).

These goals make clear that the purpose of screening procedures is to identify and remove bodies that have the potential to infect others. Noting this may seem obvious; but it is important to single out that the intent here is not primarily to identify ill travellers so that they can receive appropriate treatment. We could imagine other potential goals of screening: for example, to identify those at risk of the virus in order to provide targeted medical care and information about prevention. Instead, the focus here prioritizes 'surveillance, control and containment' as a management strategy (Nunes, 2016, p. 552). Screening technologies are not concerned with identifying which bodies *are* infected with the Ebola virus, but instead which bodies *could* infect others. Airport security practices that aim to inhibit the spread of EVD are therefore geared towards constraining and removing bodies that are considered a 'risk' in terms of their likelihood to produce Ebola vomit in the airport. It is the risk of Ebola vomit that screening technologies attempt to govern.

Once vomit is rendered a known object by screening technologies, it then becomes a material that can be contained. Vomit can be pinned down and fixed, measured and risk assessed and triaged. It becomes an object that can be ordered, rather than a disorderly and disruptive material. Visuality renders vomit a governable object. It is something that can then be pre-emptively restricted and sealed off from the general public. Failing the primary screening phase channels vomit into the secondary screening procedure. There, vomit meets a host of barriers intended to limit its spread beyond a single body: trained public health or medical staff, and a procedural chain that can lead to vomit being channelled away from the airport and into other spaces (Centers for Disease Control and Prevention, 2014, p. 5). Secondary screening procedures emerge as a way to govern vomit, to limit its mobility by channelling it into other, more easily quarantined and contained spaces.[5] Through screening technologies, the mobility of Ebola vomit can be restricted, and it can be made safe through referral and isolation procedures.

Racializing Ebola vomit

Before we can further unpack these screening assemblages, we need to understand how they connect to a wider historical assemblage of racializing/ racialized representations of EVD in Africa. This history continues to structure the encounter between security gaze, African body and vomit that emerges at the airport. Here, I turn to foundational cultural representations of Ebola in the West to unpack this representational landscape and its current affects.

White colonialism has often represented 'Africa' as the heart of darkness, an inscrutable and hostile landscape harbouring unknown dangers and threats (Bass, 1998). Ebola and Ebola vomit are also produced through these racializing/racialized discourses. Ebola is commonly represented in popular culture as leading to catastrophic haemorrhage, with sufferers dying as a result of spontaneous bleeding through the mouth, ears, eyes, etc. This representation is typified in Richard Preston's 1994 pornographic viral thriller *The Hot Zone: A Terrifying True Story* (Preston, 2014). Preston's work is significant for our discussion here, as the novel (a bestseller in its own right) and the various works it inspired, principally the 1995 medical disaster thriller *Outbreak*, were vital in introducing Ebola into American and Western European public consciousness in the mid-1990s (Haynes, 2002, p. 133; Joffe & Haarhoff, 2002, p. 956). *The Hot Zone* topped the *New York Times* bestseller list for 20 weeks, and *Outbreak* (featuring big name stars such as Morgan Freeman, Dustin Hoffman and Rene Russo, among others), grossed around US$188 million worldwide (Haase, 2007, p. 86; Joffe & Haarhoff, 2002, p. 956). Releases of both the original novel and *Outbreak* roughly coincided with a real-life outbreak of Ebola in Kikwit, Zaire (now the Democratic Republic of Congo), in which, out of 316 suspected cases of Ebola, 252 people died (Hall & Chapman, 2008, p. 448). The timing of panic-laden dramatizations of the Ebola virus alongside hundreds of EVD deaths led to the association of Ebola with a 'special dread' in the West (Ungar, 1998, p. 47).

The cultural legacy of Preston's novel can still be felt today, given its recent resurrection as a television miniseries of the same name (Uppendahl & Murphy, 2019). This was also accompanied by a companion documentary on the 2014 and 2019 Ebola outbreaks in West Africa entitled *Going Viral: Beyond the Hot Zone* (2019). These discourses of EVD continue to underpin Western fears and anxieties about the disease, and function as narrative frames in the interpretation and understanding of contemporary outbreak events (Joffe & Haarhoff, 2002; Kinsman, 2012). The special dread of Ebola that popular representations of the disease have inspired is undoubtedly related to the dramatization of what the death of an Ebola patient looks like, with 'the most grisly depictions of dying imaginable' often present in media narratives of EVD (Ungar, 1998, p. 46). Given its importance in establishing Ebola in the public consciousness, *The Hot Zone* in particular is worth interrogating further in this regard. The gruesome pleasure that Preston evidently takes in constructing his horror novel is significant for this discussion. The terror inspired by these gruesome, pornographic passages continues to permeate pop culture representations of the Ebola virus today, creating a discursive framing of EVD that centres body horror (Haynes, 2002; Schell, 1997; Weldon, 2001b).

Significantly, air travel and vomit merits special attention in *The Hot Zone*, when the book follows the journey of a man as he is infected with the virus:

> The airsickness bag fills up to the brim with a substance known as vomit negro, or the black vomit. The vomit is not really black; it is a speckled liquid of two colours, black and red, a stew of tarry granules

> mixed with fresh red arterial blood. It is hemorrhage [sic], and it smells like a slaughterhouse. The black vomit is loaded with virus. It is highly infective, lethally hot … [t]he bag is bulging and softening, threatening to leak. (Preston, 2014, p. 46)[6]

It is such cultural representations of Ebola that haunt contemporary scenes of the virus: chilling pandemic tales of spontaneous bodily combustion and the bloody, wet, oozing bodily substances that threaten to break down those who encounter them into a similar pulpy mess.[7] Crucially, these representations of Ebola are intensely racialized and heavily reliant upon discourses of anti-blackness. In this passage, a white man named Charles Monet has contracted EVD from a visit to a cave in a national park. In doing so, he becomes a 'host possessed by a life form', the pernicious Ebola virus that attempts to 'convert the host into itself' (Preston, 2014). The Ebola virus functions here as a predator, and a particularly African one at that. It is a stalking and prowling aggressor, a 'sentient being … capable of hunting and capturing prey' such as the innocent, white Charles Monet (Weldon, 2001b, p. 285).

This representation of EVD draws upon colonial Western imaginaries of Africa and African bodies as co-terminus with wildness, animalism and dangerous beasts (Haynes, 2002; Lynch, 1998; Murdocca, 2003; Ungar, 1998). The portrayal of the Ebola virus as a near sentient 'life form' (Preston, 2014, p. 45) is rooted in colonial imaginaries of African landscapes as populated by savage beasts, of which Ebola is one – a viral predator emerging from 'the last recesses of the wild' (Schell, 1997, p. 97). Even the naming of the Ebola virus (after the Ebola river, close to the location of the 1976 outbreak) links Ebola to a specifically African geography (Haynes, 2002, p. 139). Through these discourses, Ebola is positioned not just as a virus but as a particularly African virus. The fear of disease is wrapped up in notions of Africa and African bodies as natural reservoirs of disease and a danger to white colonial bodies (Lynch, 1998, p. 239). EVD is thus racialized through its incorporation into anti-African and anti-black colonial discourses, becoming a menacing predator that can come to prey upon white bodies.

That the vehicle of infection, the vomit from Ebola patients, is referred to by Preston as 'vomit negro' demonstrates to us that Ebola vomit is an assemblage that is compromised by bodies, viral disease, and narratives of anti-blackness. Not only is the vomit bloody, but it is blackened, the vomit negro. In the graphic scenes that Preston's novel creates, colour plays an important role. The blackness of the vomit mingles together with the red of blood, discursively linking blackness together with uncontrollable and uncontainable bleeding and generating a heavy affective sense of disgust and repulsion. The association of blackness and darkness here with sickness, disgust and the Ebola virus is made possible by colonial representations of Africa as a 'dark continent' of primitive and undiscovered disease and danger (Joffe & Haarhoff, 2002, p. 957). Notions of darkness/black as the colour of evil in comparison to the purity and virtue of light/white are deeply woven into European and North American culture and language, where 'the binarism of black and white might be called the originary language of racial difference' (Hall, 1995, p. 2). Issues of physical colour were hugely important to the white colonial mindset, where for white people 'the most Negro thing about the Negro was his blackness' and gradations of skin colour were used to assign slaves to particular roles (Jordan, 2012, p. 516). In representing Ebola vomit as visually black, Preston ties colonial racist discourses into the physical manifestation of EVD, rendering Ebola vomit black in a colourful and racializing/racist symbol. Ebola vomit is presented by Preston as a literal pooling of blackness upon the floor, the racialization of which can only be further cemented and rammed home through Preston's use of 'negro' as a description of darkness.

The representation of Ebola as 'natural' to the African landscape, and to black African bodies, is reflected in racist responses to the 2013–16 outbreak. Initial Western coverage of the outbreak highlighted 'bushmeat' as the key cause of Ebola, othering African diets and working to produce EVD again as an organically 'African' phenomenon, the result of unhygienic food consumption (Abeysinghe, 2016; Monson, 2017).[8] There were also numerous stigmatizing responses to black African bodies in the US in the wake of the Ebola outbreak. For example, Sarah Monson documents how a New Jersey elementary school proposed to subject two Rwandan children to three temperature checks a day for three weeks (Monson, 2017). This was a result of threats from teachers of refusing to work and from other parents that they would keep their children at home if these two children attended school, believing them to be at high risk of spreading EVD, despite the fact that Rwanda reported no Ebola cases (Monson, 2017). After a visit to Zambia (at least 3,000 miles away from the nearest confirmed Ebola cases) Lee Wannik, a principal at a school in Mississippi, agreed to take a week of leave after parents pulled their children out of school citing him as an Ebola risk (Culzac, 2014). High-school football player Ibrahim Toumkara, who had moved to Pennsylvania three years previously, had players from the opposing team at a football match chant 'Ebola' at him (Brandt, 2014). Despite having no direct or indirect contact with any Ebola patients, lacking even a physical proximity to the outbreak, being associated with 'Africa' at all was enough to generate fear of EVD. The associations drawn in these instances between Africa and black bodies with Ebola compounds the 'Africa is a place' narrative, and that Ebola is something that is a property of both Africa and black bodies – and one that can be passed on to others (Monson, 2017).

Security gazes

Now that we can see the historical racialization that has gone into the production of Ebola vomit, and the anxieties it provokes (specifically in North America), let us return to the airport. How does this fearsome fluid, the 'black vomit' of Ebola, come to be governed by security gazes? A queerfeminist curiosity requires us to think about the ways in which markers of bodily difference are produced through the interplay between multiple different axes of power; what else are these racist fears around Ebola vomit and African bodies tangled up in, and productive of?

It is important to remember that these screening technologies and security gazes at the airport are not neutral forms of technology and/or vision. Security gazes do not emerge from nowhere, but are produced by and productive of a scene that is steeped within gendered and colonial hierarchies. In this form of seeing-as-knowing, security technologies conduct a performance that is both racialized/racializing and gendered. Screening visualities are reliant upon the performance of the 'the god trick', a form of gaze that claims to be entirely objective and disembodied (Haraway, 1988). The vision deployed to 'see' vomit aims to emulate such a disembodied form of vision, where the gaze of technology (without a body, pure, rational) is directed towards and into a body. These forms of vision are made possible by masculinized discourses of science, which pursue gendered ideals of 'detached, objective, rational scientific mastery' (Franklin, 1995, p. 65). These masculinized screening gazes produce and present what they see as 'simply there' and 'utterly transparent' in its existence (Haraway, 1988). Screening assemblages create the eye of the non-contact thermometer, the questionnaire, and the screening agent as clinical and objective forms of biopolitical vision. The knowledge of risk that these gazes are imagined to produce (how likely this body is to vomit, how likely it is that this vomit is contaminated with the Ebola virus) is understood as simple, technical knowledge.

The god trick is, however, as feminist technoscience scholars have argued, an impossible ideal; the security and surveillance gaze is always already 'entangled in societal interests' (Åsberg & Lykke, 2010).[9] Screening gazes are grounded in social relations; they are not apart from them. In addition to the idea of looking-as-knowing, in this context we can understand looking as penetrating. The gaze of health screening technologies is increasingly focused not just on looking at the surface of bodies, but attempting to visualize and penetrate the *interior* of the body. These gazes attempt to seek out vomit within a space that is not immediately optically accessible to the human eye. These forms of visuality attempt to move inside the body, opening up biological matter to a security gaze. As the security gaze shifts its technological eye through and into the body, vomit is produced as visible and containable. In doing so, screening technologies make use of a particularly 'gendered erotic trope' of masculine discovery and movement into natural, hidden, feminine spaces (Haraway, 1991, p. 205). As this book has already argued, the body has historically been gendered in Western contexts as a feminized location. This is achieved through the positioning of the body within the feminized realm of 'nature', as opposed to the masculinized technological realm (Franklin, 1995). Following a queerfeminist curiosity leads us to see here that gender, race and coloniality are all forms of power at work in structuring and affecting the screening assemblage, and the bodies that must through it. Through a gendered dichotomy of space, the biological interior of the black African body is produced as a natural space, a closed and hidden biosphere. As long as it is closed to the gaze, this unknown space is imagined to seethe with hidden dangers and possibilities.

Black African bodies that emerge from this landscape are produced by airport screening practices as opaque containers that potentially harbour this dangerous Africanized vomit. Under screening protocols and technologies developed by the CDC, African travellers are therefore produced as 'opaque receptacle[s] … subject to rupture', a body that 'obscures its pathogenic contents but does not safely contain them' (Belling, 2016, p. 44). This movement of the security gaze into African bodies in order to discern whether they harbour the threatening vomit negro thus reinscribes the well-worn path of colonialism, in its attempt to penetrate and control African bodies and landscapes in order to protect the health of colonizers and assert the 'physical (and moral) well-being of the imperialists' (Bass, 1998, p. 431).

To know vomit and to secure against it requires opening this space, traversing into the body, and this journey to the interior resonates with highly gendered and colonial tropes of scientific discovery and of white masculinized conquest over native, virgin territories. The 'secret hidden insides of things' are laid bare for the masculine and colonial technological gaze (de Beauvoir, 1997, p. 208). Black African bodies shift from being imagined as closed, secretive and dangerous spaces to ones that have been penetrated and neutralized by the 'ordering mechanism' of Western technology (Franklin, 1995, p. 65). It is in this penetration that we can discern the erotics of this form of vision. As Haraway argues, the masculinized technological gaze 'fucks the world' in its looking (Haraway, 1988). The penetration of the body by security gazes reflects a similarly sexualized form of looking. The penetration and governance of these colonizing gazes generates control, and therefore safety, by rendering the possibility of racializing/racialized disease transmission 'known'. Through these security assemblages Ebola vomit, and by extension the threat posed by African bodies, can only be contained and secured through these forms of looking. In this penetration of the gaze, the interior of bodies is laid open to the colonization and governance of the body through Western screening technologies.

These practices together perform extremely important work for the production of Ebola vomit. Ebola vomit is produced as an object that *can* be controlled, channelled and restrained. It can be known and mastered through the application of masculinized technology: a box to be ticked on a questionnaire, a number on a thermometer, a bloodshot eye in a face in a queue. Once vomit is made known *before* it materializes outside of the body, the conditions of its materialization can then be selected to ensure minimum mobility on behalf of the vomit. Vomit emerges from this assemblage as something that can be bent to the will and mastery of scientific-security technologies; while it may not be prevented entirely, it can at least be channelled appropriately at the will of security agents. The ramifications this has for particular bodies are explored in the following section.

The racial politics of quarantine

How does this form of looking, this security gaze, impact relationships of life–death at the airport? And how is life–death distributed between bodies at an international level through the airport screening assemblage? In this section, I show that these security gazes (re)produce a distribution of life–death that attempts to incapacitate the mobility of African bodies in order to protect non-African bodies. Airport screening assemblages attempt to secure not only the bios of non-African bodies, but to secure them from the racializing effects of EVD.

Body boundaries and racial contagion

Despite the fears of vomiting Ebola bodies at the airport, there are very few incidents during which passengers vomited (and no documented instances in which a person with EVD vomited either at the airport or aboard a plane). Still, those handful of instances prompted a heavily securitized response. In October 2014, a passenger, who was reported to be a one-year-old child, vomited on a plane landing at McCarran Airport in Las Vegas; the child had been to the African continent, but not to any of the countries affected by the outbreak (Moore et al., 2014). Despite this, the plane was 'surrounded' by multiple ambulances on arrival (Lloyd & Arabian, 2014, para. 2). The image of the plane as 'surrounded' by emergency vehicles immediately conjures up the idea of a border erected around the plane, a medical seal intended to quarantine and stymy the movement of disease. In the Dominican Republic in the same month, a flight from the US was boarded by a 'hazmat' team after a vomiting passenger was reported to have said 'Hey, I've got Ebola, you're screwed' (Agence France-Presse, 2014, paras. 2–3). Those who were within proximity to the vomit were also subject to containment, remaining quarantined on the plane while 'checks were conducted' or until the vomiting risks (the ill travellers) had been removed (Moore et al., 2014, paras. 7–8; Reilly & Graaf, 2014, para. 26). In these instances, the vomit on board the aircraft became a national security threat. It prompted a response that centred on ideas of quarantine, of identifying and immediately shutting down the potential of vomit and vomiting bodies to move freely through national space.

As these stories demonstrate, the relationship between Ebola vomit and international air travel is crucial in situating EVD and Ebola vomit as a security threat to Western countries and populations. Airplanes magnify the infectious capabilities of Ebola vomit, transposing it to the level of entire national populations (Budd et al., 2009). EVD's mechanisms of infection are, in a sense, very limited – they require close and intimate contact and proximity with an EVD patient (unlike, for example, airborne viruses). But through the assemblage of air travel, the ability of Ebola vomit to connect bodies is magnified on a far grander scale, as the airplane facilitates close contact between vomit and numerous different bodies within a closed environment. It is vomit's entanglement with the airplane that produces it as hypermobile. The airplane enables vomit to be produced as a national security threat to countries that may otherwise count themselves at a safe distance from Ebola. Understanding Ebola vomit's production as threatening Africanized matter allows us to see how Ebola vomit is produced as a hypermobile racialized threat.

Within these discourses, Ebola vomit becomes a threat that must be secured against as it is not simply disease that is crossing international borders, but 'Africa' itself. As this chapter has argued, both Ebola vomit and virus are racialized within the West as black African matter and agent, respectively. Contact with Ebola vomit is therefore constructed as having the ability to Africanize other bodies, through transmission of the EVD virus. Produced as racialized matter, Ebola vomit can form connections between bodies, put bodies into relation with each other. Biological material is transferred and communicated between bodies through Ebola vomit, in the form of the replication and exchange of the Ebola virus itself. Within the logics of the racialization of Ebola, these relationships of connection therefore also transfer racialized material between and into bodies.

It is pertinent here to return to Preston's graphic passage in *The Hot Zone* in order to illustrate the imagined dangers of Ebola vomit within airport contexts. In falling victim to Ebola, Preston produces Charles Monet as transformed by his infection into something less than human, a walking manifestation of the animalistic EVD that forces white bodies to spew 'vomit negro'. In his infection and subsequent vomiting, the lines between 'sociability and animality' are blurred, which here is a profoundly racialized process (Isaksen, 2002, p. 803). Within Western cultures, the idealized (white masculine) body and subject are produced through the maintenance of 'rigid and absolute' boundaries between the body, the external world, and Other bodies (Martin, 1992, p. 126). White bodies that maintain these clear lines of demarcation are proper, pure bodies that are unpolluted by the contaminating stuff of Others (Douglas, 2002). In falling ill and vomiting, the figure of Charles Monet in *The Hot Zone* represents the ways in which Ebola patients are figured as bodies that threaten and transgress this social order. In failing to uphold Western ideals of selfhood that demand the exercise of control over a neatly bounded body, Charles Monet is marked not only as not-West but also as a degree of not-human. His body vomits and falls apart while he is unable to exert control over this process (Waskul & van der Riet, 2002, p. 495). In failing to achieve this mastery of self over body, mind over matter, he falls short of Western standards of personhood. These Western ideals of personhood therefore produce Charles Monet, and Ebola patients like him, as unable to maintain the white and proper 'corporeal capacity for self-containment' (Lawton, 1998, p. 136). In failing to meet white Western expectations of personhood, Ebola victims are therefore produced as less human and instead as a 'host' or vehicle for Africanized EVD. EVD patients are thus not portrayed in such narratives as suffering people, but rather dehumanized as 'objects of horror that can infect any who ... come into contact with them' (Bass, 1998, p. 442).

The vomit negro is produced as being able to come into contact with, and transform, white Western bodies through viral transmission. Coming into contact with Ebola vomit is therefore constructed as a racializing experience. Regardless of skin colour, the body that comes into contact with Ebola vomit is then seen as at risk of being possessed by the Ebola virus. Like Charles Monet, white bodies that come into contact with the vomit negro are produced as at risk of becoming the embodiment of this Africanized virus, transformed into something less than human and at risk of similarly contaminating others with EVD. Ebola vomit is therefore not only produced as racialized matter, but as racializing matter. Within Western discourses it is produced as having the potential to take over and transform bodies through transmission of the Africanized virus via the 'vomit negro'. This is a profoundly violent and racist production of Ebola vomit, which works to (re)inscribe racial binaries that produce blackness and Africa as unhygienic and dangerous to white Western bodies.

The transportation of this racialized matter via air travel therefore challenges both individual bodily boundaries as well as the differentiation between 'the West' and 'Africa'. Ebola vomit becomes a symbol for the literal 'bleeding out' of Africa into the West (Lynch, 1998, p. 241). The 'decadent emanations' of African bodies that Ebola vomit represents are transposed to spaces 'inside' Western and North American countries through assemblages of Ebola vomit and air travel (Haraway, 1991, p. 223). This is produced as threatening 'white [Western] manhood' through the contamination of 'cities, civilization, the family, [and] the white personal body' with 'African' biological material (Haraway, 1991, p. 223). It is this purity of these boundaries that are seen as at risk in regards to EVD. Ebola vomit is constructed as threatening the whiteness of both national space and body with being 'infiltrated and penetrated by savages', with EVD itself occupying the place of the African antagonist (Lynch, 1998, p. 235). Ebola vomit therefore prompts highly securitized responses precisely because it is produced as a threat to whiteness, portending the 'third-worlding' of the (imagined) whiteness of Western space and bodies (King, 2002, p. 773). Ebola vomit signifies a potentially lethal transformative experience for Western bodies. To be put into relationship with African-ness in this way risks death. This representation masks the continuing brutal reality that, for many black Africans and black Americans, it is white bodies that have consistently posed a lethal threat to black bodies; from the thousands abducted, tortured and killed by systems of slavery and settler colonialism, to the lives claimed by continued individual and institutionalized violence (hooks, 1987; Krieger, 2016; Pulido, 2016; Spillers, 1987; Weheliye, 2014).

By shifting the experience of Ebola from 'African' to 'Western' bodies, Ebola vomit is imagined to create one-directional connections between these two groups, and connections between their interior biological landscapes. Through these connections, the imagined hard border of the Western body is shown to be porous, to be penetrable. Western bodies can catch Ebola too. They are equally vulnerable to these forms of 'African' diseases in a way that skin colour does not mitigate. Ebola vomit does not discriminate between white and black bodies. That everyone can catch Ebola and die throws the racial differentiation between black African and white Western bodies into uncertainty, as Ebola moves into and across bodies regardless. That there is no biological distinction between the colour of a patient's skin and their compatibility with the virus points towards the ways in which 'race' is a socially constructed term, rather than one rooted in objective biological 'fact'. Within the context of the racialization of Ebola vomit, airport screening assemblages are therefore attempting to secure not only the biological life of the global North but also racialized modes of living, through attempts to protect and insulate white Western bodies from infection. If Ebola is an African disease that only affects African bodies, then the vulnerability of bodies to each other can be denied and racialized modes of living can be maintained through the reinstantiation of racial binaries. Ebola vomit, however, reveals the fragility of 'race' as a way of differentiating bodies.

In order to sustain 'race' as a category of bodily differentiation, then, airport screening practices reproduce logics that racialize West African transmission of the virus as natural. These screening practices attempt to confine Ebola vomit to black African bodies, and prevent it from coming into contact with white Western spaces. Through limiting the movement of black African bodies and attempting to ensure transmission does not occur within the global North, airport screening assemblages reinforce discourses that figure Ebola's existence within West Africa as natural. In turn, the wider racialization of Ebola vomit that screening assemblages reinforce serves to protect race as a form of bodily differentiation, ensuring the white bodies outside West Africa remain free from the disease. In doing so, the fiction that Ebola vomit is the property of black African bodies can be maintained, drawing attention away from the equal susceptibility of all racialized bodies to EVD, and legitimizing increased surveillance and governance of African bodies. The racialization of Ebola vomit renders race meaningful as a quantifier of risk and threat, and a form of threat that can then be governed and controlled through airport screening technologies.

Quarantining African bodies

The surveillance of vomit through airport screening assemblages reflects and reproduces a geopolitical hierarchy of life–death, in which the lives of the global North are prioritized over and against those in the global South. In the case of EVD and airport screening in particular, the lives of those in Western Europe and Northern America are privileged over the lives of West Africans. This hierarchy of living is reflected in the fact that the concern for bodies expressed in screening procedures does not revolve around a duty of care for the infected person. Screening assemblages do not primarily aim to identify and treat ill persons. Rather, the duty of care expressed here is for those not yet infected: the bodies at the other end of the plane journey. Possible Ebola patients were not allowed to travel to other countries lest they infect other populations. They were important within screening assemblages not because they were 'infec*ted*, but because they are infec*ting*' (Waldby, 1996, p. 107). Screening procedures necessitate questions around whose lives are arranged into a relational hierarchy of value, and who benefits from this arrangement at the expense of others. Through airport health screening practices, the lives of those already infected with Ebola are affirmed as less valuable than the lives of those that have yet to be infected. Under these logics, '[i]nfection in less valuable bodies does not count as infection, except in so far as they threaten to infect more valuable bodies' (Waldby, 1996, p. 105). The identification of vomit-potential at the airport is conducted in the service of quarantine, of halting chains of movement and relationship between bodies.

The logic that underpins this quarantine response is based on a profoundly racist hierarchy of life and worth. This hierarchy is further supported by colonial power dynamics. The naturalization of the West African EVD pandemic works to render invisible the conditions that made the pandemic possible. This obscures both historical and contemporary colonial practices that work to reproduce and maintain these hierarchies of living and dying. This chapter has already shown how the EVD pandemic is produced as a natural phenomenon, one that results from the unhygienic and diseased landscapes/cultures of 'Africa', and how this narrative is the result of 'legacies of imperialism and colonialism in which "tropicality" is associated with disease' (Ali et al., 2016). Such racist and colonialist narratives arguably helped to stunt international responses to 'yet another African plague'. They also worked to obscure the important role that colonial legacies of exploitation, poverty, development, urbanization, neoliberal governance and climate change played in creating the necessary conditions for such large-scale transmission of the disease and loss of life (Ali et al., 2016; Nunes, 2016). That the largest EVD outbreak since the disease was discovered spread so rapidly and quickly through West Africa, when previous outbreaks had remained relatively isolated in comparison, is testament to the ways in which people in West Africa were made vulnerable and susceptible to the spread of EVD. The virus itself has not radically changed its mode of transmission since 1976. But the conditions for wide-scale transmission, the factors necessary to produce those living in Liberia, Sierra Leone and Guinea as particularly vulnerable to a large-scale outbreak of EVD, have political origins.

It is outside the scope of this book to provide a full analysis of West African countries' responses to the pandemic. Looking briefly at the (colonial) relations of mistrust, however, serves as a valuable illustration of how Guinean, Liberian and Sierra Leonian populations were made vulnerable to EVD. Health interventions during the outbreak in some areas were met with extreme hostility. This was most notably displayed in the killing of eight government employees in Womme, Guinea. The workers were attempting to raise awareness of EVD and infection-control practices, before being killed by local residents (Dixon, 2014; see also Kinsman, 2012). Crucially, Benton and Dionne's research counters colonial framings of this hostility as 'backward' or natural to West African communities, instead arguing that people were 'unsurprisingly' mistrustful of the sudden descent of workers in hazmat suits removing the bodies of their deceased loved ones (Benton & Dionne, 2015, p. 228). Benton and Dionne's work traces how the legacy of transatlantic slavery and colonial governance has generated levels of mistrust between publics and governments along the west coast of Africa (2015). The authors draw attention to the histories of mistrust that rendered some populations particularly hostile towards government and international NGO advice around Ebola, such as the cessation of burial practices that involve washing and dressing the bodies of deceased family at home. Drawing attention to the very real and remembered violence of colonial governance situates local residents' hostility within a context of ongoing racialized violence and intervention. When viewed in light of hundreds of years of white atrocities against black Africans, beliefs that Ebola could be (in the words of a local police officer) 'an invention of white people to kill black people' is far from illogical (Dixon, 2014, para. 6). Benton and Dionne argue that it is vital to remember that colonial powers during the smallpox and flu outbreaks of World War I introduced aggressive methods of surveillance and higher taxation, and these legacies of violence and surveillance inform a variety of mistrustful and antagonistic responses to government advice in the context of EVD (Benton & Dionne, 2015). This mistrust of public authorities is only one example of how people's vulnerability to EVD is rooted in colonial histories. Other authors have pointed to the International Monetary Fund's structural adjustment programmes, international donors' preferences for vertical rather than horizontal health programmes, and widespread poverty to explain a lack of effective healthcare infrastructure to respond to the epidemic, as well as the inability of many people in affected countries to access healthcare resources and follow guidelines (Benton & Dionne, 2015; Kapiriri & Ross, 2020; Nunes, 2016).

Understanding how EVD deaths have been naturalized through colonial discourses matters when assessing how relations of life–death are governed through airport screening practices. It matters because it allows us to make sense of these practices within an international colonial terrain that has systematically prioritized the 'life' of the West at the expense of African lives and bodies. It is vital to understand airport security assemblages within a setting of the incapacitation of African bodies in order to understand how three West African countries along the 'slave coast' have been systematically put at risk in regards to a global pandemic, and how the 'precarity' of these bodies and communities has been produced and maintained (Puar, 2017b, p. xvii). The violence of this history also extends into the future, rendering future outbreaks and deaths likely as the political and economic accelerants of the outbreak (and colonial complicity in these structures) are neglected by international responses. These broader colonial discourses are at work in producing security assemblages that attempt to govern the mobility of African people internationally. The (re)production of plague stories that locate Africa as a global exporter of disease easily becomes 'a call for the global policing of African places, people and cultures' (Lynch, 1998, p. 249). This contributes to an international distribution of life–death by legitimizing the deaths of African bodies from EVD as natural, concealing the political agency that made these deaths possible. This legitimizes airport screening assemblages that attempt to secure Ebola vomit in order to protect lives in the global North.

Not only is political agency and antecedent concealed by this attempt to curtail the movement of infectious bodies; but it is also important that we point out that this curtailing of movement, this quarantining of infectious potential, impacts the mobility of black African bodies to a much greater extent than it does white Western bodies. Take the disparity in screening procedures that led to Pauline Cafferkey, a white nurse returning from working at an Ebola treatment centre in Sierra Leone, being allowed to take and record her own temperature (incorrectly) at Heathrow airport. Through collusion with two of her colleagues, despite having a slight fever, Cafferkey was able to record her temperature as normal (BBC News, 2016a, 2016c, 2017). The lack of surveillance levelled at Cafferkey's white female body – despite her fever and the fact she was at a high risk of contracting the disease – stands in stark contrast to practices at West African airports. Pauline Cafferkey was able to evade measures ostensibly designed to quarantine vomit-potential, by virtue of being a white Western medical professional. She was considered to be a more trustworthy, more honest, more reliable body. She was entrusted to take and report her own temperature. Cafferkey was positioned as a participant of airport screening technologies, and operator of such measures; she was not subject/object to the screening gaze. She was allowed to look, rather than to be simply looked at.

This is in stark contrast to many civilian travellers, and black African travellers, who passed through airports during the pandemic. As already noted, at Lungi airport in Sierra Leone, travellers were required to pass four temperature checks that were administered by medically trained staff (Robert Koch Institut, n.d., para. 10). That Pauline Cafferkey was trusted to assess her own vomit risk while West African travellers were not demonstrates that not all bodies are seen as posing a risk to others. The white body of Pauline Cafferkey, in the freedom she was allowed to assess herself, is a body that is deemed safe, honest, and low risk. In sharp contrast, the bodies of black West Africans become hyper visible within airport screening assemblages. They become uniquely 'trap[ped] as public/publicized representational forces' that are made to symbolize the threat of Ebola vomit (Sjoberg, 2012, p. 345) and, as such, become subject to increased attention and governance. Surveillance of bodies within these screening assemblages is premised upon gendered and racialized attempts to open up the interiors of black bodies to white colonial gazes, in order to inspect them and produce a determination on whether they are 'safe' or not (Belling, 2016; Browne, 2015). It is West African bodies that are produced through these assemblages as needing the greatest degree of exterior surveillance. These invasive forms of gaze are not only violent in and of themselves, but produce supposed scientific justification for limiting the movements of particular African peoples in the name of global health.

Conclusion

Following Ebola vomit – and the spectre of it – through the airport demonstrates to us that race and gender are vital in understanding security assemblages. This chapter has shown that airport screening technologies represent attempts to see within the body, in an attempt to produce and then govern Ebola vomit. Security technologies are reliant upon gendered and racialized gazes that attempt to penetrate black African bodies in order to govern them, in an attempt to confine Ebola vomit to West Africa. Such governance revolves not only around an attempt to secure life in the global North against Ebola vomit, but also to secure racialized modes of living. Airport security assemblages therefore perpetuate discourses that reinstantiate race as a meaningful form of bodily differentiation. Airport screening technologies are complicit with colonial discourses that position Ebola vomit as a racial threat to the West, an agent of dissolution and, as such, considerable security resources are directed towards it.

Chapter 5 of this book turns towards a fluid whose mobility is, in contrast to Ebola vomit, heavily encouraged by security agents, as long as it is mobilized in certain directions. It explores the movements of semen through military-medical assemblages in the case of US soldiers with genitourinary injuries. If Ebola vomit threatens a racialized reordering of relationships of life–death between bodies, the next chapter asks after the ways in which semen is used to secure the lives of particular security bodies through sexed and gendered relationships.

5

Securing Cisheterosexuality: Semen and Genitourinary Injuries*

So far, previous chapters have examined the securitized politics of plasma and vomit; now it is time to turn our attention to our final fluid of the book. In this chapter, I focus on semen, specifically the semen of US service members who have suffered genitourinary injuries (GUIs).

Between 2001 and 2013, 1,462 US service members were identified as having a GUI (Reed et al., 2018). As a result of Operation Enduring Freedom (OEF) and Operation Iraqi Freedom (OIF), there is a common discourse of an 'unprecedented increase' in the prevalence of GUIs for military personnel (Reed et al., 2018, p. 306). It may well be the case that these types of injury are not new, but surviving them is, thanks to advances in medical technologies and treatment procedures (Hudak et al., 2005, p. 1041). Regardless, the US Department of Defense (DoD) and various branches of the military have paid increasing attention to GUIs. The US Army Medical Research and Materiel Command have sponsored the ongoing Trauma Outcomes and Urogenital Health project (with the fittingly masculine acronym TOUGH). GUIs are also now included as a specific focus under the Armed Forces Institute of Regenerative Medicine's second programme (AFIRM II).

The vast majority of service members with GUIs are men; of the 1,462 service members with GUIs noted previously, only 20 of these service members were women. This is unsurprising as during both OEF and OIF women were barred from active combat roles, and vastly outnumbered by male service members (Reed et al., 2018). The prevalence of improvised explosive devices (IEDs) during OEF/OIF was responsible for a large share

---

* An abridged version of this chapter originally appeared in the journal *Review of International Studies*, as: Hobbs, J. 'Capacitating militarised masculinity: Genitourinary injuries, sex/sexuality, and US military medicine', *Review of International Studies* pp. 1–9. Copyright [2022] (Jennifer Hobbs). DOI: [10.1017/S0260210522000560].

of GUI injuries (Williams & Jezior, 2013, p. 503). IEDs create a blast pattern that radiates upwards and outwards from devices that are often located at ground level, placing the external genitalia, lower limbs and the abdomen at particular risk of injury (Williams & Jezior, 2013, p. 503). Medical staff and service members report that the status of the external genitalia is often the first thing injured service members ask about (Williams & Jezior, 2013). It is reported of one service member with a GUI, awakening from an impact blast, and realizing both his legs had been severed above the knee, that his first words were 'Hey! Check my nuts! [sic]' (Wood, 2012, para. 21). In a (very) small-scale study of service members with extensive GUIs, out of the 13 service members questioned, eight described their GUIs as having a greater impact on their lives than losing one or both legs, given that viable prosthetic options are available for missing limbs, but not for GUIs (Lucas et al., 2014). This suggests that GUIs (and specifically genital injuries) are more feared among service members than other types of severe injury (Grady, 2018; Williams & Jezior, 2013). GUIs can impact toileting and sexual function, as well as causing wider damage to the identity of the service member, and are often framed as 'spiritually and emotionally debilitating' injuries (Recovering Warrior Task Force US Department of Defense, 2013, p. 221).

Making use of media representations of GUI treatments and documents from the DoD, the Veterans Association, and medical treatment programmes, I argue that the US military makes a substantial investment in governing semen. Treatments for GUIs attempt to regulate semen, and thus the bodies of service members, in normative gendered and sexed frames. The governance of semen is therefore vital in these settings to the naturalization of the US cisgender and heterosexual male body; this happens at the expense of queer, trans, Afghan and Iraqi lives and bodies. This chapter follows a queerfeminist curiosity to unpeel the interlocking layers of gender, sex, sexuality and race that position bodies in different places both within (and outside) treatment assemblages.

This chapter begins by arguing that, through binary logics of sex/gender, service members with GUIs are produced as ambiguously sexed/gendered bodies in need of 'fixing'. I then look at how this 'fix' is performed through the governance of seminal capacity in transplant and fertility treatments. Such treatments perpetuate a violent distribution of life–death, whereby cishetero male bodies are produced as the only 'true' possessors of seminal capacity, and thus of the phallus. This production of cismale bodies as 'natural' is achieved through the debilitation of queer and trans bodily possibilities. I then turn to explore the racialized and internationalized politics of seminal capacity, attempting to track these injuries through Iraqi and Afghan civilian and military populations. Finally, I reflect on the significance of the military body's seminal capacity to the politics of militarism writ large in the US.

GUIs, trauma and emasculation

GUIs are often experienced as incredibly traumatic injuries by service members, but the specific psychological impacts of these forms of injury have not yet been fully explored in the wider literature (Lucas et al., 2014; Villareal et al., 2021; Wain et al., 2017; Wilcox et al., 2015a). However, preliminary research does indicate higher rates of post-traumatic stress disorder (PTSD), depression and suicidal behaviours in service members with GUIs (Wilcox et al., 2015b). I argue that part of the reason GUIs can have such an injurious effect on the psyche is because the penis has been constructed as central to masculinity, and any injury to the genitals therefore has the potential to trouble the subject's gender identity. As feminist scholars have taught us, normative and binary gender identities are one of the primary ways in which the subject comes into being, acquiring a sense of self and becoming legible as 'human' to others (Butler, 2010; Nash, 2010). Losing access to a gender identity that is recognized and legitimized by others can be a profoundly traumatic process for the subject.

GUIs can challenge a service member's sense of self and masculine identity by damaging the key physical attribute that is often understood as 'making' them a man. It is impossible to understand gender, sex and sexuality in isolation from each other here. The link between gender, sex and genitalia is so strong that these terms are used as if they were synonymous with each other . This is true of both popular culture and scientific literatures, which portray particular genitals as 'male' and 'female', something which trans, intersex and (some) feminist scholars have worked to challenge (Callahan, 2009; Hird, 2000; Serano, 2007; Turner, 1999; Westbrook & Schilt, 2013). Even the language we have developed to discuss these experiences and wounds points towards the symbolic merging of masculinity with the penis. The physical process of losing the penis and testes is referred to as 'emasculation', a word that joins together the Latin for 'change of state' and 'male'. Thus, to lose the penis through a GUI (whether it is total loss of the organ itself or loss of penile function) is understood as a change to maleness, to masculinity itself. This is a view commonly held among medical providers; in a survey of doctors, gender identity and sexual function were rated as the most important functions of the penis (Najari et al., 2018). The genitalia are so central to constructions of gender and sex that sustaining damage to the penis or scrotum is also to sustain a rupture to masculinity, disqualifying the body from being able to achieve the 'normal' masculine shape.

The refrain that these injuries stop men from feeling like men is common across literatures and media reporting on genital injury (BBC News, 2016b; Grady, 2015, 2018; Hendershot, 2018; Massachusetts General Hospital, n.d.; Myrttinen, 2018; Wilcox et al., 2015b; Williams & Jezior, 2013). A service member who received a penis transplant in 2018 reported that his

GUI had left him struggling to view himself 'as a man' (Grady, 2018, para. 6). The crisis these injuries commonly portend for male subjects are also frequently acknowledged by members of their medical teams, who emphasize how these injuries wound gendered embodiments, damaging the physical (genital) seat of 'your sense of self and identity as a male' (Grady, 2015, para. 17). In a social world where the penis and testes are the materialization of masculinity upon the body, with the penis in particular functioning as 'a symbol of masculinity *par excellence*', GUIs lead to a fracture within both body and sense of self (Caso, 2017, p. 223). As a doctor reported, '[t]hey say, "I want to feel whole again" … [i]t's very hard to imagine what it means if you don't feel whole' (Grady, 2015, para. 36). It is genitalia, in particular, that damages a sense of wholeness, more so than other body parts; As the 2018 transplant recipient noted, despite having to have both of his legs amputated as a result of his injuries, it was the penis transplant that restored this sense of 'wholeness' to his body (Rinkunas, 2018; see also Lucas et al., 2014).

Some scholars have suggested that service members (particularly younger service members) may be especially vulnerable to feelings of a loss of masculinity following a GUI (Williams & Jezior, 2013). Decades of feminist work has unpacked the ways in which militaries and the process of military training relies heavily on hyper-masculinized ideals, fetishizing bodily strength, hardness, and heterosexual virility (Adelman, 2007; Arkin & Dobrofsky, 1978; Dyvik & Greenwood, 2016; Welland, 2013; Williams, 1994). GUIs threaten to disqualify soldiers permanently from being able to occupy corporeal fantasies of the hetero-masculine soldier through the loss of the phallus. Not only is the damage to the genitalia extremely symbolic in and of itself, but GUIs threaten men's ability to perform a range of masculine bodily activities. These activities centre on the capacity of the penis: urinating standing up, maintaining erections, ejaculation, having penetrative sex and fathering children. All these masculine bodily capacities are potentially disrupted by GUIs. This can leave service members with feelings of both physical and social emasculation, where they are no longer able to fulfil the corporeal roles and bodily expectations that are associated with masculinity and maleness (Myrttinen, 2018). Bodies with GUIs lack the affirming hardness of the stiff phallus; the power to penetrate, the hard bodily borders that the idealized phallus signals (Höpfl, 2003; Linstead, 2000; Potts, 2000; Stephens, 2007). GUIs thus come to function as a mode of castration whereby phallic power is lost through loss of the penis. This can be seen in the comments of a urological surgeon who describes service members with GUIs as having lost 'everything they have' (Grady, 2015, para. 17). The penis is, under dominant hetero-masculine logics, everything. It signifies masculine power and serves as the justification for that power. Without it, service members and men have nothing left. They experience the 'humiliation' of loss of control over the phallus (Stephens, 2007, p. 91).

As a result, the masculinity and gender/sex of these bodies is less certain. It is not so simple as claiming that these bodies are feminized – rather, they are 'reconfigured as "rootless, dismembered"' by their GUIs, thrust into sex/gender ambiguity (Weber, 1999, p. 131). Bodies with GUIs thus exist in a limbo of signification, where the loss of the phallus is co-morbid with a softening of the body's sexually invested shape. Frequently produced by those experiencing a GUI and their attendant medical teams as being not quite a man, service members '[g]endered anatomies' become 'hard to decipher' (Cavanagh, 2013, p. 433). They 'upset' binary logics of sex (Shepherd & Sjoberg, 2012, p. 11). GUIs challenge their gendered and sexed claim to being a recognizably 'human' subject, a recognizably 'human' life.

As feminist, queer and trans scholarship has argued, conforming to dominant norms of personhood requires us to conform to binary understandings of sex/gender that privilege cisgender subjects/bodies (Butler, 2011; Spade, 2003; Turner, 1999). For service members with GUIs, semen and the phallus are vital in producing recognizable forms of human life. In failing to possess either of these capacities, service members with GUIs float outside of dominant sex/gender identities. In the next section, I argue that treatments for GUIs attempt to restore the phallus through the restoration of ejaculation and seminal capacity. The restoration of seminal capacity to the body aims to reinscribe the bodies of service members with 'gender certainty' and secure their masculine corporeality (Shepherd & Sjoberg, 2012, p. 10).

'Fixing' GUIs

As we can see, service members with GUIs are produced as fractured bodies, requiring medical intervention to render them whole again. So, how does this 'fixing' happen? And how does semen enter the picture here? This section looks at the governance of seminal capacity as a way to 'fix' GUIs.

It is not just the penis that is vital to masculinity – it is what the penis can do. To unravel the relationship between genitals, semen and masculinity, we need to talk about ejaculation. Semen and ejaculation have long been vital to hegemonic masculinities; semen, the ejaculative act, and *control* of semen have often been used to represent the phallic power of male bodies (Johnson, 2010, p. 238; Khan et al., 2008; Moore, 2002). In Western European contexts, the relationship between semen and masculinity has historically portrayed semen as the wellspring of masculinity, literally producing it. Men who were not able to control their expression of semen, or who wasted it during masturbation, were often depicted as weak and febrile as a result of losing the fluid that was understood as enlivening man with manly vigour (Stephens, 2008; Tuck, 2003). The 'ability to ejaculate, the quantity of semen produced, and the forcefulness of … ejaculation' is therefore crucial for performances of the 'hegemonic masculine ideal' (Johnson, 2010, p. 241).

This masculinity-affirming semen is often represented as a powerfully creative force, a 'high valued' fluid that contains the seed of life in contrast to the inert, passive matter of the ovum (see also Grosz, 1994, p. 199; Linstead, 2000, pp. 33–34; Martin, 1992, pp. 121–122).

Of course, there are caveats, as the way in which ejaculation happens, and who it happens in conjunction with, are vital for the relationship between masculinity and ejaculation. But when ejaculation is expressed according to dominant heterosexist logics (during sex between a man with a penis and a woman with a vagina) semen can function as 'proof' of the presence of the phallus, of masculine power (see also Cook, 2005; Khan et al., 2008; Tuck, 2003, p. 268). Ejaculation happens only because of the ultimate 'prestige of manliness', a functional penis, and semen thus comes to act as a material referent for the phallus, a physical proof of its existence (Khan et al., 2008, p. 42).

Enabling and ensuring service members can therefore produce and express semen is important to maintain the militarized masculinity of service members. This is something the US military takes seriously, as we can see in its financial investment in seminal/ejaculative treatments. We can see a consistent pattern of military investment in this area beyond treatment specifically for GUIs. In 2015, the Defense Health Agency spent around US$84 million on erectile dysfunction medicines, US$41 million of which was on Viagra (Kime, 2015). While this makes up less than 1 per cent of the Defense Health Agency's spend for that fiscal year, it is worth noting that it dwarfs the estimated costs of US$2.3–8.4 million associated with providing healthcare to trans service members, an expense that a former president decried as constituting a 'tremendous' amount, citing as a reason to ban trans servicemembers from the military (Gereben Schaefer et al., 2016; Ingraham, 2017). Drugs classed as 'genitourinary agents' rank 13th in terms of TRICARE's (the programme that provides healthcare for active service members) top drugs by days of supply, and 7th for the Veterans Health Agency (which provides healthcare for veterans); Viagra is TRICARE's 15th most supplied single source active ingredient, and the VHA's 9th (Mulcahy et al., 2021, pp. 14–15). Investment in the seminal capacity of soldiers is also not uncommon outside the US. Jasbir Puar's work on the Israeli military points to the ways in which the seminal 'capacitation' of soldiers through reproductive services supports broader assemblages of militarism (2017b, p. 117). Fitting penis transplants surgeries within a wider context of military governance of soldiers' genitals demonstrates that the establishment of seminal function is vital to the military, as it works to secure militarized masculinities through establishing a clear sense of sex/gender to service members' bodies.

It is important here to note that it is the symbolic potential of semen that is being governed under existing treatment options. This point is vital in order to understand how semen is governed through the curation of bodily capacity. For instance, the ejaculation of semen may still be impossible following transplant surgeries, depending on which tissues the service member has lost, as penis transplants do not currently include the transplantation of donor testicles (Johns Hopkins Medicine, 2018). But it is the curation of ejaculative *potential* that these surgeries aim to restore, in order to (re)masculinize the bodies of service members. Biopolitical forms of power are regimes of governance that are primarily concerned with risk, the governance of possibility and potentiality of biological life and matter (Clough, 2016; Kienscherf, 2011). We can understand biopolitical power therefore as a selective bodily 'capacitation machine' (Puar, 2017b, p. xviii) As Martin notes, under biopolitical regimes of governance, the governed object 'need not be present to be *felt* as real' (2010, p. 28). Biopolitical military-medical assemblages are therefore concerned with the governance of seminal capacity, the possibility and potential for these bodies to perform as if they *do* possess semen, regardless of whether semen *is* physically present. Semen still matters, as the logics of both/and a queerfeminist curiosity pushes it to see; it can be both absent and present at the same time. It is the masculine symbolism of semen that is governed through these treatment options. Treatment assemblages revolve around the production of seminal capacity.

There are two key ways in which the bodies of service members are produced as having seminal capacity. Firstly, through penis transplant surgeries, which attempt to produce soldiers as capable of ejaculation and therefore capable of expressing semen; it is both form and function that is the goal here, as medical providers aim to restore/preserve 'spontaneous erection and orgasm' to service members (Grady, 2018, para. 11). It is the ability to perform the motions of ejaculation that is the ideal goal of these transplant surgeries. Whether semen is actually produced/expressed or not is secondary to the ability to mimic ejaculation. The pantomime of ejaculation is often positioned as synonymous with orgasm. As Lisa Moore argues, ejaculation and the materialization of semen is often taken as 'irrefutable evidence' of men's sexuality and confirmation of orgasm (2008, p. 72). This treatment option attempts to govern the mode of seminal capacity, regulating semen by producing the conditions for it to exit the body 'normally'. The penis here functions as an essential pre-condition for the possibility of semen. It is the performance of semen that is crucial here, and it is the ability to ejaculate, or achieve ejaculative mimicry, that transplant surgeries attempt to restore. These transplant surgeries attempt to 'fix' service members with GUIs, through the production of seminal capacity. Through the restoration of seminal capacity via erection and ejaculation, these surgeries work to reaffirm 'the "natural" possibilities for male bodies … that injured bodies need to be made whole and functional again in order to be and perform a whole and functional manhood' (Hendershot, 2018).

The second type of treatment that may be offered to service members with GUIs are fertility treatments. Fertility treatments attempt to produce seminal capacity within service members through facilitating reproduction. This second treatment option attempts to govern the effect of seminal capacity, allowing the body to perform as if it were capable of reproductive heterosexual ejaculation. Fertility treatments attempt to produce service members' bodies as in possession of semen, and as fertile, regardless of how this semen achieves fertilization. Whereas transplant surgeries aim to govern and regulate semen's means of exiting the body, fertility treatments revolve around capacitation through the governance of relationships between bodies. The focus here is on facilitating seminal relationships between the bodies of service members and their partners, producing seminal capacity through reproductive abilities.

Governing semen: transplants and fertility

So, what do these two treatment options set in motion, when it comes to relationships of life–death? In the next section of this chapter, I examine these two treatment pathways in greater depth. Firstly, I argue that surgeries naturalize cisgender male bodies in opposition to trans bodies. Secondly, I argue that fertility treatments centre heterosexuality at the expense of queer modes of living. Current treatment assemblages therefore subordinate queer and trans modes of living to masculine, cishet embodiments.

Cis bodies, trans bodies and 'natural' masculinity

In attempting to restore masculinity to the bodies of soldiers with GUIs, surgical treatments are reacting to discourses of gender that link gender to sex, and sex to genitalia. These surgeries, however, not only emerge in response to these discourses, but also reaffirm said discourses as natural and inevitable. In doing so, penis transplantations cement a particular relationship between gender, sex and genitalia as natural and beyond question.

Largely speaking, the relationship between sex, gender and genitalia is (as this chapter has already briefly touched upon) often presented as natural. A penis and testicles are understood as making a body male, and there is a strong prevailing assumption that such an embodiment will also lead to feeling like a man. Conversely, being born with a vagina and ovaries makes a body female and the subject a woman. At least, these are the dominant ways in which Western societies connect bodily materialization with symbolic discourses of gender. Trans and intersex subjects have been challenging and complicating this narrative for hundreds of years, as have queer people, with the aberrant and devious lines of desire they draw between bodies and subjects. Arguably it is the ways in which some bodies cannot be read within a cisgender sex/gender/genital framework that has led to profound violences being inflicted upon trans and queer bodies. These bodies cannot be made intelligible according to dominant systems of meaning and, as such, cannot be made to fit within the bounds of 'the human', which prioritizes heterosexual and cisgender subjects (Heyes, 2003; Hird, 2000; Lamble, 2009; Thomas, 2002; Turner, 1999).

Soldiers with GUIs likewise challenge ciscentric understandings of sex and gender. Here are 'male' bodies and manly subjects that do not correspond to dominant norms of sexed bodies. As this chapter has argued, their alternate embodiment throws what counts as a 'male' body into question and, in doing so, troubles the stability of the relationship between 'man' as a subject position and 'body with penis and testes' as a sexed embodiment. This has ramifications for how we then understand not only the relationship between sex and gender, but gender itself as unmoored from a binary understanding of sex.

Surgical treatments for GUIs, however, attempt to silence this challenge, intervening in order to 'correct' these improperly male bodies. Surgical treatment options may involve reconstructive surgeries to attempt to restore the damaged genitalia or, in very recent years, genital transplants. Reconstructive surgeries are heavily dependent on the extent of the injuries. Reconstructive surgeries may attempt to reconstruct the shape of the penis if it has been damaged, and can also include the insertion of prosthetic devices into the penis to allow erections to be achieved and sustained (Williams & Jezior, 2013). Penis transplants, while still in their infancy, are currently being developed in regard to service members with GUIs. To date, there have been five successful penis transplants recorded worldwide, with two taking place in the US. In 2018 at Johns Hopkins, the first penis transplant in the US for a wounded service member took place. Despite only the most recent transplant involving a service member, the figure of the wounded soldier has been instrumental in the development of these surgeries. At Massachusetts General Hospital, where a civilian transplant took place in 2016, the transplantation programme came about as a result of a military urological surgeon, Dr Curtis Cetrulo, training at the hospital, who brought their experience 'with devastating genitourinary injuries of wounded warriors' to a team working on penile cancer survivors (Massachusetts General Hospital, n.d., para. 16). He cited early on in the project that one of the main aims of the programme was to help soldiers who had sustained GUIs in OEF and OIF (BBC News, 2016b, para. 15).

To date these surgeries are not currently covered under existing military insurance schemes. The DoD has, however, financially invested in the research for penile transplantations, and the surgeons involved in the 2018 procedure were hopeful of the possibility of grants from the Pentagon to fund future operations – perhaps not unreasonably given GUIs new priority in AFIRM II (Grady, 2018, paras. 17–18) and the DoD's existing investments in other forms of transplantation surgeries, such as hand and face transplants, and the establishment of funding for veterans to receive care for these through the VA (Fries et al., 2020). These surgeries aim to restore urinary and sexual function, but also have more symbolic goals: 'to restore a person's sense of identity and manhood' according to Dr Lee, the chair of plastic and reconstructive surgery at Johns Hopkins (Grady, 2018, para. 9). This restoration of masculinity is achieved through the acquisition of a normative penis, one that looks right and is capable (or presumed that it will become capable, in the case of transplantation surgeries) of performing masculine penile functions.

The positioning of penis transplants, in particular, as an exciting and innovative surgery for soldiers with GUIs produces non-normative phalluses as problems that require fixing. Through penis transplantations, this fix comes in the form of the surgical restoration of an ejaculating penis (or one that can pantomime this ability). This works to naturalize and solidify a particular genital configuration as 'proper' for masculinity. As the recipient of the 2018 transplant put it, penile transplants give soldiers an opportunity to have 'the real thing' (Grady, 2018, para. 31). That the genitals involved in penis transplantation are positioned as the 'real thing' establishes a hierarchy of genitalia. Penises that do not belong to cismen are produced as not real, but instead as fakes, or poor imitations of the ejaculative penis. Any alternative genital configurations are false. This has a concurrent impact for how the power of the phallus operates. Cisgender men here emerge as having 'the real thing', as owners and possessors of the 'true' and 'natural' phallus. These discourses naturalize the penises of cisgender men, and (re)produce phallocentric discourses that centre the ejaculative penis as the true, 'real' signifier of masculinity and of masculine power. The symbolic value attached to supposedly 'real' penises in penile transplant surgeries, as something 'fixing' the body, and any gender/sex confusion arising from GUIs, further solidifies the importance of the penis to masculinity.

Importantly, this (re)affirmation of the 'naturalness' of phallic masculinity is done at the expense of masculinities without penises, or masculinities with non-normative genitalia. The genital hierarchy established by transplant surgeries works to organize a hierarchy of masculinities in which some are more 'real' than others. Trans bodies, in particular, exist at the periphery of discourses around penile reconstruction and transplantation, often invoked only to establish the dominance of cis male bodies. When questioned about whether these surgeries may be developed in order to benefit trans people, a bioethicist at Johns Hopkins edged around how this would be managed in transplantation surgeries: '[w]hat do you say to the donor? A 23-year old wounded in the line of duty has a very different sound than somebody who is seeking gender reassignment' (Grady, 2015, para. 25). Similarly, service members have been recorded as rejecting any comparison between their bodies and those of trans people. As one article records, the referral of service members with GUIs at the Walter Reed National Military Medical Center to doctors who specialize in genital surgeries for trans people is 'an option not well received in the ranks' (Wood, 2012, para. 28). As a staff sergeant with a GUI is reported to have 'growled' (a word laden with masculine connotation), 'I ain't going to no sex-change doctor' (Wood, 2012, para. 29). The use of 'growled' indicates the anger (as well as gruff and aggressive masculinity) generated by the suggestion that cis bodies would ever tarnish themselves by making use of resources designed for trans people.

Trans bodies and surgeries associated with trans people are evoked here only in order to subordinate them to injured cis bodies, who are figured as more deserving of phallic surgical intervention. Surgical treatments for GUIs therefore work to (re)affirm the dominance of cis bodies above and against trans bodies. That cis male bodies should have ejaculative penises is the natural order of things, requiring no justification, whereas trans bodies and surgeries are positioned as something freakish, something that it is insulting to which to compare service members with GUIs. Surgical treatments thus assemble cis and trans bodies and lives into a hierarchical relationship. Through the intense effort made to 'restore' ejaculative capacity to soldiering bodies, cisgender male bodies are produced as natural. Their masculinity is constructed as something that can be 'restored' to them, something that pre-existed their injury and naturally belongs to these particular bodies. Surgical treatments give intensive care and attention to the production of cisgender phalluses and cismale subjects. As a result, trans masculinities and bodies are established as 'bad copies' of a supposedly natural, 'biological masculinity' (Johnson, 2010, p. 246). They are produced against soldering bodies with GUIs as less worthy, less valuable, and unnatural candidates/possessors of ejaculative capacity and the phallus.

The (re)production of phallocentric genital hierarchies here is important when considering the distribution of life–death. Within a North American context, trans folk are subject to enormous and daily amounts of violence for failing to perform binary understandings of sex/gender. The logics at work in penile transplant surgeries fit into wider structures of power through which trans bodies are produced as perverse others, as not-normal bodies. Assemblages of penile transplant surgery are thus nested within wider relations of power that devalue trans bodies and trans lives. These power relations are (re)produced through phallocentric curations of service members' semen. It is vital to connect discourses of 'the real thing' with wider patterns of transphobic violence in international politics. Doing so reveals to us how trans bodies and lives are subordinated to cisgender lives, not only through medical technologies that directly engage with trans folk, but through medical technologies that explicitly do *not* engage with trans folk. This cements a particular distribution of life–death in these settings, whereby trans possibilities must be eradicated in order to secure the naturalness of cisgender masculine life. Despite genital surgeries for service members with GUIs and trans folk seeking a penis attempting to achieve the same outcome – the creation of a penis on a body that is otherwise without one – the clear efforts to distinguish gender-affirming surgeries for trans folks from gender-affirming surgeries for service members establish a violent relationship of life–death between the two.

An intense amount of work, effort and technology is required in order to produce and graft these 'real' penises onto the bodies of service members. The need for surgical intervention renders the acquisition of this phallus far from a 'natural' process for service members with GUIs. This is a technologically mediated phallus, produced through an enmeshment of biological material with technoscientific practice. Paradoxically, however, discourses of the 'real' penis subordinate this level of artifice to the end result, producing the service member's penis transplant as a penis that 'feels normal' (Zaleski, 2019, para. 61). Such naturalness is not granted to the penises of trans subjects, however, which continue to be actively excluded from such surgical initiatives. As such, biopolitical military-medical assemblages operate as selective capacitation machines, whereby only some bodies are deemed appropriately worthy recipients of masculinizing surgeries. These surgical interventions attempt to adjust the bodies of soldiers with GUIs through the (re)production of binary, phallocentric understandings of masculinity/maleness. Through surgical treatments, we can see that the restoration of seminal capacity to some bodies and not others is crucial in reproducing hierarchical relationships of life–death.

Securing semen, securing heterosexuality

Unsurprisingly, for soldiers with GUIs there is also the attendant risk of fertility problems. Whether a GUI impairs the ability to have penetrative sex and ejaculate, or the testes themselves are damaged, there are multiple ways in which a GUI may make biological reproduction difficult, if not impossible, for service members. The military does offer some assisted reproductive services for service members who were injured on active duty, including sperm and egg retrieval, in vitro fertilization (IVF), artificial insemination, blastocyst implantation, and cryopreservation of embryos (Defense Health Agency, n.d.). For veterans, the VA covers hormonal therapies, 'surgical correction', artificial insemination and IVF for veterans with service-related injuries and their spouses (US Department of Veterans Affairs, n.d., para. 2).

While there is a lack of data as to how service members with GUIs access these services (and, indeed, whether they are able to in practice), it is important to note that these fertility treatments are organized around heterosexual childbearing practices, and the nuclear family. Infertility health cover under TRICARE and the VA is only accessible if the partner has a 'lawful spouse' (Defense Health Agency, n.d.). That the provision of fertility cover only extends to married couples demonstrates that, for the military, the nuclear family is the only type of familial arrangement that is worth financially investing in. While of course in the US same-sex couples can marry, it is impossible not to note the heterosexist presumptions that underlie a decision to set marriage as the access bar for fertility services.[1] LGB marriage rights were only secured across all 50 states in 2015 by the Supreme Court (*Obergefell v. Hodges*), meaning that prior to this decision access to fertility services for service members with GUIs were premised upon the exclusion of queer couples. Although it is now possible for married queer couples to fulfil this access criteria, that marriage is a requirement for fertility services entrenches heteronormative ideals of marriage as the most deified form of relationship arrangement, and the basic organizational unit of the family (Peterson, 2014a). This is exemplified in the Supreme Court's 2015 ruling, which stated that '[n]o union is more profound than marriage, for it embodies the highest ideals of love, fidelity, devotion, sacrifice, and family'. The privileging of marriage within existing fertility provisions therefore not only practically speaking has excluded queer couples prior to 2015, but continues to devalue queer partnerships and childrearing arrangements that exist outside heterosexist norms.

Investigating what fertility treatments are available to service members with GUIs further underscores the profound privileging of normative, cisgender heterosexual families. The available TRICARE and VA treatments, such as artificial insemination and IVF, presume that a married couple can between them supply both sperm and egg. For many queer couples wishing to have a child that is biologically related to them, a third party is needed to either supply sperm or act as a surrogate for the pregnancy. No provision is made for the acquisition of donor sperm or forms of surrogacy under TRICARE, and there is no provision made for adoption fees or support for couples electing to parent a child that is not biologically related to them (which includes both queer and heterosexual couples). Existing fertility treatments are therefore premised on an understanding that, within a married couple, one partner has ovaries and eggs and one partner has testes and sperm. These treatments thus rule out many queer couples even if they are married, along with a number of heterosexual couples where one partner may be trans, intersex, or otherwise unable to provide the necessary biological material (for example, as a result of a GUI).

The fertility treatments available, then, operate on the presumption that service members with GUIs are arranged into neat pairings of heterosexual cisgender married couples. The provision of fertility treatments is almost always publicly discussed in the context of service members' wives and girlfriends, reinforcing the central place of the heterosexual couple. At the time of writing, there is little to no reporting on queer service members with GUIs and fertility problems. There are, however, plenty of pieces discussing GUIs and fertility problems that interview heterosexual couples (Demirjian, 2016; Grady, 2016, 2017; Lawrence & Kaiser Health News, 2016). The nuclear family is pride of place here, and the constant repetition of fertility treatments that exclude queer veterans with GUIs works to sustain heterosexual relationships and families as the dominant familial ideal. It is heterosexual families that the military considers worth perpetuating, and it is these heterosexual forms of seminal exchange that the military actively works to facilitate.

Privileging heterosexual nuclear families within the military fits into a wider historical pattern of governance. As David Serlin argues, the 1944 GI bill and its mortgage provisions constituted 'a mechanic to promote and privilege family life' and to help in 'sustaining heteronormative bliss' (Serlin, 2015, p. 40). Fertility treatments work in the same way, to ease the pressures infertility brings to bear upon military couples and to conserve the conventional nuclear family (Hendershot, 2018). That fertility treatments for service members with GUIs are premised upon the heterosexual couple and the nuclear family demonstrates how the military is highly invested in the governance of service members' semen in particular ways, and in heterosexual orientations. As this chapter has already argued in its exploration of surgical treatments, the military-medical bureaucracy invests in endowing soldiers with ejaculative capacity. This capacity is granted with particular heterosexual goals in mind, as this two-pronged strategy of surgical intervention/fertility treatments demonstrates. The governance of service members' semen revolves around an image of the soldier as a heterosexual, cisgender male; this is who the treatments cater to, and these are the bodies and sexualities that occupy the central place in discourses of GUIs.

Fertility treatments offered under the VA and TRICARE do not work to enable veterans simply to raise children. Were this the case, the acquisition of donor sperm, forms of surrogacy, and adoption fees would be covered under existing insurance programmes. However, it is only forms of reproductive technologies that involve sperm and egg from married, cisgender couples that are covered. It is only these specific forms of childbearing and familial arrangements that current military insurance plans work to perpetuate. This secures the centrality of the hetero-nuclear family. Heterosexual modes of living are (re)enforced as natural, normal and dominant through the curation and governance of semen under military fertility treatments.

In doing so, queer bodies and queer lives are produced as unworthy of similar levels of support through their total exclusion from such treatments. As such, fertility treatments attempt to mobilize semen in heterosexual directions. Even when the penis cannot physically ejaculate semen, medical intervention produces the soldiering phallus by exporting ejaculative capabilities to reproductive technologies. The service member's reproductive phallus is thus intact in the form of technical intervention, and ejaculative mimicry is performed in conjunction between body and medical technology. This desire to facilitate biological reproduction arguably works to secure the hetero-masculinity of service members' bodies through controlling and extending their seminal flows. The governance of soldiers' semen in the case of fertility treatments validates and reproduces heterosexual biological reproduction and heterosexual forms of life and living as the dominant norm. Queer lives and families are rendered invisible in these discourses. The governance of semen for the purpose of heterosexual reproduction instantiates family, reproduction and future as the property of heterosexuality.

This feeds into a wider politics of anti-queerness, which associates queerness not with temporal futures, but with the end of them. As Edelman argues when he reminds us that queerness 'is understood as bringing children … to an end', queerness is often figured within dominant heterosexual cultures as anti-life, as portending species death (Edelman, 1998, p. 25). Fertility treatments for GUIs thus partake in a distribution of life–death that protects and values heterosexual forms of life at the expense of queer possibilities. This chapter has already argued that surgical treatments for GUIs necessitate the killing of trans possibilities in order to protect embodied cisgender forms of life. Fertility treatments perform the same function within the broader parameters of queerness. These treatments actively attempt to distribute and perpetuate heterosexual life, through the replication of heterosexual families. In order for this to happen, queer possibilities and queer forms of family and kinship must become invisible. They are made to fade away from fields of possibilities through an active distribution of resources that prioritizes heterosexual lives.

The racialized distribution of injury

This chapter has thus far focused on the sexual and gendered distribution of life–death that is affected through the treatment of US service members. US service members, however, are of course not the only bodies to experience GUIs. Curiosity compels us to ask what else is happening in the production, distribution and treatment of GUIs. There is also a profoundly racialized dimension to the international distribution of injury and seminal capacity. Given that the rise in GUI occurrence in service members is often associated with the wars in Iraq and Afghanistan, and the increased use of IEDs within these wars, I want to explore here how the production of US service members' seminal capacity sits in tension with the huge numbers of injured service members and civilians in Iraq and Afghanistan.

Before we think about how these bodies relate to each other, and where a distribution of life–death enters the frame, a comparison would be useful to assess the scale of GUIs in Iraq and Afghanistan. Unfortunately, this is also difficult to offer. Understanding the impact and treatment of GUIs upon Iraqi and Afghan populations is much harder than following the seminal trails of US service members. As many others have noted about the wars in Iraq and Afghanistan, authoritative data sources about the prevalence of death and injury among Iraqi and Afghan communities are scarce. The devastation both wars wrought upon civilian and military administration has made the collection of reliable and verifiable statistics about injury and mortality difficult to come by. Some of the most reliable estimates come from the Costs of War project, which draws upon data from a variety of governmental, NGO and international institutions. The Costs of War project estimate that, between 2001 and 2014, direct war-related violence killed around 92,000 Afghan people, with an additional estimated 61,970 war-related injuries in Afghanistan during these years (Crawford, 2015). In Iraq, estimates suggest 250,000 civilian injuries between 2003 and 2012 (Lafta & Al-Nuaimi, 2019, p. 217).

There is no publicly available data on injuries among Iraqi or Afghan military personnel, either government forces or insurgents. And there is no data that can help us describe or attempt to quantify the numbers of GUIs, either. The closest we can get to an appraisal of the numbers of GUIs in Afghan and Iraqi populations, as a direct result of war, is to circle around the edges of the (estimated) number of injuries. We know that in Iraq in 2014 around 56 per cent of civilians who were injured in 2014 experienced a disability as a result of these injuries; and that after 2008, the nature of injuries changed from primarily gunshots to blasts and explosions, in line with the broader pattern of conflict (Lafta et al., 2015, p. 12). Between 2003 and 2014, in Baghdad, injuries to the abdomen and pelvis accounted for 12.7 per cent of reported civilian injuries (Lafta et al., 2015, p. 9). In Afghanistan, the number of civilian casualties caused by IEDs has risen since 2009 (Crawford, 2015, p. 4). The Afghan National Disability Survey estimates that around 17 per cent of all disabilities in the country are directly related to the war (Crawford, 2015, p. 7).

Despite the lack of data around GUIs, based on the existing estimates of injury prevalence, disability rates, and the cause of these injuries, it is therefore very reasonable to suggest that there are likely substantial numbers of people in Iraq and Afghanistan living with GUIs. These populations have also been exposed to and wounded by the same devices that have led to an increased GUI prevalence among US service members. Of course, given that civilians are highly unlikely to be wearing the protective body armour that US service personnel have access to, and may lack access to a similar level of medical care and resource, these injuries are likely to have a higher fatality rate among civilian populations. But it is feasible and realistic to suggest that people in Iraq and Afghanistan have also suffered from these injuries and may be experiencing a resulting lack of seminal capacity.

How to understand the relationship, then, between the US service member with a GUI and the unknown numbers of civilian and military personnel, spread across two countries, who might have similar injuries? The very lack of an ability to clearly see and identify the scale of these injuries is significant. When we follow trails and circulations of seminal capacity, absence speaks as loudly as presence. The fact that we know so little about the impact of these injuries upon Afghan and Iraqi people is testament to a distribution of life–death where the seminal capacity of US service members is protected, monitored and (re)produced with a much greater level of care than that which is given to the populations they declare war upon. The US invasion of Iraq is particularly instructive here for highlighting that a lack of data is not an inevitable consequence of armed conflict. With regards to Iraq, the US Department of State and the Agency for International Development (USAID) signed contracts with both the World Health Organization (WHO) and the United Nations Children's Fund (UNICEF) to implement a programme of health surveillance, training and monitoring post-invasion; these responsibilities were then moved to the DoD, based on the US presumption that US forces would be welcomed by the Iraqi people as 'liberators', and OEF would therefore be completed within three weeks, leaving no need for a prolonged health plan (Burkle & Garfield, 2013). Following this incredible presumption, the budget for humanitarian aid was cut in half, and various experienced members of the State Department were dismissed from their posts in Iraq following a drive for 'ideological loyalty' by Donald Rumsfeld; this included the interim minister of health, Frederick Burkle Junior, who was dismissed after declaring Baghdad to a be a public health emergency (Terry, 2017). As a result of the Bush administration's imperial presumption that they would be welcomed as great white liberators of poor brown Iraqis, the US rejected opportunities to systematically monitor and assess the health consequences of the US invasion. To this end, the WHO and UNICEF contracts were never implemented, and USAID did not receive any funds for conducting public health surveillance (Burkle & Garfield, 2013; Terry, 2017). The opportunity to gather data and information about the injury rates in the Iraqi population was therefore not so much missed as refused.

The extreme inequalities in the distribution of life–death between US service members and the people they were sent to fight is also evident in Afghanistan. Among a general picture of high civilian casualties as the result of the 'war on terror', the bombing of the Kunduz Trauma centre in Afghanistan stands as a particularly traumatizing episode in which the lives of Afghan people were treated as 'available for maiming' (Puar, 2017b, p. xvii). The Kunduz Trauma Centre was a hospital run by Médecins Sans Frontières (MSF), which had treated general trauma patients since 2011, providing surgical care in a country where public health infrastructure had been decimated by a near constant state of war since 1979. In 2002, only 9 per cent of the population had access to healthcare (Collins, 2015, p. 28); close to 20 per cent of the population had either a close relative or friend who had died as a result of being unable to quickly reach or afford medical care (Médecins Sans Frontières, n.d., p. 8). The Kunduz Trauma Centre therefore provided vital surgical care to those with severe injuries, amid a context in which access to healthcare was severely circumscribed. On 3 October 2015, however, the hospital was bombed by US aerial forces. In the bombing attack, which lasted approximately one hour, at least 30 people died – 10 identified patients, 13 identified staff members, and seven who were burned beyond recognition (Médecins Sans Frontières, 2015, p. 12). Having been operating for four years, the location of the hospital was well known, and given an escalation in fighting in Kunduz in the preceding week, the hospital had recently reconfirmed its GPS co-ordinates with the DoD, the Afghan Ministry of Interior and Defense and the US army in Kabul (Médecins Sans Frontières, 2015, p. 5). The US military initially claimed that the attack was to protect US troops engaged in a firefight; it has since claimed that the bombing was a 'mistake', caused by 'human error', and that they did not knowingly and intentionally target a military hospital (BBC News, 2015). The US army eventually offered condolence payments to those who were injured in the strike and to the families of those who were killed in the attack – around US$3,000 and US$6,000, respectively (Ackerman & Rasmussen, 2016).

Neither of these stories tells us about the prevalence, or experience, or treatment of GUIs among Iraqi and Afghan populations. But they do tell us a lot about why it is difficult to even conduct a conversation about GUIs within these countries. When following trails of bodily fluids through assemblages, sometimes that trail is interrupted. We are led to an impossibility of a story. The trail of seminal fluid that we attempt to track in this chapter disappears into the warren of US military imperialism, a tangled assemblage that redirects seminal fluids towards US service members. Our concern, our attention, our critique, our focus is therefore only sustained in relation to US bodies and their relative capacities and debilities. In doing so, a thorough critique of the distribution of seminal debilitation among Iraqi and Afghan communities is interrupted. These fluids, these capacities, become invisible. They are obscured by a set of decisions not to undertake medical surveillance. They are obscured by a set of imperial attitudes that presumed the US military would be welcomed with open arms by the Iraqi population. They are obscured by chains of command, failures of communication and a lack of care, which considered Afghan lives worth so little that people burned to death in their beds in a hospital that was being repeatedly bombed for an hour, despite multiple calls to the DoD and its allies by desperate medical staff (Médecins Sans Frontières, 2015, p. 8).

But in failing to follow these trails of semen to the bodies that lack or possess it, we are still led to something that it is important to know. The fact that this trail is wilfully obscured by a set of decisions from US defence officials reveals much to us about the distribution of life–death in these spaces. Both the failure to conduct medical surveillance in Iraq and the bombing of Kunduz Trauma Centre in Afghanistan demonstrate to us that an unequal distribution of life–death was set in motion in Iraq and Afghanistan. This was a distribution in which the life and capacity of US service members was protected and promoted through the exposure of Iraqi and Afghan populations to higher levels of death and debilitation. The arguments about the unequal distribution of risk in both these wars has been made thoroughly by other scholars, so I will not repeat them there (Owens, 2003; Shaw, 2002). But beyond the unsurprising fact that warfighting actively attempts to inflict an unequal distribution of life–death, the difficulty we have in following seminal fluids and the management of capacity-debility in relation to GUIs in Iraq and Afghanistan shows us how capacities in US service members are maintained through the production of Iraqi and Afghan bodies as available for debilitation. That seminal capacity is diverted away from Afghan and Iraqi bodies towards US bodies (and only certain US bodies) shows us that the production of seminal capacity for US service members allows the US to '[displace] the production of debilitation … through practices both "here" [the US] and in the "elsewhere" [Iraq and Afghanistan]' (Puar, 2017b, p. 92). Afghan and Iraqi bodies are therefore produced as 'objects of un-care' in this equation (Puar, 2017b, p. 92). We cannot even accurately and precisely recognize the ways in which these populations are debilitated and capacitated through GUIs, because US military imperialism redirects our attention towards only US service members, the only bodies represented, considered and cared for in the literature and research around these types of injuries. So, when we think about the distribution of life–death in Iraq and Afghanistan, the absence of information and data around GUIs effects an 'elision' of the role of US imperialism in producing GUIs, erasing a thorough consideration and critique of how wounding and injury similarly affects populations 'over there' (Puar, 2017b, p. 93). This demonstrates how the distribution of life–death, achieved through practices of governing bodily fluids, is premised upon a racialized hierarchy that situates Afghan and Iraqi bodies as 'available' for debilitation in contrast to the bodies of select US service members, which are produced as 'available' for (re)capacitation.

GUIs and the politics of militarism

Why is the seminal capacity of service members important for the US military? I turn to this question now, and seek to untangle the relationship between seminal capacity, GUI and US militarism as a discourse and practice.

Within media discourses, service members are produced as bodies uniquely deserving of treatment for their GUIs. In the case of penis transplantation for example, one medical professional reports that, when family members of possible donors 'hear that the goal is to help wounded veterans, many consent' (Grady, 2018, para. 35). It is the service member's wounded body that leverages this consent. Indeed, in the case of the 2018 penis transplant, the donor's family offered a message of support to the recipient, writing that they are 'very proud' to be able to help someone who 'served this country', and expressed their gratitude at 'the job [he] did for this nation' (Grady, 2018, para. 36). And it is not just the families of donors who are moved, emotionally, by the act of soldiering; it is also medical professionals. In a study assessing attitudes to penile transplantations among health professionals, the health professionals surveyed were more likely to take a positive and supportive view of penile transplantations after reading a short excerpt about service members' fears and feelings about GUIs (Najari et al., 2018). When it comes to service members with GUIs, it is their soldiering that marks them as those bodies particularly deserving of help.

GUIs are portrayed as the ultimate sacrifice, where service members gamble their heterosexual masculine identities (and attendant privileges) in order to serve their country. They have given 'everything they have', and have offered up the phallus and thus their masculine power and identity on behalf of the nation (Grady, 2015, para. 17). The benefit of their sacrifice is somewhat unclear; it is never specified exactly what it is that service members have laid down their hetero-masculine power for, other than a generalized sense that it has been done while 'defending their country' (Demirjian, 2016, para. 23). The lack of clarity over what this sacrifice has been done for allows grand narratives of militaristic heroics to be invoked, and thus the GUI is more than a wound to an individual; it is an injury aimed at the nation, but absorbed by the individual body of the service members – a sacrifice: a stigmata, suffered on behalf of us all. These types of stories invoke the nation in order to offer familiar militaristic tales of heroic martyrdom. The sacrifice of the phallus becomes discussed as almost a romantic, poignant tragedy (though I am not suggesting it feels this way to service members); giving up the most valuable thing a man possesses for the sake of the nation.

In understanding why these particular bodies elicit more emotional responses than other bodies with genital wounds (or trans bodies requesting similar surgeries), it is vital to understand the fetishism of service members' bodies as hard, tough, reliable and virile. Through the submission and surrender of their bodies to the state, the bodies of service members become potent objects of desire, embodying the symbolic power of the state and being 'rewarded with the sex appeal that only massive symbolic power can bestow' (Crane-Seeber, 2016). The romanticism of sacrifice is reliant upon these sexualized narratives, which position the body of the service member as the ultimate object of desire, on both an individual and national level (Hendershot, 2018). Service members' bodies are supposed to be reliable and consistent: to function like well-oiled machines, to transcend human (and feminized) weakness, to embody the previously discussed masculine qualities of 'hardness' (Masters, 2005; Meeuf, 2018; Williams, 1994). Basic training practices in the US military are premised upon these elimination of softness and vulnerability, of driving the 'weakness' from service members' bodies (Arkin & Dobrofsky, 1978; Woodward, 1998).

The sacrifice and destruction of the service member's phallus is then poignant not just as the embodiment of individual and personal struggle. It is the story of the ultimate object of desire, the much-fetishized body of the nation, failing. Through GUIs, service members' bodies are revealed to be precisely what they are supposed to repudiate. The borders of these bodies are revealed as open and permeable through GUIs; their 'corporeal stability' is no longer dependable and, instead of embodying an unchanging, unyielding hardness, they are suddenly revealed to be mutable and open 'to metamorphosis' (Stephens, 2007, p. 95). The romantic and sexualized loss of these bodies is thus an issue of national pain; and it is made all the more so as threatening the hard and fastness of service members' bodies threatens not only archetypal masculinities, but also discourses of militarism more broadly.

The instability that GUIs pose to masculine embodiments has a knock-on effect. When the bodies of service members are revealed as lacking the phallus, the attendant power of militarism – which is reliant upon these bodies – is also challenged and disrupted. This is a problem for the US military, which is reliant upon phallic discourses of power to present an image of the military as a producer of 'hypermasculinist, all-American, patriotic, hard guy[s]' (Pin-Fat & Stern, 2005, p. 27). The bodies that are imagined to populate the military are part of the production of militarism, and the state, as tough, hard, righteous, virile and, ultimately, an institution endowed with these forms of phallic power (Caso, 2017; Serlin, 2015; Weber, 1999). As such, the bodies of services members are vital to the maintenance of militarism and the state. If these bodies fail to meet the hyper-masculine and hyper-sexualized corporeal fantasies that the institution of militarism is premised upon, the US military also runs the risk of being de-phallicized. Locating service members with GUIs in relation to militarism is therefore vital in understanding how these bodies are produced as 'objects of care' in need of rehabilitation, as opposed to 'economic burden[s]/social pariahs', a frame disabled folks are often trapped within (Puar, 2017b, p. 84).

Cynthia Weber's work is invaluable here in unpacking the implications GUIs have for military and state power. In her book *Faking It: US Hegemony in a 'Post-Phallic' Era*, Weber unpacks how US attachments to and policy towards the Caribbean are premised on US anxieties around the status of US phallic power (Weber, 1999). In analysing these relationships, Weber argues that 'subjects engaged in relationships with the symbolically disempowered (castrated) end up losing their own power' (1999, p. 23). It is this phallic loss, generated through binary logics of sex/gender, that GUIs threaten to transfer to the military. The bodies of service members, stripped of their own phallic power through the lack of seminal capacity, trouble the fantasy of the US military as having the power to produce 'war heroes', glorious figures of phallic manhood (Caso, 2017, p. 223). Instead, these bodies are revealed as vulnerable, fragile, prone to injury. Feminist work has long pointed out the impossibility of fantasies of the military as an ultra-masculine, heterosexual space. Figures of femininity and of queerness necessarily constitute the military, which depends upon the existence of these subjects and bodies in order to generate phallic power through their imagined opposition and expulsion (Caso, 2017; Pin-Fat & Stern, 2005; Welland, 2013). In the failing of bodies with GUIs to conform to masculine ideals, the phallic power of the US military is exposed as lacking. Draw back the curtain and, instead of finding an institution packed to the gills with Rambos, we find human bodies that are vulnerable, fallible, and potentially lacking seminal capacity and thus the symbolic phallus.

The irony of GUIs is thus not only a revelation that the US military, embodied through service members, has lost its phallic power, but that 'it never "had" the phallus in the first place' (Weber, 1999, p. 134). GUIs point to the impossibility of these masculinized ideals of power, the impossibility of their complete and total embodiment. GUIs thus require intervention from the US military, and the bodies of service members must be re-phallicized, in order to conceal this essential lack. GUIs do not strip away an already existing source of power from the US military, but instead reveal that there is no hard (exactly) objectively existing source of power there. In attempting to (re)produce the phallus, GUI treatments highlight the phallus as performative. Rather than affirming the masculinity of bodies with GUIs, the fact that treatments must conjure seminal capacity in order to strap the phallus onto the body reveals the contingency and unnaturalness of the phallus in the first place. GUI treatments reveal phallic masculinity not as a stable and inherent state of being, but one that is only created in the performance of seminal capacity. Rather than stripping the phallus from the US military, GUIs threaten phallic power by undermining its very existence.

In the experience of GUIs, both service members and the US military are confronted by 'the horror of its own lack' (Weber, 1999, p. 8). The production of masculinity and heterosexuality in US soldiers through GUI treatments are thus best understood as an instantiation of these qualities, rather than a restoration. Instead of returning these essential qualities to the bodies of service members, GUI treatments produce masculinity and heterosexuality at the same time as they produce service members' bodies as lacking them. It is the queer both/and of our queerfeminist curiosity that allows us to recognize this – that GUIs proffer something to bodies at the same time as they take it away. It is the continuous performance of this contradiction that keeps the assemblage in motion. When we press pause on this interchange in our analysis, we can recognize the fault lines written into the dance. The US military as a powerful institution is dependent upon service members' bodies. The military's power is produced and naturalized through the production and maintenance of sex/gender binaries, and such attempts to fit the bodies of service members into them. Securing masculine, cisgender, heterosexual lives for service members at the expense of queer/trans lives thus also attempts to secure the 'life' and continued existence and vitality of US militarism.

Conclusion

GUIs, on the rise in contemporary combat operations, are produced as an emasculating and feminizing injury. These injuries can leave the bodies of service members in an ambiguously gendered/sexed position. In response, military medical assemblages attempt to 'fix' these injured bodies through the governance of their seminal capacity. Both penis transplant surgeries and fertility treatments set in motion a violent relationship of life–death between cishet male bodies and queer and trans bodies, affirming the cishetero service member as the true normal and natural possessor of seminal capacity. There is also a racialized and internationalized distribution of seminal capacity at play. US military imperialism and its attendant lack of care towards 'others' makes following seminal fluids in Iraq and Afghanistan nearly impossible. The presence of data on US service members with GUIs, and the lack of similar data for Iraqi and Afghanistan military forces and civilians, works to conceal the role that racial military imperialism plays in the (unequal) distribution of seminal capacity. These injuries are important to the US military precisely because they threaten to destabilize the masculinized underpinning of US militarism more broadly. Following our curiosity to explore the possibility of multiplicity and contradiction shows us something interesting; that attempting to neutralize this 'threat' is, however, a failing process. In following semen through military medical assemblages, we can ultimately discover the fragility and lack of the phallus in the first place.

By approaching the site from the perspective of semen, this chapter demonstrates that, by asking how fluids are governed and how bodies are 'broken' and 'fixed' in particular ways, we are able to begin to investigate how life–death is distributed in the capacitation and rehabilitation of certain bodies and not others. It is certain racialized, gendered and sexed lives that are considered worthy of seminal capacitation, and not others.

At this point, we have together followed three fluids through a variety of securitized assemblages, in order to see what we can discover about international politics and the distribution of life–death among populations. Chapter 6 of this book presents the final 'research finding' of this project; this act of following the fluid. I now turn to unpack this practice in greater detail.

6

Finding, Following, Fluids

The previous three chapters show what an analysis that follows bodily fluids through assemblages might look like, and what it can reveal to us about life and death. Chapter 7 summarizes and ties these three contexts together. But before we move onto this concluding work, this chapter lays out and reflects upon the process of producing these arguments and ideas in conjunction with a focus on bodily fluids.

I have chosen to do this at the end of the book, rather than the beginning, because the method of thinking about the world with and through bodily fluids emerged in the doing of this research project. When beginning this research project, 'methods' felt like the biggest, looming obstacle to overcome. My research training had largely focused on quantitative and qualitative methods, statistical analysis, participant observation, interviewing, and so on. This training was interesting and enlivening, but none of it fitted the way I thought about conducting research. I got the distinct impression from my research training that, when it came to the question of methods, the field of possibility seemed to narrow intensely, and that 'methods' meant it was time to 'get serious' and pick something rational.

As multiple critical scholars have pointed out, however, the research process is in practice 'inevitably messy'; it involves 'loops, spirals, and even cul-de-sacs' (Baaz & Stern, 2016, p. 118; see also Lather, 2009; Law, 2004; Squire, 2012; Zalewski, 2006). At the start of this research project, there were some questions my education and training up until that point had failed to answer. How do feminists produce knowledge about the world? How do critical race scholars do it? How do critical perspectives go about *enacting* their critical sense of the world, when we might be suspicious of the ways this has traditionally been done? How do you *choose* a methodology? Of course, there is no one answer to any of these questions. But in what follows, I lay out how a method and methodology emerged from the process of doing this research, based on the advice from critical researchers (particularly feminists) to follow the 'the lost thoughts, the glimpsed insights … the things that seemed to matter once, even if fleetingly' (Zalewski, 2006, p. 52).

Taking a cue from Harcourt et al., I use method/ology in an attempt to capture the ways in which I take 'method' and 'methodology' as inseparable (2015, p. 159). Traditional positioning of methods and methodologies take methodology as the larger, philosophical framing of the process of conducting research, and methods as the tools we rely upon in order to conduct such research (Harding, 1987). As a result, methods come to be understood as apolitical tools that we pick and choose between, before 'applying' to the world. Grounded in feminist technoscience studies, however, this book rejects such masculinized and positivist understandings of methods as neat scalpels that can make incisions on a world that is objectively 'out there'. Instead I take them as mutually imbricated processes and reject the 'traditional philosophical fetishizations of distinctions' that has traditionally attempted to keep methods and methodologies separate (Harding, 1987). Methods and methodologies are conjoined practices that are 'within worlds and partake in their shaping' (Aradau & Huysmans, 2014, p. 598).

The first section of this chapter tells the story of how this project began, outlining how I initially attempted to argue that bodily fluids constitute feminized threats to the social order of international politics. Beginning with an honest accounting of what did not work matters for building less disciplined forms of knowledge and rejecting the image of the researcher as all seeing and all knowing. In refusing such a linear and logical methodological account, we can see the value of paying attention to gut feeling as a way to begin thinking about the world. The second section of this chapter then unpacks this book's understanding of a fluid method/ology. I argue that a fluid method/ology uses bodily fluids to think international security with. Thinking with bodily fluids means paying attention to the ways bodily fluids complicate distinctions between bodies and subjects, and are themselves caught up as objects of governance. I show how a fluid method/ology therefore emphasizes experimentation, mobilizing different research assemblages in different contexts to interfere in these patterns of governance. Finally, I detail how this book practices these ideas about research through the concept of 'following the fluid'. I show how following bodily fluids as agential assemblages can allow us to map the relational distribution of life–death in security practices.

Beginnings

Why include the initial ideas and a failure to carry them out? Why not just begin at the end and save you from experiencing my own frustrated attempts to make fluids orderly? The answer is that telling an honest story about how this book has attempted to know things about assemblages of bodies, security and fluids matters. Knowing that this book's author changed her mind matters not because it helps clarify the end result, but because explicating what went wrong is a crucial part of this book's commitment to queerfeminist method/ologies. Such method/ologies reject 'normalized, linear, tidy' research stories, instead seeking to build messier and less disciplined forms of 'knowing' that cannot be summed up in terms of right/wrong (Zalewski, 2006, p. 50). In offering an honest account of this book's method/ological journey, then, this book contributes to queerfeminist attempts to move past the idea of the researcher as a producer of right/wrong facts, instead attempting to generate ways of thinking about and being in the world that have more complex and contradictory answers.

The earliest drafts of this book attempted to tell a different story about bodily fluids than the one that runs through these pages now. I started this project by thinking about disgust, and why bodily fluids are able to elicit this feeling. I suspected that bodily fluids are so provocative because they have come to be associated with the grotesque and feminine material. Drawing on feminist scholars, I argued that women's bodies have traditionally been produced as wet, unstable, leaky and porous, and that bodily fluids have been subsumed within this category (Cavanagh, 2013; Grosz, 1994; Shildrick, 1997). My book did not initially employ bodily fluids in order to rescue them from the dark, viscous matter of the feminine. My purpose was not to elevate them to the status of serious objects of study in international politics, but to positively revel in the feminized affective power I believed they had. If this was the disgusting feminine, then I was going to embrace it. I was going to build a research project that was grounded in entirely feminized objects of impropriety, and I was going to (frankly) rub people's noses in it. I began by arguing that following the profoundly gendered mind/body split that emerged in Enlightenment philosophy (Andreescu & Shapiro, 2014; Linstead, 2000; Stephens, 2008), bodily fluids emerged as feminized objects of disgust due to their abilities to move within and between bodies. This, I argued, threatened the collapse of masculine body ideals where the body functioned as a discrete, enclosed and impermeable container for the individual rational subject (Aretxaga, 1997, pp. 122–145; Linke, 1997; Longhurst, 2001; Shildrick, 1996). Bodily fluids were disgusting because dominant imaginaries within Western Europe in particular understood bodily fluids as the emergence of feminized mess that threatened to blur the boundaries between self and Other. I argued that bodily fluids had been implicitly aligned with femininity, leading to fluids prompting disgust as they constituted a feminized threat to the masculinized boundaries of social life.

Problems quickly emerged from attempting to talk about fluids in these ways, however. For a start, I was simply wrong in insisting bodily fluids always provoke disgust. Bodily fluids were difficult to affectively 'fix' in any one register. While my initial desire was to root out 'the disgusting' and use 'disgust' as a method of framing bodily fluids, bodily fluids generate other affective reactions. Much as is the case with their relationship to gender, bodily fluids are not all disgusting, at all times, in all settings. Urine in a public street might generate disgust from some, but in a laboratory setting urine within a sample pot may generate different feelings. A stranger vomiting in your lap might be disgusting, but your baby's milk spit might not upset you in the same ways. Secondly, bodily fluids were also very difficult to fix in terms of gender. There were many times, for example, where bodily fluids were at work in producing heterosexual masculinity, as Chapter 5 demonstrates. In fixing on bodily fluids as feminine, I was missing opportunities to see bodily fluids as gendered/gendering more broadly – and, even more importantly, I was missing opportunities to focus on instances where gender/gendering was not the primary form of politics at work. As Chapters 3 and 4 demonstrate, often it was more useful to frame bodily fluids in terms of racializing practices. These are gendered too, of course, but taking gender and particularly femininity as the lens for reading fluids was only working to obstruct a fuller analysis of the racializing politics of fluids.

These problems would not go away. They appeared and reappeared in the redlined draft material my (cherished and infinitely wiser) supervisors returned to me. They announced themselves in my stuttering defences and frustrated silences when I was pressed to answer for the (irritatingly) numerous instances where my grand claims about gender, fluids and self/Other did not work. This became clearer and clearer as I pressed on with my empirical analysis, as I struggled to restrain fluids in the place of the feminine. This struggle was ultimately a doomed practice, as this current version of the book you handle now demonstrates. In the end, fluids exceeded my attempts to tame them into grotesque femininity and I stopped fighting a losing battle. I could not make fluids signify monolithically. I could not restrict them to either/or meanings, and instead was overpowered by them as they flooded out from this form of binary analysis and swept me with them to 'the (pluralized) and/or' (Weber, 2016, p. 42).

Bodily fluids, and the ways in which they entangle with assemblages of bodies and security, were working in more complex and contradictory ways than I had initially thought. Attempts to 'straighten' (indeed) out where these fluids belonged in relation to gender, and in relation to bodily differentiation, quickly came undone. My attempts to get fluids to function as a method/ological frame for the project felt profoundly troubled by the difficulties of plotting fluids' relationships with gender, bodies and processes of bodily differentiation. At this point I wondered whether giving them up entirely was the more productive path. After all, I had three case studies at this point and plenty to say without insisting on fluids as method/ology for approaching my reading of these assemblages. So, why stick with fluids as method/ology?

Queerfeminist guts

Even though my earliest attempts at making use of bodily fluids had gone awry, I was not yet done with them. As such I made the decision to keep working with the idea of bodily fluids as a method/ology. This was not for reasons I could clearly identify but because I had a sense, a gut feeling, that following this idea through would lead me to something interesting and useful. As Sara Ahmed teaches us, feminism 'often begins with intensity: you are aroused by what you come up against. You register something in the sharpness of an impression. Something can be sharp without it being clear what the point is' (Ahmed, 2017, p. 22). Bodily fluids did arouse me intellectually – they called to a tactile sense of absence I had within international relations, of a lack of touch when it came to discussions on bodies. While feminist international relations literatures have contributed an incredible wealth of knowledge around the body and the idea of embodiment, I sensed that texture was missing from some of these discussions. Bodies were often put together and pulled apart by theorists in ways that neglected the sticky, clinging textures of the fleshy body. There was something 'strangely tidy' about the bodies under discussion; attention was not paid to the sticky, messy, uncomfortable parts of bodies, the fluids that regularly leak and gush from them (Longhurst, 2001, p. 4). Why were verbs like leak and gush, and the matter that leaked and gushed, so absent (and why did they feel so revolting?)? It was nausea and discomfort that bodily fluids aroused in myself when considering the body and, as a feminist-in-training, I knew that spending time with discomfort is a vital part of learning about power – it is where most of the work of feminism takes place (Harcourt et al., 2015, p. 161). Bodily fluids were absent in literatures surrounding the body, and my sense that this lack was an important one continued to grow. I felt that focusing on 'the organs, the hormones and bodily fluids, the bones … the "messy" bits' of the body could bring something to our understanding of international security and the body; I felt it could reveal something new about practices of governance and the distribution of life–death, even if I was unsure precisely what this was (Hall, 2000, p. 27).

To return to Sara Ahmed's counsel, '[a] gut has its own intelligence', and my guts were refusing to leave the idea of fluids alone, even despite my profound inability to order them in relation to gender and bodies (2017, p. 27). As Joe Dumit wrote, in advocating for the role of substances in ethnographic accounts, I had been stumped by fluids; but because I was obsessed, I was compelled to 'rethink [my] own concepts and tools' (2021, p. 177). In advocating for thus following your guts as a method/ological principle, I am not suggesting that guts and gut instinct are right, that they engage with the world on a level that is somehow 'deeper' or 'truer' than formal academic logics. Guts are just as much a part of the world as our brains, and they too absorb and soak in our social environment. My gut is frequently wrong. It makes judgements about fear and safety based on my own racism and classism, for example. There is much for my guts to unlearn. I want to argue therefore not that our gut instincts are always right and correct, but that it is worth paying attention to this question of feeling, and questioning how these senses of affect and appetite are political. I am not suggesting that we necessarily leave it up to our gut feelings to resolve questions, but rather that paying attention to them can offer a starting point; they can provoke, and open up questions to us. Feminists, after all, have done much work to highlight and identify the importance of *feeling* to practices of knowledge production (Åhäll, 2018; Brinkema, 2014). My guts yearned for the inclusion of the messy materialities of the body in our research and theorizing, pointing me towards a sense of absence in our existing theories. Paying attention to this feeling, asking why and how these absences were emerging, led to me feel that there was something – whatever this something was – that could work in the idea of fluids as method/ology. My gut called for a kind of analysis that embraced these disgusting and improper objects, and analysis that tried to build knowledge from bodily fluids as opposed to ignoring them or rendering them invisible.

My gut, then, in pulling me towards bodily fluids as a method/ology was expressing for me a particular queerfeminist hunger. My desire to build a way of thinking about my own research and the world from the position of bodily fluids was based on a queerfeminist affective lurch towards what is often considered disgusting. Queer folk have long been cast as disgusting in heteronormative Western cultures and, as such, many queer performers and artists have attempted to play with a sense of disgust and the grotesque, to embrace it and explore what possibilities for subversion it entails. John Waters' 1972 film *Pink Flamingos* is perhaps the paradigmatic example of this queer aesthetic of disgust (Breckon, 2013). Based on a homophobic construction of queer people and queer lives as perverse, disgusting, 'not normal', both queers and queer theorists have often strived to embrace these positions, in attempts to challenge and unsettle those good and normal things that constitute the (profoundly exclusionary) boundary of the human (Breckon, 2013; Caserio et al., 2006; Edelman, 1998). While queer theorists have done so to consciously destabilize heteronormative humanistic discourses, queers outside the academy have been busy demonstrating these principles in the pursuit and care of their 'unnatural' lives, finding worlds within their 'disgusting' and 'aberrant' communities, partnerships and practices that have nurtured them. Queer folk themselves know and understand that embracing that which is considered disgusting can lead to the discovery and creation of new and unexpected ways of thinking and living. That queerness is deemed disgusting by heteronormative orders makes objects and practices of disgust (queer sex, love, family, relationships, bodies) necessary for queer folks. They can be profoundly nourishing, and we are sustained by seeking out these disgusting ways of being and living. In seeking to embrace bodily fluids as disgusting objects that could inform this book's method/ology, then, my guts were pulling me in queer directions towards objects that are often absented from work on the body and embodiment, based on a sense and suspicion that there may be something useful in them.

Yet following this queer gut hunger for 'disgusting' matter became an opening up of bodily fluids, pointing me not towards a singular affective reaction as I anticipated but instead highlighting the work that bodily fluids are performing as they generate actions and reactions. As Mary Douglas teaches us, matter that is considered to be disgusting (or 'dirty' in her parlance) is never matter that is inherently this way, but instead matter that is produced as such because it both orders and disorders patterns of social hierarchy (2002). Douglas argues that feelings of disgust or revulsion towards bodily matter are an exercise in maintaining bodily boundaries, in an attempt to secure a social bodily hierarchy. Drawing from Douglas' work, this book therefore takes the position that disgust points us not towards a totalizing analysis of how bodily fluids are always understood and received, but instead point us towards *some* of the many possible ways in which body boundaries are governed in order to secure particular social orders. As this book goes on to show, bodily fluids are engaged in the governance of bodies and life–death not only through negative reactions of disgust but also through positive attempts to curate relationships through fluid connections. For example, while sexually active queer men are banned from donating blood in the UK, heterosexual black donors are actively recruited. While queer male bodies are barred from participating in relations that prolong life, there is an attempt to actively include heterosexual black bodies within these assemblages. Beginning rather than ending with disgust was therefore important in this book's attempt to open up the ways in which bodily fluids are governed, not only in a 'negative moment' to secure certain orders, but also as part of a 'positive effort to organize the [security] environment' through bodily relations (Douglas, 2002, p. 2; insertion my own).

Disgust thus served as a starting point to open up the range of affective responses bodily fluids can and do prompt. Paying attention to the different and contingent ways people respond to bodily fluids demonstrates how for 'feminists, affect, simply, generates [queer] feminist questions' (Åhäll, 2018, p. 50; insertion my own). Paying attention not only to disgust, but also to the complex and ambiguous range of affective responses bodily fluids provoke, opens up the deeper set of queerfeminist questions this book pursues. What are bodily fluids doing in international security? What forms of politics are they engaged with producing and challenging? How are bodily fluids bound up in materializations of race, sexuality, sex and gender? This book therefore attempts not to explore an affective politics of disgust, but instead to investigate how the governance of bodily fluids helps to reinforce/destabilize particular hierarchies of life–death in international politics. The next section of this chapter details how this book has made use of fluids in order to do so.

A fluid method/ology

Following a gut sense led me to continue to explore bodily fluids not only *in* international politics, but as a way of thinking *about* international politics. In this section I offer a definition of a fluid method/ology, arguing that bodily fluids can be used as a way to analyse the distribution of life–death in international security. I begin by showing that bodily fluids complicate relationships between bodies/subjects, and act as a point of connection between assemblages of bodies, security, gender, race, sexuality and life–death. In order to study these complex relationships and how security is organized through them, I argue that a fluid method/ology requires us to take a 'fluid' approach to research that focuses on experimentation and is responsive to change. Finally, I outline the idea of 'following the fluid' that this book practises in order to conduct this work.

Throughout the book, whether it is plasma, vomit, or semen, I show how bodily fluids work to forge connections and relationships between various bodies. Fluids are able not only to mark the surface of our skin, but to move between the interior of me to the interior of you. That fluids are able to move into and between bodies challenges the concept of bodies as bounded spaces. That we can share the intimate stuff of our bodies, can incorporate something from the inside of your body into the inside of mine reveals the precarity of our distinctions of self/Other, interior/exterior. When fluids move in and out of bodies, they trouble the boundary of the self. Take blood transfusions, for example. Following a transfusion, can we say that a part of someone else's body is inside you? At what point does part of their body become part of your body, and where/how do we then locate you both after this? Bodily fluids have the potential to challenge our notions of self/Other, prompting us to question the arbitrariness of these binaries and to think anew about the boundaries of our bodies and ourselves (Haraway, 1991). Bodily fluids show the impossibility of enforcing impermeable boundaries through their easy movements across and into others; 'the substance becomes its own metaphor' in the ways fluids demand a fluid understanding of the world (Dumit, 2021, p. 177). What bodily fluids are doing in connecting bodies together is drawing attention to the way your body may touch and affect my body, how permeable I am to you, and how uncertain the distinction between you and me really is.

As the book demonstrates, however, bodily fluids are simultaneously put to work in order to produce and maintain distinctions between bodies. These distinctions are often produced through notions of racial/

gender/sexed differentiation between bodies. When bodily fluids point to the arbitrariness of perceived body boundaries, then, they also threaten these power structures, which are dependent upon notions of corporeal differentiation. Racism, sexism, homophobia, transphobia and dis/ableism are reliant upon the production and ordering of corporeal hierarchies, of structured and unequal relations of power between differentiated bodies. In connecting bodies regardless of these differences, bodily fluids threaten to reveal that the systems of bodily differentiation that our worlds are built upon are also arbitrary. In Chapter 3, for example, the ability of plasma to move from the inside of Mexican bodies to the inside of white American bodies threatens the perceived racial purity of white bodies. If white American bodies can contain Mexican bodily fluids, how 'white' are these bodies? What do 'white' and 'Mexican' mean if these bodies are mingled together? Can we meaningfully differentiate between the two and enforce these categories in the context of plasma donation – and what kinds of racist politics are furthered by attempts to do so? Fluids can generate these questions through their ability to connect bodies together at a biological level. As an effect of living within racial, heteronormative capitalist orders, this ability demands the careful policing of bodily fluids to make sure that existing corporeal hierarchies are maintained.

Their potential to collapse differences between bodies thus also renders bodily fluids as crucial sites for the production of difference. Controlling bodily fluids allows the relationships they generate to be controlled too. The successful control and governance of bodily fluids suggests the possibility of maintaining differentiated bodies and subjects through their continual (re)production. It is for this reason that we see policies and practices in place in a variety of security sites that attend to bodily fluids. This book shows how a variety of practices that aim to govern the flows of fluids are crucial in (re)producing corporeal hierarchies of difference, by attempting to incorporate bodily fluids into gendering, sexing and racializing assemblages. In Chapter 5, for instance, we see how attempts to govern the flow of soldiers' semen following genitourinary injuries are vital in attempts to produce cisgender masculine heterosexual subjects, in opposition to non-normative sexed and gendered bodies and practices. Bodily fluids are thus produced as political substances in particular contingent contexts. It is through their contact with certain bodies, in certain places, and at certain times, that leads to their entanglement within security assemblages, where they are made to become vital in producing and regulating bodies and subjectivities within international security. Studying international politics through examining the play of fluids thus orients this book towards queer logics of and/or in the governance and regulation of bodies and subjectivities. They are a medium through which bodies, life, death, governance and security assemblages intertwine and wrap around each other. They are a locus of action and inter-action, of the joining together and breaking apart of bodily assemblages through various practices of governance.

The possibilities that fluids hold, their plural nature in regard to being able to both challenge and secure bodily distinctions, renders them a vital object of governance. A fluid method/ology must therefore be capable of studying and attending to the queer logics of and/or that bodily fluids can set into motion. Bodily fluids perform duplicitous actions. The doings of bodily fluids move in multiple contradictory directions, often at the same time. A fluid method/ology, then, is a way of thinking about the world that attempts to capture these messy, contingent movements of rupture and connection. Rather than tidy up the research story to present a linear narrative, a fluid method/ology seeks to create knowledge that is particular, situated, and contradictory, a story about the world that may lack clear plot lines and endings. In order to do so, we must adopt a similarly 'fluid' way of thinking about research. We need a way of thinking that is able to engage this sense of fluidity, change and movement.

Rather than prescribing fixed tools (methods) that must be applied 'correctly' to the world, a fluid method/ology instead adopts an approach centred on experimentation. It is not a prescriptive technique with a clear set of steps, but instead centres on the mobilization of a loose assemblage of ideas, techniques and concepts. These are based upon the particular thing/practice/site that we are attempting to engage. This conception of method/ology is influenced by critical approaches that emphasize the importance of 'method assemblages' that 'detect, resonate with, and amplify particular patterns of relations in the excessive and overwhelming fluxes of the real' (Law, 2004, p. 14). In particular, I draw upon Aradau et al.'s conceptualization of 'bricolage' as a method/ological approach, which takes method/ology as 'a way of experimenting with an assemblage of concepts, methods and empirical objects' (Aradau et al., 2014, p. 7). In order to understand how relationships of life–death are produced and governed in international security, this book draws together a host of concepts, ideas and objects; feminist technoscience studies, gender, queerfeminist curiosities, race, sexuality, security practices, bodies and subjectivity. Inspired by the idea of bricolage, I attempt to explore the relationships between these different assemblages to understand how they are mediated and effected through bodily fluids. The exact configuration of these different elements changes depending on the context. The objects, actors, practices and concepts depend upon which security setting we investigate. What is helpful and prominent in one setting may not be relevant in the next. A fluid method/ology therefore utilizes a sense of bricolage and experimentation to vary its analytical objects depending on specific security assemblages. It is not a one-size-fits-all approach to understanding the world, but instead emphasizes experimentation and change to engage contextually specific security assemblages.

Bricolage requires not only a changeable and situated choice of methods and concepts, but also prioritizes methods as a form of 'situated interference' (Aradau et al., 2014, p. 8). A fluid method/ology actualizes this through attention to bodily fluids. This book offers an analysis of 'the processes and conditions through which insecurities are made politically significant' by the governance of connections between fluids, bodies, and security assemblages (Aradau et al., 2014, p. 9). Disrupting violent modes of governance in these spaces and challenging the way in which life–death is unevenly and hierarchically distributed means highlighting the modes in which bodily fluids are caught up in distributing life–death. It also requires us to locate and identify the contradictions and tensions within these relationships. Fluid method/ologies therefore mobilize a range of concepts that are tailored towards a particular setting, and do so in order to disrupt harmful and violent security practices by identifying the ways in which these practices are always already failing. The next section of this chapter looks at how this challenge and engagement is achieved through the practice of 'following' bodily fluids.

Following the fluid

Following the fluid is (and has been) a difficult business throughout this book project. Following bodily fluids requires us to explore fluids as assemblages that elicit particular situated responses. Following the fluid therefore requires us to follow fluids in and out of other assemblages, mapping the relationships they form and disrupt along the way in order to situate them within, and understand their effects upon, a wider security 'field of play' (Lather, 2001, p. 204).

This book draws inspiration from both Jane Bennett's work on matter and Donna Haraway's work on string figures to think about both the agency of fluids and how we might track the relationships they form (Bennett, 2010; Haraway, 2016). In order to explore the agency of physical matter and how we may begin to gesture towards a theory of agency that is not limited to the human, Bennett takes a variety of objects and follows them through particular events – electricity in the 2003 North American blackout, food in eating practices, stem cells in anti-abortion debates. To follow them, she enquires after the relationships they establish and engage along the way. Her work on the 2003 blackout explores the assemblage of the electrical grid, examining the role human agency played in the blackout, as well as nonhuman agency – the 'looseness and slipperiness' of electricity, which 'sometimes goes where we send it, and sometimes ... chooses its path on the spot' (Bennett, 2010, p. 28). Bennett tracks electricity from power plant to power line, through deregulation and energy traders, attempting to understand how these relationships culminated in the 2003 blackout. But this understanding is not geared towards finding the causal agent behind the blackout. Instead of attempting to find the 'doer … behind the deed', Bennet proposes that there is no doer, but 'a doing and an effecting by a human–nonhuman assemblage' (Bennett, 2010, p. 28). This posthuman understanding of agency that Bennett constructs is brought about by her careful attention to the tangle of differential relationships that make up any given assemblage. As such, rather than attempting to identify the cause of a particular event, Bennett's work focuses on the 'collaboration, cooperation, or interactive interference of many bodies and forces' that comprises assemblages (Bennett, 2010, p. 21).

In doing so, Bennett adopts a methodological principle of 'follow the object' (Aradau et al., 2014, p. 79). Bennet tracks a given object through an event in order to understand the relationships it is engaged in, and ultimately draw wider conclusions about agency and matter (Bennett, 2010). While drawing inspiration from the way Bennett follows particular objects, and her understanding of agency, this book takes two important breaks away from Jane Bennett's work. Firstly, whereas Bennett's primary purpose is in exploring physical matter and reaching towards a posthuman construction of agency, this book's aim is to explore the physical matter of the human body. In doing so, the borders of the human body are challenged, and nonhuman objects have an agential role to play; but I am not so concerned here with decentring the human as I am with showing how the human body is a porous assemblage (one that does encompass nonhuman elements). Secondly, Bennett's work draws (critically) upon the vitalist tradition, exploring questions of what *life* means. Rather than attempt to understand how matter is animate, this book instead looks to the implications agential matter has for practices of gendered/sexed/raced (in)security and the body. As such, the main currents of Bennett's work that I engage with in this book are her ideas of following an object (though I follow fluids) and her understanding of matter as agential. I have attempted to bring these insights together with international politics, (in)security, race/sex/gender and the body, asking how following bodily fluids through particular security assemblages can help us understand the relationships between these elements.

Following a fluid requires understanding fluids as affective and agential matter in international politics. This does not mean that I take bodily fluids as conscious and scheming actors, but rather understanding their capacity for 'activity and responsiveness' (Bennett, 2010, p. xii). Bodily fluids are able to affect others as well as be affected by them. Plasma, for example, when introduced to the interior of a person's body, can cause an allergic reaction, anaphylactic shock, transfusion-related acute lung injury, as well as a host of viral affects, such as HIV transmission (MacLennan & Barbara, 2006). Close contact with the vomit of someone with Ebola can result in viral infection, as well as more prosaic but still noteworthy effects: if you tread in it, you may slip and fall. Semen, upon entry into the vagina, will make their way towards an egg, guided by (probably) temperature gradients and chemotactic signalling from the egg, causing (if this journey is successful) fertilization (Bahat & Eisenbach, 2006; Kaupp et al., 2008; Spehr, 2003). These bodily fluids all have the capacity to act and respond to other assemblages, to set certain things in motion. Bodily fluids are therefore agential matter in international politics, able to move and do things in chorus with a host of other elements.[1]

Donna Haraway's *Staying with the Trouble: Making Kin in the Chthulucene* provides us with a roadmap for a method/ology of following. As Jane Bennett explores what objects can do, Donna Haraway mobilizes an assemblage of various figures in order to follow (or 'trace', in her vocabulary) these 'doings' of objects in order to understand 'who lives and who dies and how' in the current political moment (Haraway, 2016, p. 3). Haraway's chosen mode of following is to look at what she terms string figures. String figures refer both to a loose ensemble cast of entanglements (Haraway identifies science fiction, speculative feminism, science fact and speculative fabulation) and to a mode of following. For Haraway, the idea of string figures is a way of picturing the linkages between differently assembled elements, the webbed relationships that constitute 'the actual thing, that pattern and assembly that solicits response, the thing that is not oneself but with which one must go on' (2016, p. 3). In employing string figures Haraway commits to an undecidability of the object. Her swarm of string figures change, with different configurations occupying her catch-all abbreviation 'SF', allowing her to account for the interdependency of the objects she studies upon each other. For Haraway, following is all about 'passing on and receiving, picking up threads and dropping them' (Haraway, 2016, p. 3).

An example is helpful here to demonstrate what it means to follow an object that is interdependent, malleable and changing alongside our attempts to track them. One of the string figures Haraway follows is the urine of her dog, Cayenne (Haraway, 2016, pp. 104–116). In Cayenne's old age, the lack of oestrogen in her body leads to the weakening of muscles in her urethra, leading to her experiencing a leaky bladder. Following Cayenne's urine in order to think about the ways in which humans, animals and technology are enmeshed in relations with each other, Haraway finds her dog's urine exists in relation to/with pregnant horses in Canada and menopausal women in the US, through the manufacture of Cayenne's synthetic oestrogen capsules. In tracking Cayenne's urine, Haraway ultimately brings to light the 'conglobulation of interlinked research, marketing, medical and veterinary, activist, agricultural, and scholarly body- and subject-making apparatuses' (2016, p. 114). Following Cayenne's urine here entails following it through and into the other assemblages it connects to and forms relationship with. It is a form of following that traces urine into and through its other connections, a following that gives into and accepts that following also requires us, at some points, to get lost. Following Cayenne's urine for Haraway means paying attention not only to urine as an object itself, but also to the other assemblages it joins up with and the types of connection, exchange and transformation that proceed from there. Through its entanglement with other assemblages, urine here acts as a node connecting bodies together.

No research project is easy to undertake, and a practice of following fluids is no exception. Bodily fluids are tricky substances. They are able to cross borders, to show up where they should not be found, to overwhelm the frameworks we use to make sense of the world. Following them, then, means giving oneself up to a research process that is 'slow and uncertain … risky and troubling' (Law, 2004, p. 10). Following a fluid requires us to be curious, to wander off the beaten path and go wherever the slimy and viscous trails lead us in our journey through international politics. We must pay close attention to the relationships and connections these bodily fluids form with national borders, the body, gender, race, and security practices. Following these fluids means paying attention to the ways they draw in/are drawn into actors, matter and discourses. These other assemblages they come into contact with are not just conduits for fluids to move through. Bodily fluids change these assemblages as they interact with them, in a reciprocal and mutual relationship where everyone and everything involved is thrown slightly off-kilter by this contact. The relationships formed between these various assemblages change and shift at this point of contact, and following a fluid means studying how these moments of connection alter the state of play for all involved.

Conclusion

As such, this book follows fluids into security assemblages in order to identify how life–death are distributed through the connections between bodies that bodily fluids establish. Following fluids allows us to make use of fluids as 'nodal points' that both 'glue' and separate bodies with/from each other, and exchange life–death differentially between them (Baaz & Stern, 2005). Importantly, when we follow fluids as objects that have the capacity to 'do' things, we are able to see that this is only a capacity, a potential. Fluids are dependent on wider assemblages in order for this capacity to be actualized. Following fluids therefore makes visible how security assemblages attempt to mobilize fluids in this way, and also how these relationships are both formed and disrupted through fluid connections. Fluids, therefore, offer a useful object to 'think with', as they allow us to make our way into wider security assemblages and examine how relationships of life–death between bodies are established through the governance of fluid connections (Lather, 2001, p. 217). Following fluids allows us to see 'the connections that must exist' for security practices to govern life–death, by following 'the contingent connections' between fluids, bodies and other assemblages that render these practices of governance meaningful (Aradau et al., 2014, p. 68).

In the preceding work, I follow bodily fluids both in their presence and absence. I follow them in and out of bodies, and as they splatter their way across various discussions, practices and policies in order to understand how it is these fluid relationships are vital to the distribution of life–death in international security settings. There is no set list of directions for how to 'properly' follow a fluid. The other things, bodies, objects, practices and assemblages we need to engage are contingent, dependent upon the specific following we are attempting to conduct. The specific sources this book draws upon depend upon the fluid and site in question. The source selection reflects the particularities of each assemblage examined within this book, and changes depending on which security actors are involved, where public discourse around these fluids are located, and the relevant historical context that these assemblages emerge from. Chapter 2 utilizes a variety of media articles on plasma donation, as well as material produced by plasma collection companies and industry journals. Chapter 3 again draws from news media as well as policy documents, guidelines from the World Health Organization and Centers for Disease Control and Prevention, novels and films. Chapter 4 combines documents from the Department of Defense (DoD), data collected by the Costs of War project, various DoD-funded projects looking into genitourinary injuries (GUIs) and news media around GUIs. In using these documents, this book tracks the movements of fluids into and out of the various structures designed to govern their movements, asking how fluids are understood and made meaningful within these assemblages.

Focusing on a particular fluid acts as a guide to understanding these complex and entangled relationships and doings. Vomit, semen and plasma all function as guiding objects within this book. By attempting to locate and follow them as they make their way into and through a variety of assemblages, we are able to track and map the points at which biopolitical governance attempts to secure these relationships. Looking to a certain fluid and attempting to follow it as it disperses into a particular web of relationships highlights the ways in which biopolitics operates through the (attempted) regulation and control of these fluid exchanges. Following fluids thus takes us on unexpected journeys. Bodily fluids may dis/re/connect bodies in ways we do not predict. A commitment to following our queerfeminist noses along slimy bodily trails and seeing where they lead means relinquishing our sense of control. All masculinized hopes of mastery over 'the field' must be dispensed with; instead, we must feel our way, asking questions at every turn, and be willing to go off-track, to be led astray. We must commit to seeing what bodily fluids might bring us to, what kinds of bodies they might work with/through, and what kinds of politics they may entangle themselves in. In following bodily fluids, then, we must propose to 'lose our ways … and possibly our minds', in the hope that we may 'find another way of making meaning' that disturbs our ideas about the body, about sex/gender, race, and about international politics and security (Halberstam, 2011, p. 147).

7

Concluding Is the Wrong Verb

Telling stories about international politics with bodily fluids matters. As Donna Haraway suggests, '[i]t matters what matters we use to think other matters with; it matters what stories we tell to tell other stories with … [i]t matters what stories make worlds, what worlds make stories' (Haraway, 2016, p. 12). Using them to study international politics matters. It matters because where we start our stories, where we begin our thinking, takes us to different places. It can make the familiar unfamiliar, and it can show us familiar settings in new lights. This book has revisited ground that is well trodden in the study of international security (the airport, the border, the soldier), but in focusing on fluids bodies are brought uniquely into view. Starting these stories with bodily fluids changes our understanding of how biopolitical governance is conducted within these spaces. Beginning with bodily fluids allows us to see how the distribution of life–death and the governance of bodies in international politics are affected in mundane, daily encounters between loose groupings of assemblages; race, sex, gender, sexuality, security, biopolitics, bodies.

Starting with fluids shows how relationships between these assemblages are established, (re)produced and challenged through snaking trails of fluid. These fluids relations take different forms and shapes in different security sites. Chapter 2 of this book introduced feminist technoscience studies (FTS) and assemblage theory, combining the two to argue that body-assemblages are always contextual and specific assemblages that are never 'prior' to race, gender or sex. Bodily fluids are vital to the governance of bodily assemblages, by distributing relationships of life–death among them. The subsequent chapters of this book plug these understandings into three different empirical contexts. Chapter 3 analysed how assemblages of plasma donation are caught up in the governance of bodies at borders, arguing that plasma is involved in the racialized production and differentiation of bodies at the border, through the valuing of Mexicana/o donors only in relation to the effect they may have upon non-Mexican lives. Chapter 4 focused on vomit at the airport during the 2013–16 Ebola outbreak, arguing that security practices make use of a masculinized, colonial gaze to generate a racialized dichotomy of risk, producing and subordinating black African lives to white Western bodies. Chapter 5 explored how treatments for service members with genitourinary injuries secure the life of cisgender, masculine militarism over and against queer and trans possibilities, and the lives of Afghan and Iraqi people. Finally, Chapter 6 outlined the fluid method/ology this book utilized to study such relationships, outlining a method/ological approach motivated by gut feeling and actualized in the concept of 'following' bodily fluids through assemblages.

Taken together, these case studies demonstrate that the governance of bodily fluids is central to biopolitical security practices. In each setting bodily fluids establish various relationships of life–death between different bodies. By controlling the fluids that put these bodies in relation with each other, practices of international security attempt to govern these bodies, ordering them into a hierarchy that establishes some bodies as more valuable than others. These hierarchies are, however, simultaneously threatened by bodily fluids, which establish relational flows of life–death between bodies in ways that both (re)produce and challenge these hierarchies. In this final chapter, I reflect upon the significance of FTS in conjunction with a focus on bodily fluids. An FTS approach is uniquely valuable for showing us that biopolitics operates in the mundane, and pushing us to recognize that bios is always already raced/sexed/gendered. I then offer some final thoughts on bodily fluids and relationships of life–death. I finish by then briefly pointing to the utility of following the fluid in other situations, sketching some possible future directions for analysing COVID-19 governance through following fluids.

Mundane matters matter

Feminist international relations theory has, for decades, shown that a focus on the mundane and the everyday is vital in engaging international politics, with the mantra the personal is international and the international is personal (Enloe, 2014, p. 343). Feminism's attention to that which is considered mundane and not the proper 'stuff' of international politics reveals to us how that which is considered to be an appropriate object of study in international politics is profoundly gendered. Paying attention to the potentially prosaic spaces of everyday living is, therefore, one of the 'core lessons of feminist international investigation', as Cynthia Enloe writes, because without doing so we end up with a malnourished conception of power that misses 'who wields power and for what ends' (2014, p. 9).

Paying attention to the ways power is reproduced in everyday life therefore has much to tell us about how the distribution of life–death functions at the everyday level. This is where FTS specifically becomes valuable to us.

FTS builds from feminist insights into the value of the personal to explore how human-technology assemblages in the space of everyday life work to reproduce gender, race and the body. The 'intimately personal and individualized body' is understood by FTS as 'vibrat[ing] in the same field with global high-tension' politics (Haraway, 1988, p. 588). Chapter 3 follows plasma donation at the US–Mexico border in order to understand the ways in which Mexican bodies are produced as life-giving and life-threatening in relation to American bodies. Chapter 4 follows vomit at the airport to see how health screening procedures attempt to govern the mobility of black African bodies in order to preserve the life of white bodies. And Chapter 5 follows semen in the surgical and medical rehabilitation of soldiers with genitourinary injuries (GUIs) to explore how the American soldier is made to 'live' at the expense of queer/trans possibilities.

Such settings – the border, the airport, the soldiering body – are all common security sites. The security sites that populate this book – the border, the airport, the soldiering body – are, of course, familiar sites of enquiry for international relations. Thanks to the legacy of critical scholarship, they stand out to us as obvious sites where the stuff of security is happening. We expect issues about identity and race and migration and surveillance to materialize at the border, because decades of critical scholarship have done the painstaking work of drawing attention to these spaces and what is happening within them (Anzaldúa, 2012; Doty, 1999; Nevins, 2007; Redden & Terry, 2013; Shepherd & Sjoberg, 2012; Sparke, 2006). We expect to find issues about militarism, gender, sexuality and race at the site of the soldiering body, thanks to decades of feminist work in this area (Dyvik & Greenwood, 2016; Khalili, 2011; Masters, 2005; Whitworth, 2005; Woodward, 2000).

But bodily fluids are profoundly everyday objects. They often go unremarked in literatures that attend explicitly to the body, or often go ignored and unwritten about (Longhurst, 2001). While the border is a common feature in critical security studies, plasma is not. Plasma is an everyday object for plasma donors, and Mexican donors regularly cross the border in order to donate. It is a mundane and repetitive event for many donors, involving repeated travel through border security and into a building where they will queue, sit in chairs, and answer the same questions they are asked each time. It is a formulaic chore that donors may perform twice a week. Vomit at the airport and aboard airplanes is, likewise, a mundane and common substance in that setting. It is such a common occurrence aboard airplanes in particular that airlines specifically provide handy, waxed paper bags for people to vomit into. It is not a surprising substance to find in that setting. And when it comes to semen, while the experience of a traumatic GUI injury during wartime may not be an everyday event, sex and ejaculation are. It is an everyday occurrence, a mundane happening.

Like the rest of the bodily fluids discussed in this book, it does not attract the attention of theorists of international politics precisely because it is so common that it becomes invisible, something easy to pass over.

To focus on the mundane in these settings, as we are pushed to by FTS, matters because it has the potential to bring us to a richer understanding of how security assemblages engage life–death through body–technology relationships in a whole variety of settings and conditions that have previously been invisible. Using FTS to explore biopolitics enriches our understanding of where these politics are affected, how they are affected, and through which relations. As all three case studies within this book show, biopolitics is at work through connections that we may often ignore or fail to connect with the politics of securitization. FTS has the potential to make these relationships visible, and to enable us to ask both who is living and dying at a mundane level, but also why and who they are living and dying for, and how these relationships are affected through everyday body–technology assemblages.

Noting the importance of these mundane practices locates an important level of theoretical tension between the exceptionalized spaces, objects and practices often attracting the attention of scholars, and the prosaic daily activities that these exceptional events and sites are reliant upon. Naming these practices of governance as mundane is not an attempt to claim that these empirical contexts are necessarily dull and flat events for the subjects and bodies embroiled in them. There are many potential affective atmospheres generated by plasma donation, vomit at the airport, and the experience of GUIs. Noting fluids and the practices that surround them as mundane is not an attempt to claim otherwise, or even to offer a claim about the emotional and affective responses bodily fluids can generate. Instead, noting the ways in which these experiences are often mundane shows us that the grand politics of security, the distribution of life and death, are produced and generated by small daily practices. Life–death is not only distributed through the grand theatre of war but through hospitals, the waiting around in airports, the ticking off of boxes on a form. It is distributed through assemblages that involve people eating breakfast, getting into their cars, and sitting down in treatment rooms for hours at a time. Drawing on FTS to look at bodily fluids demonstrates the ways in which security politics and modes of biopolitical governance are enmeshed within the mundane and everyday stuff of people's lives.

Trick questions: which came first, the body or race-gender-sex?

As Chapter 1 argued, FTS begins from a position that takes bodies as always already raced, gendered and sexed. This is not to say that FTS takes any of these forms of bodily marking as natural or fixed. Rather it is to point out that bodily assemblages are always already in the process of being located somewhere in relation to sex, gender and race. Bodies are not first and foremost generically human, and they cannot become specific configurations of human/unhuman without being identified and positioned in relation to sex, gender and race. FTS takes the position that there is no 'human', no 'body' that does not already function without relation to forms of corporeal marking, and that that which is paraded as 'the human' are often the bodies of white men that are allowed to transcend their whiteness and maleness and be (falsely) represented as universal. For those outside these privileged subject positions, transcendence into the universal is not allowed (Haraway, 1988).

In relation to biopolitics, then, feminist technoscience reminds us that the 'bios' of biopolitics, the life that is managed and governed, is not prior to gender, race or sexuality. As Alexander Weheliye argues, biopolitical analyses often figure bios as 'an indivisible substance anterior to racialization' (Weheliye, 2014, p. 4). Imagining biopolitics thus as 'the installation of epistemic and political technics through which "human life" emerges' risks instantiating a universalist understanding of 'the human', and imagining that there is a generic 'human' form of life out there that exists before such troublesome additions such as race, gender, sex and sexuality (Athanasiou, 2005, p. 143). Trading in a universalist conception of life results in a profound neglect of the ways in which 'racialization and different axes of domination cooperate' in the structuring of life and body assemblages (Weheliye, 2014, p. 49). Imagining biopolitical governance as curating and managing human life, a bios that is complete before it is then stratified by race and gender, fails to recognize the ways in which race and gender are central in constructing the category of the human. As Donna Haraway argues, 'there is no pan-human, no pan-machine, no pan-nature, no pan-culture … [t]here are only specific worlds, and these are irreducibly tropic and contingent' (Haraway, 1994, p. 64). This book takes up the proposition of FTS scholars that picturing bios as prior to race and gender ignores the ways in which racializing and gendering assemblages are responsible for generating bios as plural, as a spectrum of bodies that are made possible through their relationships with each other. Taking bios not as prior to race and gender but as produced in conjunction with race and gender refuses to take what constitutes bios/life/the human as natural or inevitable, instead demonstrating that what counts as 'life' 'is not given by definition, but only by relation, by engagement in situated, worldly encounters' (Haraway, 1994, p. 64). FTS engagements with biopolitics therefore return us to a feminist technoscience engagement with assemblage theory where life itself is not 'pre-formed before the counter' but comes into being through differentiating relationships with other assemblages (Puar, 2009, p. 168). FTS's contribution to biopolitics reminds us that 'bios' is a profoundly qualified term rather than a universal referent. FTS takes the importance of race and gender seriously as profoundly generative of life, rather than treating them as superficial additions to it. As a corpus of literature, it demonstrates that there is no 'universally-conceptualized "basic" body, onto which are layered social meanings and identities ... [i]nstead, the body [and life] itself and what it represents may be very differently conceived' (Thomas, 2002, p. 24).

Pulling feminist technoscience together with a practice of following bodily fluids thus changes our understanding of where the boundaries of biopolitics lie. If biopolitics relates to the governance of life–death, feminist scholars have already been doing biopolitical analysis for years, while sometimes using different lexicons in order to tackle these questions. Donna Haraway, for example, has written on the governance of life through enmeshment with technoscience using the figure of OncoMouse, a transgenic mouse, and its relation to a figure Haraway dubs FemaleMan, charting what spirals from holding these two assemblages in relation with each other (Haraway, 1997). Elizabeth Grosz examines how life is governed through the production of biology and gender/sex (Grosz, 1994). Hortense Spillers pulled on the ways in which the violence of slavery points to a distinction between body and flesh, and engages with 'the flesh' (particularly the female flesh of black enslaved women) as a 'text for living and dying' (Spillers, 1987, p. 68). Jasbir Puar explores how bodily debility and capacity work to blur boundaries between living and dying (Puar, 2017b). Catherine Waldby and Cindy Patton have both argued that particular materializations of the AIDS virus are used to produce and govern gay/straight and male/female bodies and populations (Patton, 1985; Waldby, 1996). Jennifer Nash has written about the ways in which doulas are drawn into birthing arrangements and expected to address the disproportionate chance of death and complication black birthing people face (2019). As such, this book grounds its engagement with biopolitics in the work of feminist technoscience, which has been engaging with and analysing forms of biopolitical governance for years. FTS's analysis of biopolitics draws on the two principles outlined previously: (1) an appraisal of the value of the mundane, and (2) a positioning of life as produced through gendered and racializing assemblages, rather than existing as a universally 'human' referent. Drawing from feminist technoscience engagements with biopolitics therefore not only works to build a rich and nuanced analysis that takes race, gender and the mundane seriously, but draws attention to the fact that space within biopolitical literatures is already occupied by feminist technoscience scholars.

One last chorus: life–death and bodily fluids

Studying international security through bodily fluids teaches us lessons about where biopolitics happens. In doing so, bodily fluids critically open up our understanding of both 'life' and 'death' by complicating the relationship between them. Looking at bodily fluids shows us that the politics of life–death are achieved not only in zero-sum exchanges through which some die so that others may live. This book has demonstrated the ways in which biopolitics are conducted through relationships that require specific and particular groups to live for others. Studying fluids therefore makes it easier for us to recognize relational patterns of living in international politics. Bodily fluids show us that we must not only enquire after who dies but who is required to live, for whom, and in what way. This book has shown how 'life' is not a singular process but always a situated mode of being that is enabled and generated through its relationships with other forms of life–death.

Rather than thinking in binary terms about the politics of life–death, this book has made use of bodily fluids to push life–death into the plural and queer logics of both/and. Studying these relationships therefore opens up the relationship between life and death, requiring us not to only investigate these two terms as discrete opposites, but to make visible the breadth and nuance of the spaces in-between. Bodily fluids do not only work in zero-sum biopolitical equations, whereby one dies so that another lives. They are also embroiled in circulatory flows of life–death. Bodily fluids and life are not necessarily subtracted from one body and added to another. They also pulse continually around assemblages, coming and going between bodies and being continually siphoned off and put back. We can often map these two modes of relationship in the same instance, at the same time. Within plasma donation, as this book has demonstrated, life is extracted from Mexicana/o donors and transferred into other bodies through the medium of plasma. At the same time, this 'life' is replenished by Mexicana/o donors. It is continually being produced and pushed through donation assemblages, being renewed again within the bodies of donors. Plasma donors within this system are not dying so that others might live. Rather, this book has shown that studying fluids draws our attention to how life–death is governed through requiring some populations to live for others. This book thus contributes a critical questioning of biopolitical modes of governance that pushes beyond understanding life only in relation to death, instead making visible the ways in which different forms of 'life' are constituted by relationships between particular and specific bodies.

But, of course, at the same time, people and particular subjects are dying within these relationships. The queer logics of both/and bite both ways simultaneously. Studying bodily fluids also complicates the way in which we understand death, by highlighting the various differential speeds of dying. Dying is, when we look at bodily fluids, not only something absolute whereby a specific individual's heart stops and their brain ceases functioning. Bodily fluids show us how this process can be distributed at the level of population in much smaller increments whereby the life of particular subjects and bodies becomes unimportant, lacks value. Death is not only the cessation of particular bodies, a precise moment, but can also function as a slow and structural field of being that kills through the steady decreasing of the value of some lives. Death is what happens when some lives are made to matter less, and dying is a process conducted at a variety of different speeds, dependent on the specific assemblage in question.

Understanding how practices of governance distribute life–death through ordering relationships between bodies matters, because it makes visible how these violent and unequal practices operate. Understanding the distribution of life–death as happening through the governance of bodily fluids, and thus the relationships bodies form with others, is a vital step in working to disrupt these relationships. Challenging the practices that make some lives more valuable and worthy than others requires us to understand where and how these practices are at work. Bodily fluids allow us to map these relationships of life–death. They are the radioactive dye that moves through security assemblages, allowing us to plot the pathways through which life–death are produced and circulated between bodies. By telling stories that begin with bodily fluids, this book has been able to produce a roadmap of how fluids are governed in order to distribute life–death between bodies, as well as demonstrating how this process is bound up in violent (re)productions of particularly raced/sexed/gendered forms of humans. Discovering these pathways is an essential first step in working to disrupt them. If we want to work towards different ways of being with each other in international politics, we need to know what we have to change.

Bodily fluids help us produce a map of life–death in international politics, and help identify pre-existing fissures in these relationships. As this book has shown, bodily fluids do not necessarily enable smooth and seamless patterns of governance. Rather, they are often affecting multiple, contradictory forms of politics at the same time. They are differentiating raced bodies at the same time as they are collapsing the notion of racial difference. They are both profoundly challenging to cishet masculinities at the same time as they are helping to secure them. The stability and instability that bodily fluids generate allows us to identify pressure points in the system, to show how these practices of governance are always already a delicate balancing act, a see-sawing motion that produces its image of stability only by remaining in perpetual motion. Conjoining FTS with bodily fluids thus provides us with a way to tell stories about international security without sedimenting the practices we wish to challenge. If we can keep them liquid, keep them fluid, we can see that the picture of an unchangeable and unchanging violent exercise of power is an illusion. Repetitive violences can only be shored up by constant change, by constant multiplicity and negotiation. In recognizing that, we can see where the fault lines are in the pattern, where there is the potential for other possibilities. And we can press upon them.

Future followings: COVID-19

As the title of this final chapter suggests, I am ambivalent about the idea of concluding, and all the finiteness and neatness that is implied in this term. That does not sit well with an ontology of assemblage. So, instead, I want to end by suggesting ways in which this project on bodily fluids could very well stretch and sprawl into areas of research beyond the confines of this book. We began with a story about COVID-19, and I want to end by pointing out the ways in which bodily fluids and feminist technoscience may help us understand the destruction that COVID-19 has brought to our lives and communities (and some lives and some communities much, much more than others).

There is a pull towards talking about COVID-19 as if it is exceptional. In many ways, it is – it was a novel virus among the human population, it spread incredibly quickly around the world, and it has already killed millions of people. But where I want to push away from understanding COVID-19 as exceptional is in our framing of the problem. As Lauren Berlant has pointed out, when we apply the framework of 'crisis', we risk losing sight of the ways in which crisis is a 'process embedded in the ordinary that unfolds in stories about navigating what is overwhelming' (2011, p. 10). SARS-CoV-2 is a novel coronavirus virus, yes. But the effects that COVID-19 had were, in many ways, entirely predictable. And that is what I think bodily fluids can help us to map and understand.

COVID-19 is a virus spread through contact with bodily fluids, and minute traces of them at that – the droplets that we exhale, that we sneeze, that we emit when we speak (Salian et al., 2021). Tracking these bodily fluids and attempting to sever the (dangerous, harmful) relationships that they create – between infected and uninfected bodies, between human body and viral body – was the centrepiece of many public health strategies that emphasized minimizing the spread of disease among given populations. Following a bodily fluid in this setting requires us to understand how a bodily fluid becomes infectious; what it can contain within itself; how it becomes either able or unable to pass between bodies; and which bodies are most vulnerable to becoming embroiled in transmission chains. So far so obvious. But following bodily fluids and seriously considering the assemblages they conjoin with, and transform, may also help point us towards the deep-rooted historical structures that made so much of what happened during COVID-19 so totally and depressingly unsurprising.

If you live in the UK, you may well remember Belly Mujinga. Belly was 47 years old and employed by Govia Thameslink Railway. She was working at the concourse on Victoria station in central London on 22 March 2020 when a white man claimed he had COVID-19, and coughed and spat at both Belly and a colleague. Within days, both Belly and her colleague fell ill with the virus. Belly was admitted to Barnet Hospital, where she died on 5 April.

It is unclear whether the assault a white man subjected Belly, a black woman, to on that day was the incident that led to her contracting coronavirus. But following the fluid that the unnamed man coughed, spat and exhaled in Belly's direction requires us to understand how all parties came to be present in that interaction in the first place. We need to understand whether and how Belly's employers viewed the risk to her, a person with existing respiratory problems who had raised concerns and objections about working in close proximity to the general public, without PPE, was an acceptable level of risk (Weaver & Dodd, 2023). This requires us to understand the nature of racial capitalism, and the treatment of black subjects under these structures as 'available for maiming' (Puar, 2017, p. xvii; see also Papamichail, 2023). It requires us to understand the racialized nature of the violence committed against Belly, and the history that underpins a white man spitting at a black woman. It requires us to understand why Belly was working in that role, and the gendered and ethnic distribution of key worker roles among various populations. To follow that saliva, and to really understand the conditions for its materialization, we have to think about how the bodies that came to be involved in this interaction were made to present in the ways that they were, to see the political and historical assemblages that put Belly and her attacker in that place, in that interaction, under specific circumstances. We need to account for the legal framework (or lack of it) for managing COVID-19 as a public health problem, and why a government that ranked an infectious disease outbreak as both a highly likely and severe risk to the UK in 2017 had no discernible plan in place for dealing with such an eventuality (Cabinet Office, 2017). And following the fluid from this point forward, as it passed from the man whose name we are not allowed to know to the body of Belly as he spat and coughed at her, requires us to follow it beyond the railway station and into the hospital with Belly, into the assemblage of medical technology and the protocols that governed the delivery of COVID-19 treatment.

And in following the reverberations of this interaction, we are led to the interconnected assemblages of violence that permeated that train station concourse. What happened to Belly happened to other rail and transport workers, and the acquisition of COVID-19 and fatal consequences happened disproportionately within marginalized communities. In the UK, people of marginalized ethnicities were more likely to test positive for COVID, and more likely to be hospitalized with the disease (Haque et al., 2020, p. 6). After controlling for factors such as age and geography, the deaths of black African hospital patients with COVID-19 were 3.7 times higher than white British patients; that figure is 2.9 for Pakistani patients and 2.0 for Bangladeshi patients (Platt & Warwick, 2020, p. 3). People of marginalized ethnicities were more likely to report not being given adequate PPE at work (Haque et al., 2020, p. 3). And of all the deaths involving COVID-19 between January 2020 and February 2021, the majority of those who died (around 56 per cent) were disabled (Bosworth et al., 2021, p. e820). It is crucial that we recognize the painful and violent individual contours of what was done to Belly; and that we also set her attack within a wider scene of violently unequal risks during the COVID-19 pandemic.

Following the fluid can lead us to see the many, many (political) choices and governance practices that worked to violently curtail the possibilities of a life; and to see that many of these choices predate the COVID-19 virus making the jump from other animal life to humans. Fluids can point us towards the social, economic and historical assemblages that COVID-19 emerged into; and chart the divergent ways in which some bodies were actively 'protected' from bodily fluids during this time, while others were consciously and intentionally exposed to them. Bodily fluids – and an ontology of the world rooted in FTS – can point to how these practices and decisions were rooted in existing assemblages of racialized misogyny, disableism and capitalism. It is these messy, congealed webs of violence that we need to keep pulling and picking at.

Notes

Chapter 1
1. See also Rahul Rao's work on the ways in which 'the woman question' and 'the homosexual question' interact with and disrupt each other (Rao, 2014).
2. I use the umbrella term 'queer' in this section to refer to the LGBT community, while recognizing that some LGBT people may not identify their sexuality as queer, and that some members of the community have no warm feelings towards this particular word (for a brief introduction, see Segal, 2016).

Chapter 2
1. This is an ethical problem with Deleuze and Guattari's text, which continually abducts vulnerable subjects and their bodies for the purposes of making grand theoretical statements. In this case, the empty and dreary bodies under discussion are those of hypochondriacs, people suffering from extreme paranoia, schizophrenics (sensitively referred to as the 'schizo body'), and drug addicts (Deleuze & Guattari, 1980, pp. 174–175; 178). Deleuze and Guattari have little problem with referring to the bodies of vulnerable social groups as 'sucked-dry, catatonicized, vitrified', which at best can be described as mean-spirited, and at worst as a tendency of the theorists to act as though the bodies they happily deploy at will to advance their arguments are purely figurative and do not feel or suffer the consequences of theory (Deleuze & Guattari, 1980, p. 175).
2. While they do make a brief acknowledgement that molar politics is 'indispensable' for women in order to win 'back their own organism, their own history, their own subjectivity', this statement is also immediately undermined by the warning that this is a 'dangerous' form of politics, which forecloses valuable relational possibilities (Deleuze & Guattari, 1980, p. 321).

Chapter 3
1. The FTC originally named five companies. One of these, Talecris, is now owned by Grifols, and Baxter's collection centres are operated under the banner of BioLife Plasma Services. As such, I focus here on the above companies, and refer to 'BioLife' centres instead of 'Baxter' centres.
2. As a measure of distance, the centre furthest from the border included in this group of 29 is the Grifols donation centre on East University Drive in Edinburgh, Texas; it is less than a 20-mile journey from the McAllen-Hidalgo Bridge, or just over 20 miles from the Pharr-Reynosa International Bridge, the two closest border crossing points.
3. Donation centre information is retrieved from company websites and correct at the time of writing; these numbers omit plasma donation centres not operated by Grifols, CSL Plasma, BioLife and Octapharma (CSL Plasma, n.d.-a; Grifols, n.d.-a; Octapharma, n.d.-a).

4. Hispanic or Latino origin are the terms I use here as these are the terms the American Community Survey uses; while they do not necessarily correspond to numbers of Mexicana/os or Chicana/os, these communities are encompassed in aggregate measures of Hispanic/Latino poverty.
5. Viral marker rates are a measure used to track the incidence of viral disease among donors.
6. In particular, the article attributes this statement to a report by the US–Mexico Health commission, although no citation is provided for this.
7. 'Mexican' was defined as a racial category in the US census of 1930. While it is outside the scope of this book to unpack this set of issues fully, it is worth noting that the terms of this debate are already heavily reliant upon white colonial categories of racial difference (de León, 1983; Stern, 1999).
8. Of course, this is not always the case. 'American' is not always automatically a safe category of bodies within plasma donation assemblages. The furore and confusion around queer and trans American folk donating plasma is testament to this (see Ennis, 2015; Smith, 2019).
9. For more on the ways in which discourses of disease have been used to support American white supremacy in relation to Mexico, see Alemán (2006), de León (1983), P. Mitchell (2005), Stern (1999), and Volkow et al. (1998).
10. The FDA has now moved away from lifetime bans on men who have sex with men, instead requiring that only people who report a new sexual partner/more than one sexual partner with whom they have had also had anal sex in the last three months are deferred for blood and plasma donation (US Food and Drug Administration, 2023). While this is a welcome change from the previous lifelong bans for men who are sexually active, when we look at the previously excluded sections of the queer community, we can see that it is only queer men who participate in sexually monogamous relationships who are covered under these new rules; many queer men and men who have sex with men will continue to be excluded on the grounds that anal sex is constructed as a high-risk activity, along with many heterosexual donors on the same grounds.

Chapter 4

1. In this chapter, I use 'Western countries' to refer to Western European and North American countries. I take neither 'the West' nor 'Africa' as unproblematic terms in their groupings of diverse communities, but engage these terms here to evoke the imagined communities these terms refer to (Anderson, 2006).
2. For a list of the therapeutic treatments utilized during the outbreak, see Boisen et al. (2016).
3. Cases were severely limited outside the three primary West African countries affected, with the highest confirmed number of cases (Nigeria) standing at 20 as of March 2016 (Shultz et al., 2016, p. 85).
4. Looking 'sick' is obviously a highly subjective measure of measuring a person's EVD infectivity, and the anxieties and stress of flying are likely to produce the same physical effects.
5. Where vomit goes after leaving the airport is beyond the scope of this chapter, but those failing primary and secondary screening may be referred for further public health or medical evaluation, potentially within a specialist Ebola treatment centre (Centers for Disease Control and Prevention, 2014, p. 10).
6. Interestingly, Preston's novel about the Ebola virus begins with this account of Charles Monet as a man suffering from Marburg virus, another haemorrhagic filovirus, in Kenya. Despite this, I focus on Preston's description of Monet here as it has 'profoundly influenced public perceptions of Ebola', due in large part to Preston's narration of both viruses which 'without quite misinforming us, seamlessly elides the geographical and biological distinctions in these displacements' (Belling, 2016, p. 48). The discursive

slippage between these two viruses serves only to reinforce racist homogenizing 'Africa-is-a-country' narratives (Monson, 2017).

7   It is prudent to note here that, despite representations of Ebola ripping through the body and causing blood to pour out of every available orifice, the presence of haemorrhagic symptoms may depend on the precise strain of EVD, but are estimated to be present in less than half of patients (Feldmann & Geisbert, 2011, p. 851; Rougeron et al., 2015, p. 115). When haemorrhage does occur, it is mainly limited to the gastro-intestinal tract, and is not severe enough to cause death (Feldmann & Geisbert, 2011, p. 855). Most patients who die will die of multi-organ failure and shock – not due to blood loss, but because the body struggles to secrete enzymes (Ansari, 2015; Feldmann & Geisbert, 2011; Goeijenbier et al., 2014).

8   This rhetoric of 'unhygienic' diets has been mirrored in contemporary discourses around COVID-19 and Chinese wet markets (Briggs, 2020; Maron, 2020; Pavel & Engelke, 2020)

9   See also Fox Keller, 1982; Haraway, 1997; Wajcman, 2000, 2007.

Chapter 5

1   Marriage as an institution has not only been historically designed to exclude LGBT couples, but a plethora of 'other' sexed/racialized/disabled subjects (see Kandaswamy, 2008; Peterson, 2014a; Rainey, 2017).

Chapter 6

1   This method/ology of following fluids is not about unveiling bodily fluids as prime movers of international politics, nor about tracing events backwards to find the original pesky fluid that functions as the source of action. Instead, bodily fluids as agential is about giving up the search for a primary cause and instead attempting to understand how bodily fluids are able to affect other elements within a given assemblage, how the interplay between these elements and assemblages creates motion. Rather than attempting to position plasma, or vomit, or semen as the primary object or agent in international politics, we are instead concerned with studying the 'swarm' of elements at play and their interactions with each other (Bennett, 2010, p. 32). While plasma, for example, has the ability to affect people's bodies, it can only come into being as a medical product through an assemblage that involves a medical technician, a needle, a centrifuge, a donation centre, etc. All elements in this assemblage are important in allowing plasma to affect bodies.

References

Abeysinghe, S. (2016). Ebola at the borders: newspaper representations and the politics of border control. *Third World Quarterly*, *37*(3), 452–467. https://doi.org/10.1080/01436597.2015.1111753

Ackerman, S., & Rasmussen, S. E. (2016). Kunduz hospital attack: MSF's questions remain as US military seeks no charges. *The Guardian*. https://www.theguardian.com/us-news/2016/apr/29/kunduz-hospital-attack-msf-us-military-charges

Ackleson, J. (2005). Constructing security on the US–Mexico border. *Political Geography*, *24*(2), 165–184. https://doi.org/10.1016/j.polgeo.2004.09.017

Adelman, R. A. (2007). Sold(i)ering masculinity: photographing the coalition's male soldiers. *Men and Masculinities*, *11*(3), 259–285. https://doi.org/10.1177/1097184X06291886

Adey, P. (2003). Secured and sorted mobilities: examples from the airport. *Surveillance and Society*, *1*(4), 500–519.

Adey, P. (2004). Surveillance at the airport: surveilling mobility/mobilising surveillance. *Environment and Planning A*, *36*(8), 1365–1380. https://doi.org/10.1068/a36159

Adey, P. (2009). Facing airport security: affect, biopolitics, and the preemptive securitisation of the mobile body. *Environment and Planning D: Society and Space*, *27*(2), 274–295. https://doi.org/10.1068/d0208

Agamben, G. (1998). *Homo Sacer: Sovereign Power and Bare Life* (D. Heller-Roazen (trans.)). Stanford University Press.

Agathangelou, A. M. (2013). Neoliberal geopolitical order and value: queerness as a speculative economy and anti-blackness as terror. *International Feminist Journal of Politics*, *15*(4), 453–476. https://doi.org/10.1080/14616742.2013.841560

Agence France-Presse (2014). Ebola joke, vomiting passenger spark scares in US. *Ndtv.com*. https://www.ndtv.com/world-news/ebola-joke-vomiting-passenger-spark-scares-in-us-677875

Åhäll, L. (2018). Affect as methodology: feminism and the politics of emotion. *International Political Sociology*, *12*(1), 36–52. https://doi.org/10.1093/ips/olx024

Ahmed, S. (2017). *Living a Feminist Life*. Duke University Press.

Aldama, A. J. (2003). Borders, violence, and the struggle for Chicana and Chicano subjectivity. In A. J. Aldama (ed.), *Violence and the Body: Race, Gender, and the State* (pp. 19–38). Indiana University Press.

Alemán, J. (2006). The other country: Mexico, the United States, and the gothic history of conquest. *American Literary History*, *18*(3), 406–426. https://doi.org/10.1093/alh/ajl006

Ali, H., Dumbuya, B., Hynie, M., Idahosa, P., Keil, R., & Perkins, P. (2016). The social and political dimensions of the Ebola response: global inequality, climate change, and infectious disease. In W. L. Filho & U. M. Azeiteiro (eds.), *Climate Change and Health. Improving Resilience and Reducing Risks* (pp. 151–169). Springer International Publishing. https://doi.org/10.1007/978-3-319-24660-4

Amar, P. (2013). *The Security Archipelago: Human-Security States, Sexuality Politics, and the End of Neoliberalism*. Duke University Press.

Amoore, L. (2006). Biometric borders: governing mobilities in the war on terror. *Political Geography*, *25*(3), 336–351. https://doi.org/10.1016/j.polgeo.2006.02.001

Amoore, L., & de Goede, M. D. E. (2005). Governance, risk and dataveillance in the war on terror. *Crime, Law & Social Change*, *43*, 149–173. https://doi.org/10.1007/s10611-005-1717-8

Amrein, K., Valentin, A., Lanzer, G., & Drexler, C. (2012). Adverse events and safety issues in blood donation – a comprehensive review. *Blood Reviews*, *26*(1), 33–42. https://doi.org/10.1016/j.blre.2011.09.003

Anderson, B. (2006). *Imagined Communities: Reflections on the Origin and Spread of Nationalism* (3rd revise). Verso.

Andreescu, F. C., & Shapiro, M. J. (2014). Narcissism and abject aesthetics. *Journal for Cultural Research*, *18*(1), 44–59. https://doi.org/10.1080/14797585.2013.826443

Ansari, A. A. (2015). Clinical features and pathobiology of Ebolavirus infection. *Journal of Autoimmunity*, *55*(1), 1–9. https://doi.org/10.1016/j.jaut.2014.09.001

Anzaldúa, G. (2012). *Borderlands/La Frontera: The New Mestiza* (4th edn). Aunt Lute.

Aradau, C., & Huysmans, J. (2014). Critical methods in international relations: the politics of techniques, devices and acts. *European Journal of International Relations*, *20*(3), 596–619. https://doi.org/10.1177/1354066112474479

Aradau, C., Coward, M., Herschinger, E., Thomas, O. D., & Voelkner, N. (2014). Discourse/materiality. In C. Aradau, J. Huysmans, A. Neal, & N. Voelkner (eds.), *Critical Security Methods: New Frameworks for Analysis* (pp. 57–84). Routledge.

REFERENCES

Aradau, C., Huysmans, J., Neal, A., & Voelkner, N. (2014). Introducing critical security methods. In C. Aradau, J. Huysmans, A. Neal, & N. Voelkner (eds.), *Critical Security Methods: New Frameworks for Analysis* (pp. 1–22). Routledge.

Aretxaga, B. (1997). *Shattering Silence: Women, Nationalism, and Political Subjectivity in Northern Ireland*. Princeton University Press.

Arkin, W., & Dobrofsky, L. R. (1978). Military socialization and masculinity. *Journal of Social Issues*, *34*(1), 151–168. https://doi.org/10.1111/j.1540-4560.1978.tb02546.x

Åsberg, C. (2010). Enter the cyborg: tracing the historiography and ontological turn of feminist technoscience studies. *International Journal of Feminist Technoscience*, 1–25. https://www.academia.edu/603854/Enter_cyborg_tracing_the_historiography_and_ontological_turn_of_feminist_technoscience_studies

Åsberg, C., & Lykke, N. (2010). Feminist technoscience studies. *European Journal of Women's Studies*, *17*(4), 299–305. https://doi.org/10.1177/1350506810377692

Athanasiou, A. (2005). Technologies of humanness, aporias of biopolitics, and the cut body of humanity. *Differences: A Journal of Feminist Cultural Studies*, *14*(1), 125–162. https://doi.org/10.1215/10407391-14-1-125

Baaz, M., & Stern, M. (2005). Why do soldiers rape? Masculinity, violence, and sexuality in the armed forces in the Congo (DRC). *International Studies Quarterly*, *53*(2), 495–518.

Baaz, M. E., & Stern, M. (2016). Researching wartime rape in the Democratic Republic of Congo: a methodology of unease. In A. T. R. Wibben (ed.), *Researching War: Feminist Methods, Ethics and Politics* (pp. 117–140). Routledge.

Bahat, A., & Eisenbach, M. (2006). Sperm thermotaxis. *Molecular and Cellular Endocrinology*, *252*(1–2), 115–119. https://doi.org/10.1016/j.mce.2006.03.027

Bailey, M. (2010). They aren't talking about me… *Crunkfeministcollective.com*. http://www.crunkfeministcollective.com/2010/03/14/they-arent-talking-about-me/

Bailey, M., & Trudy (2018). On misogynoir: citation, erasure, and plagiarism. *Feminist Media Studies*, *18*(4), 762–768. https://doi.org/10.1080/14680777.2018.1447395

Baker, D. (2014). Why they are made this way – plasma derivatives. *The Source*, *8*(3), 28–31.

Barad, K. (2003). Posthumanist performativity: toward an understanding of how matter comes to matter. *Signs*, *28*(3), 801–831.

Bashford, A. (2000). 'Is White Australia possible?' Race, colonialism and tropical medicine. *Ethnic and Racial Studies*, *23*(2), 248–271. https://doi.org/10.1080/014198700329042

Bass, J. D. (1998). Hearts of darkness and hot zones: the ideologeme of imperial contagion in recent accounts of viral outbreaks. *Quarterly Journal of Speech*, *84*(4), 430–447. https://doi.org/10.1080/00335639809384231

BBC News (2014). Ebola screening begins at Heathrow Airport. *BBC News*. http://www.bbc.Co.Uk/News. http://www.bbc.co.uk/news/uk-29616724

BBC News (2015). Kunduz bombing: US attacked MSF clinic 'in error.' *BBC News*. https://www.bbc.co.uk/news/world-asia-34925237

BBC News (2016a). Ebola nurse banned for hiding Pauline Cafferkey's high temperature. *BBC News*. https://www.bbc.co.uk/news/health-38095295

BBC News (2016b). Man receives penis transplant in US. *BBC News*. https://www.bbc.co.uk/news/world-us-canada-36304320

BBC News (2016c). UK Ebola nurse Pauline Cafferkey cleared of misconduct. *BBC News*. https://www.bbc.co.uk/news/uk-scotland-glasgow-west-37364497

BBC News (2017). Medic suspended for 'dishonesty' over Ebola temperature. *BBC News*. https://www.bbc.co.uk/news/health-39446355

BCC Publishing (2023). Global markets for blood plasma products. *bccresearch.com*. https://www.bccresearch.com/market-research/healthcare/global-markets-for-blood-plasma-products.html

Beauchamp, T. (2009). Artful concealment and strategic visibility: transgender bodies and U.S. state surveillance after 9/11. *Surveillance & Society*, *6*(4), 356–366.

Belling, C. (2016). Dark zones: the Ebola body as a configuration of horror. In K. Nixon & L. Servitje (eds.), *Endemic: Essays in Contagion Theory* (pp. 43–66). Macmillan.

Bennett, J. (2010). *Vibrant Matter: A Political Ecology of Things*. Duke University Press.

Benton, A., & Dionne, K. Y. (2015). International political economy and the 2014 West African Ebola outbreak. *African Studies Review*, *58*(1), 223–236. https://doi.org/10.1017/asr.2015.11

Berlant, L. (2007). Slow death (sovereignty, obesity, lateral agency). *Critical Inquiry*, *33*(4), 754–780. https://doi.org/10.1086/521568

Berlant, L. (2011). *Cruel Optimism*. Duke University Press.

Berlant, L., & Warner, M. (1998). Sex in public. *Critical Inquiry*, *24*(2), 547–566.

BioLife Plasma (n.d.). Donor testimonials. *Biolifeplasma.com*. Retrieved 21 August 2017, from https://biolifeplasma.com/us/#/become-donor/donor-testimonials

Blencowe, C. (2012). *Biopolitical Experience: Foucault, Power and Positive Critique*. Palgrave Macmillan.

Blundell, R., Costa Dias, M., Joyce, R., & Xu, X. (2020). COVID-19 and inequalities. *Fiscal Studies*, *41*(2), 291–319. https://doi.org/10.1111/1475-5890.12232

Boisen, M. L., Hartnett, J. N., Goba, A., Vandi, M. A., Grant, D. S., Schieffelin, J. S., et al. (2016). Epidemiology and management of the 2013–16 West African Ebola outbreak. *Annual Review of Virology*, *3*, 147–171. https://doi.org/10.1146/annurev-virology-110615-040056

Bosworth, M. L., Ayoubkhani, D., Nafilyan, V., Foubert, J., Glickman, M., Davey, C., et al. (2021). Deaths involving COVID-19 by self-reported disability status during the first two waves of the COVID-19 pandemic in England: a retrospective, population-based cohort study. *The Lancet Public Health*, *6*(11), e817–e825. https://doi.org/10.1016/S2468-2667(21)00206-1

Brah, A., & Phoenix, A. (2004). Ain't I a woman? Revisiting intersectionality. *Journal of International Women's Studies*, *5*(3), 75–86.

Braidotti, R. (2003). Becoming woman: or sexual difference revisited. *Theory, Culture & Society*, *20*(3), 43–64.

Brandt, A. (2014). HS coaches resign after players' Ebola taunt. *Athletic Business*. https://www.athleticbusiness.com/high-school/hs-coaches-resign-after-players-taunt-opponent-with-ebola.html

Braun, B. (2007). Biopolitics and the molecularization of life. *Cultural Geographies*, *14*(1), 6–28. https://doi.org/10.1177/1474474007072817

Breckon, A. (2013). The erotic politics of disgust: *Pink Flamingos* as queer political cinema. *Screen*, *54*(4), 514–533. https://doi.org/10.1093/screen/hjt041

Briggs, H. (2020). Coronavirus: WHO developing guidance on wet markets. *BBC News*. https://www.bbc.co.uk/news/science-environment-52369878

Brinkema, E. (2011). Laura Dern's vomit, or, Kant and Derrida in Oz. *Film-Philosophy*, *15*(2), 51–69. http://www.film-philosophy.com/index.php/f-p/article/view/276

Brinkema, E. (2014). *The Forms of the Affects*. Duke University Press.

Brown, C., Aranas, A., Benenson, G., Brunette, G., Cetron, M., Chen, T., et al. (2014). Airport exit and entry screening for Ebola – August – November 10, 2014. *cdc*. www.cdc.gov. https://wwww.cdc.gov/mmwr/preview/mmwrhtml/mm6349a5.htm?s_cid=mm6349a5_w

Browne, S. (2015). *Dark Matters: on the Surveillance of Blackness*. Duke University Press.

Budd, L., Bell, M., & Brown, T. (2009). Of plagues, planes and politics: controlling the global spread of infectious diseases by air. *Political Geography*, *28*(7), 426–435. https://doi.org/10.1016/j.polgeo.2009.10.006

Bult, J. M. (2007). Source plasma collection in the USA. *The Source*, *1*(5), 4–7.

Burkle Jr, F., & Garfield, R. (2013). Civilian mortality after the 2003 invasion of Iraq. *Prehospital and Disaster Medicine*, *28*(3), 223–229. https://doi.org/10.1017/S1049023X13000113

Butler, J. (2003). Violence, mourning, politics. *Studies in Gender and Sexuality*, *4*(1), 9–37. https://doi.org/10.1080/15240650409349213

Butler, J. (2010). *Gender Trouble* (2nd edn). Routledge.

Butler, J. (2011). *Bodies That Matter: On the Discursive Limits of Sex* (2nd edn). Routledge Classics.

Cabinet Office (2017). *National Risk Register 2017 edition* [online]. London: Cabinet Office. Available at: https://assets.publishing.service.gov.uk/media/5a82a189e5274a2e8ab5887d/UK_National_Risk_Register_2017.pdf [Accessed 15 January 2024].

Cabinet Office (2020). Coronavirus outbreak FAQS: what you can and can't do / Published 29 March 2020. . *Cabinet Office*. www.gov.uk.

Calderon, H., & Saldívar, J. D. (1991). *Criticism in the Borderlands: Chicano Literature, Culture and Ideology*. Duke University Press.

Callahan, G. (2009). *Between XX and XY: Intersexuality and the Myth of Two Sexes*. Chicago Review Press.

Caserio, R. L., Edelman, L., Halberstam, J., Muñoz, J. E., & Dean, T. (2006). The antisocial thesis in queer theory. *PMLA*, *121*(3), 819–828. https://doi.org/10.1632/pmla.2009.124.1.273

Caso, F. (2017). Sexing the disabled veteran: the homoerotic aesthetics of militarism. *Critical Military Studies*, *3*(3), 217–234. https://doi.org/10.1080/23337486.2016.1184420

Cavanagh, S. (2013). Touching gender: abjection and the hygienic imagination. In S. Stryker & A. Azuira (eds.), *The Transgender Studies Reader* (2nd edn, pp. 426–442). Routledge.

Centers for Disease Control and Prevention (2014). Ebola Virus Disease (Ebola) pre-departure/exit screening at points of departure in affected countries. *CDC*. https://wwwnc.cdc.gov/travel?action=NotFound&controller=Utility

Chen, M. Y. (2012). *Animacies: Biopolitics, Racial Mattering, and Queer Affect*. Duke University Press.

Clough, P. T. (2016). The affective turn: political economy, biomedia and bodies. *Theory, Culture & Society*, *25*(1), 1–22. https://doi.org/10.1177/0263276407085156

Cohen, L. (2005). Operability, bioavailability, and exception. In A. Ong & S. J. Collier (eds.), *Global Assemblages: Technology, Politics and Ethics as Anthropological Problems* (pp. 79–90). Blackwell.

Coker, R., & Ingram, A. (2007). Passports and pestilence: migration, security and contemporary border control of infectious diseases. In A. Bashford (ed.), *Medicine at the Border: Disease, Globalization and Security, 1850 to the Present* (pp. 159–176). Palgrave Macmillan UK. https://doi.org/10.1057/9780230288904_9

Coleman, M. (2005). US statecraft and the US–Mexico border as security/economy nexus. *Political Geography*, *24*(2), 185–209. https://doi.org/10.1016/j.polgeo.2004.09.016

REFERENCES

Collins, J. (2015). Initial planning and execution in Afghanistan and Iraq. In R. Hooker Jr. & J. Collins (eds.), *Lessons Encountered: Learning from the Long War* (pp. 21–88). National Defense University Press.

Collins, P. H. (2000). *Black Feminist Thought: Knowledge, Consciousness, and the Politics of Empower.* Routledge.

Collins, P. H., & Bilge, S. (2016). *Intersectionality.* Polity Press.

Comité Fronterizo de Obrer@s (n.d.). Open letter to the president of Mexico Felipe Calderón Hinojosa on the 15th anniversary of the North American Free Trade Agreement. *Cfomagquiladoras.org.* Retrieved 18 September 2019, from cfamaquiladoras.org/english site/carta_presidente_tlean.en.html

Connell, P. (1997). Understanding victimization and agency: considerations of race, class and gender. *Political and Legal Anthropology Review, 20*(2), 115–143.

Cook, I. (2005). Western heterosexual masculinity, anxiety, and web porn. *The Journal of Men's Studies, 14*(1), 47–63. https://doi.org/10.3149/jms.1401.47

Cox, R. W. (1981). Social forces, states and world orders: beyond international relations theory. *Millennium: Journal of International Studies, 10*(2), 126–155.

Crane-Seeber, J. P. (2016). Sexy warriors: the politics and pleasures of submission to the state. *Critical Military Studies, 2*(1–2), 41–55. https://doi.org/10.1080/23337486.2016.1144402

Crawford, N. C. (2015). *War-related Death, Injury, and Displacement in Afghanistan and Pakistan 2001–2014.* Watson Institute for International Studies [online]. Available from: https://reliefweb.int/attachments/69364812-d819-39a4-b11f-bc541a53533d/War%20Related%20Casualties%20Afghanistan%20and%20Pakistan%202001-2014%20FIN.pdf [Accessed 15 January 2023].

Crenshaw, K. (1991). Mapping the margins: intersectionality, identity politics, and violence against women of color. *Stanford Law Review, 43*(6), 1241–1299.

CSL Plasma (n.d.-a). Donate plasma today at a location near you. *www.Cslplasma.com.* Retrieved 27 June 2023, from https://www.cslplasma.com/find-a-donation-center

CSL Plasma (n.d.-b). iGive Rewards. *www.Cslplasma.com.* Retrieved 18 August 2017, from https://www.cslplasma.com/current-donor-rewards/iGive-rewards

CSL Plasma Inc v. US Customs and Border Protection, 21-5282 (D.C. Cir. 2022). Available from: https://law.justia.com/cases/federal/appellate-courts/cadc/21-5282/21-5282-2022-05-10.html> [Accessed 15 January 2024].

Culzac, N. (2014). Ebola outbreak: hundreds of parents remove schoolchildren after principal visits Zambia. *Independent.* https://www.independent.co.uk/news/world/americas/ebola-outbreak-hundreds-of-parents-remove-schoolchildren-after-principal-visits-zambia-9806397.html

Currier, D. (2003). Feminist technological futures: Deleuze and body/technology assemblages. *Feminist Theory*, *4*(3), 321–338.

Daggett, C. (2015). Drone disorientations. *International Feminist Journal of Politics*, *17*(3), 361–379. https://doi.org/10.1080/14616742.2015.1075317

Daily Mail (2011). Mexican 'blood smugglers' cross border twice a month to sell their plasma for $260. *MailOnline*. http://www.dailymail.co.uk/news/article-2065508/Mexican-blood-smugglers-crossing-border-twice-month-sell-plasma-260.html

Davies, S., Harman, S., Manjoo, R., Tanyag, M., & Wenham, C. (2019). Why it must be a feminist global health agenda. *The Lancet*, *393*(10171), 601–603.

Davies, S. E., Kamradt-Scott, A., & Rushton, S. (2015). *Disease Diplomacy: International Norms and Global Health Security*. Johns Hopkins University Press.

de Beauvoir, S. (1997). *The Second Sex*. Vintage.

de León, A. (1983). *They Called Them Greasers: Anglo Attitudes towards Mexicans in Texas, 1821–1900*. University of Texas Press.

Defense Health Agency (n.d.). Assisted reproductive services. *www.Tricare.Mil*. Retrieved 17 September 2018, from https://www.tricare.mil/CoveredServices/IsItCovered/AssistedReproductiveServices

Deleuze, G., & Guattari, F. (1980). *A Thousand Plateaus: Capitalism & Schizophrenia* (B. Massumi (trans.)). University of Minnesota Press.

Demirjian, K. (2016). Congress wrestles with providing fertility benefits for injured veterans and servicemembers. *The Washington Post*. https://www.washingtonpost.com/news/powerpost/wp/2016/07/27/congress-wrestles-with-providing-fertility-benefits-for-injured-veterans-and-service members/?noredirect=on&utm_term=.e17a15d5fb5b

Department for Education, & Williamson, G. (2020). Further deals on exams and grades announced. *gov.uk*. https://www.gov.uk/government/news/further-details-on-exams-and-grades-announced

Dillon, M. (2007). Governing terror: the state of emergency of biopolitical emergence. *International Political Sociology*, *1*(1), 7–28.

Dillon, M., & Lobo-Guerrero, L. (2008). Biopolitics of security in the 21st century: an introduction. *Review of International Studies*, *34*(2), 265–292. https://doi.org/10.1017/S0260210508008024

Dixon, R. (2014). Eight reported dead in attack on Ebola workers in Guinea. *Los Angeles Times*. https://www.latimes.com/world/africa/la-fg-attack-ebola-guinea-outreach-20140918-story.html

donatingplasma.org (n.d.). Donor compensation. *Donatingplasma.org*. Retrieved 22 October 2019, from http://www.donatingplasma.org/donation/donor-compensation

Doty, R. L. (1996). *Imperial Encounters: the Politics of Representation in North-South Relations*. University of Minnesota Press.

Doty, R. L. (1999). Racism, desire and the politics of immigration. *Millennium: Journal of International Studies*, *28*(3), 585–606.

Doty, R. L. (2007). States of exception on the Mexico–US border: security, 'decisions,' and civilian border patrols. *International Political Sociology*, *1*(2), 113–137. https://doi.org/10.1111/j.1749-5687.2007.00008.x

Doty, R. L. (2011). Bare life: border-crossing deaths and spaces of moral alibi. *Environment and Planning D: Society and Space*, *29*(4), 599–612. https://doi.org/10.1068/d3110

Douglas, M. (2002). *Purity and Danger: An Analysis of Concept of Pollution and Taboo* (2nd edn). Routledge.

Duffield, M. (2005). Getting savages to fight barbarians: development, security and the colonial present. *Conflict, Security & Development*, *5*(2), 141–159. https://doi.org/10.1080/14678800500170068

Dumit, J. (2021). Substance as method (shaking up your practice). In A. Ballestero & B. Winthereik (eds.), *Experimenting with Ethnography: A Companion to Analysis* (pp. 175–185). Duke University Press.

Dyvik, S. L., & Greenwood, L. (2016). Embodying militarism: exploring the spaces and bodies in-between. *Critical Military Studies*, *2*(1–2), 1–6. https://doi.org/10.1080/23337486.2016.1184469

Edelman, L. (1998). The future is kid stuff: queer theory, disidentification, and the death drive. *Narrative*, *6*(1), 18–30.

Edin, K., & Schaefer, L. (2015). Blood plasma, sweat, and tears. *The Atlantic*. https://www.theatlantic.com/business/archive/2015/09/poor-sell-blood/403012

Elbe, S. (2005). AIDS, security, biopolitics. *International Relations*, *19*(4), 403–419. https://doi.org/10.1177/0047117805058532

Elbe, S. (2006). Should HIV/AIDS be securitized? The ethical dilemmas of linking HIV/AIDS and security. *International Studies Quarterly*, *50*(1), 119–144. https://doi.org/10.1111/j.1468-2478.2006.00395.x

Enloe, C. (2014). *Bananas, Beaches, and Bases: Making Feminist Sense of International Politics* (2nd rev edn). University of California Press.

Ennis, D. (2015). To the FDA, everyone transgender is a gay man. *Advocate.com*. https://www.advocate.com/health/2015/02/02/fda-everyone-transgender-gay-man

Epstein, C. (2007). Guilty bodies, productive bodies, destructive bodies: crossing the biometric borders. *International Political Sociology*, *1*(2), 149–164. https://doi.org/10.1111/j.1749-5687.2007.00010.x

Epstein, S. (1996). *Impure Science: AIDS, Activism and the Politics of Knowledge*. University of California Press.

Esposito, R., & Campbell, T. (2009). *Bíos: Biopolitics and Philosophy* (T. Campbell (trans.)). University of Minnesota Press.

Farrugia, A., Gustafson, M., & Hoegen, I. (2009). 'Decades of Safety Measures', in K. Flynn (ed.) *The Source* (pp. 2–3), Annapolis: PPTA.

Federal Trade Commission (2009). *United States of America before the Federal Trade Commission. www.ftc.gov.* https://www.ftc.gov/sites/default/files/documents/cases/2009/05/090527cslcmpt.pdf

Feldmann, H., & Geisbert, T. W. (2011). Ebola haemorrhagic fever. *The Lancet*, *377*(9768), 849–862. https://doi.org/10.1016/S0140-6736(10)60667-8

Flint, A., & Hewitt, V. (2015). Colonial tropes and HIV/AIDS in Africa: sex, disease and race. *Commonwealth and Comparative Politics*, *53*(3), 294–314. https://doi.org/10.1080/14662043.2015.1051284

Foucault, M. (2008). *The Birth of Biopolitics: Lectures at the Collège de France, 1978-1979* (A. Davidson (ed.); G. Burchell (trans.)). Palgrave Macmillan.

Fox, N. J. (2002). Refracting 'health': Deleuze, Guattari and body-self. *Health: an Interdisciplinary Journal for the Social Study of Health, Illness and Medicine*, *6*(3), 347–363. https://doi.org/10.1177/136345930200600306

Fox, S., & Spektor, F. (2021). Hormonal advantage: retracing exploitative histories of workplace menstrual tracking. *Catalyst: Feminism, Theory, Technoscience*, *7*(1), 1–23. https://doi.org/10.28968/cftt.v7i1.34506

Fox Keller, E. (1982). Feminism and science. *Signs*, *7*(3), 589–602.

Fox Keller, E. (1992). *Secrets of Life, Secrets of Death: Essays on Language, Gender and Science.* Routledge.

Franklin, S. (1995). Romancing the helix: nature and scientific discovery. In L. Pearce & J. Stacey (eds.), *Romance Revisited* (pp. 63–77). Lawrence & Wishart.

Franklin, S. (2006). The cyborg embryo: our path to transbiology. *Theory, Culture & Society*, *23*(7–8), 167–187. https://doi.org/10.1177/0263276406069230

Fries, C. A., Tuder, D., Gorantla, V. S., Chan, R. K., & Davis, M. R. (2020). Military VCA in the world. *Current Transplantation Reports*, *7*(4), 246–250. https://doi.org/10.1007/s40472-020-00294-y

Fuentes, C. M., Peña, S., & Hernández, V. (2018). The multidimensional measure of poverty at the intraurban level in Cuidad Juarez, Chihuahua (2012). *Estudios Fronterizos*, *19*, 1–25. https://doi.org/10.21670/ref.1801001

Gereben Schaefer, A., Iyengar, R., Kadiyala, S., Kavanagh, J., Engel, C. C., Williams, K. M., et al. (2016). *Assessing the Implications of Allowing Transgender Personnel to Serve Openly.* RAND Corporation.

Gibson, M. F., & Douglas, P. (2018). Disturbing behaviors: Ole Ivar Lovaas and the queer history of autism science. *Catalyst: Feminism, Theory, Technoscience*, *4*(2), 1–28.

Gilbert, E. (2007). Leaky borders and solid citizens: governing security, prosperity and quality of life in a North American partnership. *Antipode*, *39*(1), 77–98. https://doi.org/10.1111/j.1467-8330.2007.00507.x

Giroux, H. A. (2006). Reading Hurricane Katrina: race, class, and the biopolitics of disposability. *College Literature*, *33*(3), 171–196.

Goeijenbier, M., van Kampen, J. J., Reusken, C. B. E., Koopmans, M. P., & van Gorp, E. C. (2014). Ebola virus disease: a review on epidemiology, symptoms, treatment and pathogenesis. *Netherlands Journal of Medicine* 72(9), 442–448. https://pubmed.ncbi.nlm.nih.gov/25387613/

Going Viral: Beyond the Hot Zone (2019). National Geographic.

Grady, D. (2015). Penis transplants being planned to help wounded troops. *The New York Times*. https://www.nytimes.com/2015/12/07/health/penis-transplants-being-planned-to-heal-troops-hidden-wounds.html?_r=0

Grady, D. (2016). Veterans seek help for infertility inflicted by wounds of war. *The New York Times*. https://www.nytimes.com/2016/03/01/health/veterans-infertility-benefits.html

Grady, D. (2017). Study maps 'uniquely devastating' genital injuries among troops. *The New York Times*. https://www.nytimes.com/2017/01/13/health/genital-injuries-among-us-troops.html

Grady, D. (2018). 'Whole again': a vet maimed by an I.E.D. receives a transplanted penis. *The New York Times*. https://www.nytimes.com/2018/04/23/health/soldier-penis-transplant-ied.html

Grifols (n.d.-a). Find a donation center. *www.Grifolsplasma.com*. www.Grifolsplasma.com.

Grifols (n.d.-b). How to donate plasma. *www.Grifolsplasma.com*. Retrieved 18 August 2017, from https://www.grifolsplasma.com/en/web/plasma/plasma-donor/how-to-donate/donation-requirements

Grifols (n.d.-c). Plasma: a source of life. Retrieved 25 May 2018, from https://www.grifolsplasma.com/en/web/plasma/about-plasma-donation/plasma-a-source-of-life

Grifols (n.d.-d). Why donate plasma? *www.Grifolsplasma.com*. Retrieved 21 August 2017, from https://www.grifolsplasma.com/en/web/plasma/plasma-donor/why-donate

Grosz, E. (1994). *Volatile Bodies: Towards a Corporeal Feminism*. Indiana University Press.

Haase, C. (2007). *When Heimat Meets Hollywood: German Filmmakers and America, 1985–2005*. Camden House.

Halberstam, J. (2011). *The Queer Art of Failure*. Duke University Press.

Hall, E. (2000). 'Blood, brain and bones': taking the body seriously in the geography of health and impairment. *Area*, 32(1), 21–29. https://doi.org/10.1111/j.1475-4762.2000.tb00111.x

Hall, K. (1995). *Things of Darkness: Economies of Race and Gender in Early Modern England*. Cornell University Press.

Hall, R., & Chapman, M. (2008). The 1995 Kikwit Ebola outbreak: lessons hospitals and physicians can apply to future viral epidemics. *General Hospital Psychiatry*, 30(5), 446–452. https://doi.org/10.1016/j.genhosppsych.2008.05.003

Halperin, D. M. (2003). The normalization of queer theory. *Journal of Homosexuality, 45*(2–4), 339–343. https://doi.org/10.1300/J082v45n02

Hammonds, E. (1997). Seeing AIDS: race, gender and representation. In N. Goldstein & J. Manlow (eds.), *The Gender Politics of HIV/AIDS in Women: Perspectives on the Pandemic in the United States* (pp. 113–126). New York University Press.

Hammonds, E., & Subramaniam, B. (2003). A conversation on feminist science studies. *Signs: Journal of Women in Culture and Society, 28*(3), 923–944. https://doi.org/10.1086/345455

Haque, Z., Becares, L., & Treloar, N. (2020). Over-exposed and under-protected: the devastating impact of COVID-19 on black and minority ethnic communities in Great Britain. *Runnymede.* https://www.runnymedetrust.org/uploads/Runnymede Covid19 Survey report v3.pdf

Haraway, D. (1988). Situated knowledges: the science question in feminism and the privilege of partial perspective. *Feminist Studies, 14*(3), 575–599. https://doi.org/10.2307/3178066

Haraway, D. (1989). *Primate Visions: Gender, Race and Nature in the World of Modern Science*. Routledge.

Haraway, D. (1990). A manifesto for cyborgs: science, technology, and socialist feminism in the 1980s. In L. J. Nicholson (ed.), *Feminism/Postmodernism* (pp. 190–233). Routledge.

Haraway, D. (1991). *Simians, Cyborgs, and Women: the Reinvention of Nature*. Free Association Books.

Haraway, D. (1994). A game of cat's cradle: science studies, feminist theory, cultural studies. *Configurations, 2*(1), 59–72.

Haraway, D. (1997). *Modest_Witness@Second_Millennium.FemaleMan©_Meets_OncoMouse™: Feminism and Technoscience*. Routledge.

Haraway, D. (2016). *Staying with the Trouble: Making Kin in the Chthulucene*. Duke University Press.

Harcourt, W., Ling, L. H. M., Zalewski, M., & Swiss International Relations Collective (2015). Assessing, engaging, and enacting worlds: tensions in feminist method/ologies. *International Feminist Journal of Politics, 17*(1), 158–172. https://doi.org/10.1080/14616742.2014.988451

Harding, S. (1987). The method question. *Hypatia: a Journal of Feminist Philosophy, 2*(3), 19–35.

Harding, S. (1991). *Whose Science? Whose Knowledge?: Thinking from Women's Lives*. Cornell University Press.

Haritaworn, J. (2015). *Queer Lovers and Hateful Others: Regenerating Violent Times and Places*. Pluto Press.

Haritaworn, J., Kuntsman, A., & Posocco, S. (eds.) (2014). *Queer Necropolitics*. Routledge.

Harman, S. (ed.) (2011). *Global Health Governance*. Routledge.

Harman, S. (2016). Ebola, gender and conspicuously invisible women in global health governance. *Third World Quarterly*, *37*(3), 525–542. https://doi.org/10.1080/01436597.2015.1108827

Harris, R., Brennan, E., & Clark, N. (2014). New Ebola screening measures. *The New York Times*. https://www.nytimes.com/2014/10/24/travel/new-ebola-screening-measures.html

Hawkesworth, M. E. (1989). Knowers, knowing, known: feminist theory and claims of truth. *Signs*, *14*(3), 533–557.

Haynes, D. M. (2002). Still the heart of darkness: the Ebola virus and the meta-narrative of disease in the hot zone. *Journal of Medical Humanities*, *23*(2), 133–145. https://doi.org/10.1023/A:1014846131921

Hendershot, C. (2018). Battle-induced urotrauma, sexual violence, and American servicemen. In M. Zalewski, P. Drumond, E. Prügl, & M. Stern (eds.), *Sexual Violence Against Men in Global Politics* (pp. 43–56). Routledge.

Henderson, E. F. (2014). Bringing up gender: academic abjection? *Pedagogy, Culture and Society*, *22*(1), 21–38. https://doi.org/10.1080/14681366.2013.877202

Heyes, C. J. (2003). Feminist solidarity after queer theory: the case of transgender. *Signs*, *28*(4), 1093–1120.

Heymann, D. L., Chen, L., Takemi, K., Fidler, D. P., Tappero, J. W., Thomas, M. J., et al. (2015). Global health security: the wider lessons from the west African Ebola virus disease epidemic. *The Lancet*, *385*(9980), 1884–1899. https://doi.org/10.1016/S0140-6736(15)60858-3

Hird, M. J. (2000). Gender's nature: intersexuality, transsexualism and the 'sex'/'gender' binary. *Feminist Theory*, *1*(3), 347–364.

Hobbs, J. (2021). Plasma donation at the border: feminist technoscience, bodies and race. *Security Dialogue*, *52*(1), 45–61. https://doi.org/10.1177/0967010620906749

Hogle, L. F. (1999). *Recovering the Nation's Body: Cultural Memory, Medicine, and the Politics of Redemption*. Rutgers University Press.

hooks, b. (1987). *Ain't I A Woman: Black Women and Feminism*. Pluto Press.

Höpfl, H. J. (2003). Becoming a (virile) member: women and the military body. *Body & Society*, *9*(4), 13–30. https://doi.org/10.1177/1357034X0394003

Hudak, S. J., Morey, A. F., Rozanski, T. A., & Fox, C. W. (2005). Battlefield urogenital injuries: changing patterns during the past century. *Urology*, *65*(6), 1041–1046. https://doi.org/10.1016/j.urology.2004.11.031

Ingraham, C. (2017). The military spends five times as much on Viagra as it would on transgender troops' medical care. *The Washington Post*. https://www.washingtonpost.com/news/wonk/wp/2017/07/26/the-military-spends-five-times-as-much-on-viagra-as-it-would-on-transgender-troops-medical-care/

Ingram, A. (2005). The new geopolitics of disease: between global health and global security. *Geopolitics*, *10*(3), 522–545. https://doi.org/10.1080/14650040591003516

Ingram, A. (2009). The geopolitics of disease. *Geography Compass*, *3*(6), 2084–2097. https://doi.org/10.1111/j.1749-8198.2009.00284.x

Isaksen, L. W. (2002). Toward a sociology of (gendered) disgust: images of bodily decay and the social organization of care work. *Journal of Family Issues*, *23*(7), 791–811. https://doi.org/10.1177/019251302236595

James, R. C., & Mustard, C. A. (2004). Geographic location of commercial plasma donation clinics in the United States, 1980–1995. *American Journal of Public Health*, *94*(7), 1224–1229.

Joffe, H., & Haarhoff, G. (2002). Representations of far-flung illnesses: the case of Ebola in Britain. *Social Science and Medicine*, *54*(6), 955–969. https://doi.org/10.1016/S0277-9536(01)00068-5

Johar Schueller, M. (2005). Analogy and (white) feminist theory: thinking race and the color of the cyborg body. *Signs: Journal of Women in Culture and Society*, *31*(1), 63–92. https://doi.org/10.1086/431372

Johns Hopkins Medicine (2018). Johns Hopkins Performs first total penis and scrotum transplant in the world. *www.Hopkinsmedicine.org*. https://www.hopkinsmedicine.org/news/media/releases/johns_hopkins_performs_first_total_penis_and_scrotum_transplant_in_the_world

Johnson, M. (2010). 'Just getting off': the inseparability of ejaculation and hegemonic masculinity. *The Journal of Men's Studies*, *18*(3), 238–248. https://doi.org/10.3149/jms.1803.238

Jonvallen, P. (2010). Sex differentiation and body fat: local biologies and gender transgressions. *European Journal of Women's Studies*, *17*(4), 379–391. https://doi.org/10.1177/1350506810377697

Joralemon, D. (1995). Organ wars: the battle for body parts. *Medical Anthropology Quarterly*, *9*(3), 335–356. https://doi.org/10.2307/649344

Jordan, W. (2012). *White Over Black: American Attitudes toward the Negro, 1550–1812* (2nd edn). The University of North Carolina Press.

Kamradt-Scott, A. (2016). WHO's to blame? The World Health Organization and the 2014 Ebola outbreak in West Africa. *Third World Quarterly*, *37*(3), 401–418. https://doi.org/10.1080/01436597.2015.1112232

Kandaswamy, P. (2008). State austerity and the racial politics of same-sex marriage in the US. *Sexualities*, *11*(6), 706–725.

Kapiriri, L., & Ross, A. (2020). The politics of disease epidemics: a comparative analysis of the SARS, Zika, and Ebola outbreaks. *Global Social Welfare*, *7*(1), 33–45. https://doi.org/10.1007/s40609-018-0123-y

Kaupp, U. B., Kashikar, N. D., & Weyand, I. (2008). Mechanisms of sperm chemotaxis. *Annual Review of Physiology*, *70*, 93–117. https://doi.org/10.1146/annurev.physiol.70.113006.100654

Khalili, L. (2011). Gendered practices of counterinsurgency. *Review of International Studies*, *37*(4), 1471–1491.

Khan, S. I., Hudson-Rodd, N., Saggers, S., Bhuiyan, M. I., Bhuiya, A., Karim, S. A., et al. (2008). Phallus, performance and power: crisis of masculinity. *Sexual and Relationship Therapy*, *23*(1), 37–49. https://doi.org/10.1080/14681990701790635

Kienscherf, M. (2011). A programme of global pacification: US counterinsurgency doctrine and the biopolitics of human (in)security. *Security Dialogue*, *42*(6), 517–535. https://doi.org/10.1177/0967010611423268

Kime, P. (2015). DoD spends $84M a year on Viagra, similar meds. *Military Times*. https://www.militarytimes.com/pay-benefits/military-benefits/health-care/2015/02/13/dod-spends-84m-a-year-on-viagra-similar-meds/

King, N. B. (2002). Security, disease, commerce: ideologies of postcolonial global health. *Social Studies of Science*, *32*(5–6), 763–789. https://doi.org/10.1177/030631270203200507

Kinsman, J. (2012). 'A time of fear': local, national, and international responses to a large Ebola outbreak in Uganda. *Globalization and Health*, *8*(15). https://doi.org/10.1186/1744-8603-8-15

Kocherga, A. (2016). Plasma is big business along the border. *KVIA*. http://www.kvia.com/news/plasma-is-big-business-along-the-border/53247859

Krieger, N. (2016). Living and dying at the crossroads: racism, embodiment, and why theory is essential for a public health of consequence. *American Journal of Public Health*, *106*(5), 832–833. https://doi.org/10.2105/AJPH.2016.303100

Lafta, R., Al-Shatari, S., Cherewick, M., Galway, L., Mock, C., Hagopian, A., et al. (2015). Injuries, death, and disability associated with 11 years of conflict in Baghdad, Iraq: a randomized household cluster survey. *PLoS ONE*, *10*(8), e0131834. https://doi.org/10.1371/journal.pone.0131834

Lafta, R. K., & Al-Nuaimi, M. A. (2019). War or health: a four-decade armed conflict in Iraq. *Medicine, Conflict and Survival*, *35*(3), 209–226. https://doi.org/10.1080/13623699.2019.1670431

Lamble, S. (2009). Unknowable bodies, unthinkable sexualities: lesbian and transgender legal invisibility in the Toronto Women's Bathhouse raid. *Social & Legal Studies*, *18*(1), 111–130. https://doi.org/10.1177/0964663908100336

Latham, R. (2014). The governance of visibility: bodies, information, and the politics of anonymity across the US–Mexico borderlands. *Alternatives: Global, Local, Political*, *39*(1), 17–36. https://doi.org/10.1177/0304375414560279

Lather, P. (2001). Postbook: working the ruins of feminist ethnography. *Signs*, *27*(1), 199–227.

Lather, P. (2009). Getting lost: feminist efforts toward a double(d) science. *Frontiers: a Journal of Women Studies*, *30*(1), 222–230. https://doi.org/10.1353/fro.0.0032

Law, J. (2004). *After Method: Mess in Social Science Research*. Routledge.

Lawlor, L. (2008). Following the rats: becoming-animal in Deleuze and Guattari. *SubStance*, *37*(3), 169–187. https://doi.org/10.1353/sub.0.0016

Lawrence, Q., & Kaiser Health News (2016). Why Fertility Treatments Aren't Covered for Veterans. *The Atlantic*. https://www.theatlantic.com/health/archive/2016/02/veterans-fertility-treatments/470862/

Lawton, J. (1998). Contemporary hospice care: the sequestration of the unbounded body and 'dirty dying.' *Sociology of Health & Illness*, *20*(2), 121–143.

Lemke, T. (2001). 'The birth of bio-politics': Michel Foucault's lecture at the Collège de France on neo-liberal governmentality. *Economy and Society*, *30*(2), 190–207. https://doi.org/10.1080/03085140120042271

Lilburn, T. (2022). PPTA Urges policymakers to recognize the importance of plasma donation along the southern US border. *The Source*, *12*(3), 22–23. https://drive.google.com/file/d/1YYNlKYft6GGiSCcPDRt-OaopCQ9e8xOR/view

Lind, D. (2019). Pharmaceutical companies are luring Mexicans across the US border to donate blood plasma. *Probpublica.org*. https://www.propublica.org/article/pharmaceutical-companies-are-luring-mexicans-across-the-US–border-to-donate-blood-plasma

Lind, D., & Dodt, S. (2021). The US is closing a loophole that lured Mexicans over the border to donate blood plasma for cash. *Probpublica.org*. https://www.propublica.org/article/the-us-is-closing-a-loophole-that-lured-mexicans-over-the-border-to-donate-blood-plasma-for-cash

Linke, U. (1997). Gendered difference, violent imagination: blood, race, nation. *American Anthropologist*, *99*(3), 559–573.

Linstead, S. (2000). Dangerous fluids and the organization-without-organs. In J. Hassard, R. Holliday, & H. Willmott (eds.), *Body and Organization* (pp. 31–51). SAGE Publications.

Lippert, R., & O'Connor, D. (2003). Security assemblages: airport security, flexible work, and liberal governance. *Alternatives: Global, Local, Political*, *28*(3), 331–358.

Lloyd, J., & Arabian, N. (2014). Plane briefly quarantined at Las Vegas airport after Ebola scare. *Nbclosangeles.com*. https://www.nbclosangeles.com/news/local/Las-Vegas-New-York-Flight-Plane-Quarantine_Ebola-Symptoms-278826091.html

Lock, M. (2001). The alienation of body tissue and the biopolitics of immortalized cell lines. *Body & Society*, *7*(2–3), 63–91.

Longhurst, R. (2001). *Bodies: Exploring Fluid Boundaries*. Routledge.

Lucas, P. A., Page, P. R. J., Phillip, R. D., & Bennett, A. N. (2014). The impact of genital trauma on wounded servicemen: qualitative study. *Injury: International Journal of the Care of the Injured, 45*(5), 825–829.

Lugo, A. (2008). *Fragmented Lives, Assembled Parts: Culture, Capitalism, and Conquest at the US–Mexico Border*. University of Texas Press.

Lynch, L. (1998). The neo/bio/colonial hot zone: African viruses, American fairytales. *International Journal of Cultural Studies, 1*(2), 233–252.

Macey, D. (2009). Rethinking biopolitics, race and power in the wake of Foucault. *Theory, Culture & Society, 26*(6), 186–205. https://doi.org/10.1177/0263276409349278

MacLennan, S., & Barbara, J. A. J. (2006). Risks and side effects of therapy with plasma and plasma fractions. *Best Practice and Research: Clinical Haematology, 19*(1), 169–189. https://doi.org/10.1016/j.beha.2005.01.033

Manchanda, N. (2014). Queering the Pashtun: Afghan sexuality in the homo-nationalist imaginary. *Third World Quarterly, 36*(1), 130–146. https://doi.org/10.1080/01436597.2014.974378

Markel, H., & Stern, A. M. (1999). Which face? Whose nation? Immigration, public health, and the construction of disease at America's ports and borders, 1891–1920. *American Behavioral Scientist, 42*(9), 1314–1331.

Maron, D. (2020). 'Wet markets' likely launched the coronavirus. Here's what you need to know. *National Geographic*. https://www.nationalgeographic.co.uk/science-and-technology/2020/04/wet-markets-likely-launched-coronavirus-heres-what-you-need-know

Martin, E. (1992). The end of the body? *American Ethnologist, 19*(1), 121–140.

Martin, L. (2010). Bombs, bodies, and biopolitics: securitizing the subject at the airport security checkpoint. *Social and Cultural Geography, 11*(1), 17–34. https://doi.org/10.1080/14649360903414585

Massachusetts General Hospital (n.d.). MGH genito-urinary vascularized composite allograft (penile) transplant FAQs. *www.Massgeneral.org*. Retrieved 5 September 2018, from https://www.massgeneral.org/News/assets/pdf/penile-transplant-faq-051616.pdf

Masters, C. (2005). Bodies of technology: cyborg soldiers and militarized masculinities. *International Feminist Journal of Politics, 7*(1), 112–132. https://doi.org/10.1080/1461674042000324718

Masters, C. (2015). Gaga feminism and baroque visualities. *Critical Studies on Security, 3*(2), 220–222. https://doi.org/10.1080/21624887.2015.1047159

May, T. (2003). When is a Deleuzian becoming? *Continental Philosophy Review, 36*(2), 139–153. https://doi.org/10.1023/A:1026036516963

Mbembé, J. A. (2015). Necropolitics. *Public Culture, 15*(1), 11–40.

McInnes, C., & Lee, K. (2006). Health, security and foreign policy. *Review of International Studies, 32*(1), 5–23.

Médecins Sans Frontières (n.d.). Between rhetoric and reality: the ongoing struggle to access healthcare in Afghanistan. *msf*. https://www.msf.org/sites/msf.org/files/msf_afghanistan_report_final.pdf

Médecins Sans Frontières (2015). Initial MSF internal review: attack of Kunduz trauma centre, Afghanistan. *msf*. https://www.msf.org/sites/msf.org/files/msf_kunduz_review_041115_for_public_release.pdf

Meeuf, R. (2018). John Wayne as 'supercrip': disabled bodies and the construction of 'hard' masculinity in 'the wings of eagles.' *Cinema, 48*(2), 88–113.

Mitchell, P. (2005). *Coyote Nation: Sexuality, Race and Conquest in Modernizing New Mexico, 1880–1920*. University of Chicago Press.

Mitchell, R., & Waldby, C. (2010). National biobanks: clinical labor, risk production, and the creation of biovalue. *Science, Technology and Human Values, 35*(3), 330–355. https://doi.org/10.1177/0162243909340267

Molina, N. (2011). Borders, laborers, and racialized medicalization: Mexican immigration and US public health practices in the 20th century. *American Journal of Public Health, 101*(6), 1024–1031. https://doi.org/10.2105/AJPH.2010.300056

Monson, S. (2017). Ebola as African: American media discourses of panic and otherization. *Africa Today, 63*(3), 2–27. https://doi.org/10.2979/africatoday.63.3.02

Moore, L. J. (2002). Extracting men from semen masculinity in scientific representations of sperm. *Social Text, 20*(4), 91–119. https://doi.org/10.1215/01642472-20-4_73-91

Moore, L. J. (2008). *Sperm Counts: Overcome by Man's Most Precious Fluid*. New York University Press.

Moore, S., Taloma, C., & Laux, K. (2014). Ebola threat ruled out after plane quarantined in Las Vegas. *Reviewjournal.com*. https://www.reviewjournal.com/local/local-las-vegas/ebola-threat-ruled-out-after-plane-quarantined-in-las-vegas/

Moraga, C. (1981). Introduction. In C. Moraga & G. Anzaldúa (eds.), *This Bridge Called My Back: Writing by Radical Women of Color* (pp. xiii–xix). Persephone Press.

Mulcahy, A., Phillips, B., & Whaley, C. (2021). *Balancing Access and Cost Control in the TRICARE Prescription Drug Benefit*. RAND Corporation.

Murdocca, C. (2003). When Ebola came to Canada: race and the making of the respectable body. *Atlantis, 27*(2), 1–13.

Murray, R. (2011). Mexicans cross US border to sell plasma. *New York Daily News*. http://www.nydailynews.com/news/world/mexicans-flee-cities-devastated-drug-wars-cross-border-sell-plasma-united-states-article-1.982192

Myrttinen, H. (2018). Languages of castration – male genital mutilation in conflict and its embedded messages. *Sexual Violence Against Men in Global Politics*, 71–88. https://doi.org/10.4324/9781315456492-6

Najari, B., Flannigan, R., Hobgood, J., & Paduch, D. (2018). Attitudes toward penile transplantation among urologists and health professionals. *Sexual Medicine*, *6*(4), 316–323. https://doi.org/10.1016/j.esxm.2018.06.003

Nash, C. J. (2010). Trans geographies, embodiment and experience. *Gender, Place & Culture*, *17*(5), 579–595. https://doi.org/10.1080/0966369X.2010.503112

Nash, J. (2017). Black anality. In C. Cipolla, K. Gupta, D. A. Rubin, & A. Willey (eds.), *Queer Feminist Science Studies: a Reader* (pp. 102–113). University of Washington Press.

Nash, J. C. (2019). Birthing black mothers: birth work and the making of black maternal political subjects. *Women's Studies Quarterly*, *47*(3–4), 29–50. https://doi.org/10.1353/WSQ.2019.0054

Nevins, J. (2007). Dying for a cup of coffee? Migrant deaths in the US-Mexico border region in a neoliberal age. *Geopolitics*, *12*(2), 228–247.

Noyes, R. (2007). Profile of a hero. *The Source*, *1*(5), 6–7.

Nunes, J. (2016). Ebola and the production of neglect in global health. *Third World Quarterly*, *37*(3), 542–556. https://doi.org/10.1080/01436597.2015.1124724

Octapharma (n.d.-a). Find your plasma donation center. *Octapharmaplasma.com*. Retrieved 27 June 2023, from https://www.octapharmaplasma.com/plasma-donation-centers/

Octapharma (n.d.-b). Payment & rewards. *Octapharmaplasma.com*. Retrieved 18 August 2017, from https://octapharmaplasma.com/donor/payment-rewards

Octapharma (2017). Plasma. *Octapharmaplasma.com*. http://www.octapharma.com/en/about/production/plasma.html

Owens, D. C. (2017). *Medical Bondage: Race, Gender, and the Origins of American Gynecology*. University of Georgia Press.

Owens, P. (2003). 'Accidents don't just happen: the liberal politics of high-tech humanitarian war.' *Millennium – Journal of International Studies*, *32*(3), 595–616. https://doi.org/10.1177/03058298030320031101

Papamichail, A. (2023). Reinscribing global hierarchies: COVID–19, racial capitalism and the liberal international order. *International Affairs*, *4*, 1673–1691. https://doi.org/10.1093/ia/iiad091

Patton, C. (1985). *Sex and Germs: The Politics of AIDS*. South End Press.

Pavel, B., & Engelke, P. (2020). Irresponsible wet market practices led to COVID-19. China hasn't learned its lesson. *Euronews.com*. https://www.euronews.com/2020/04/30/irresponsible-wet-market-practices-led-to-covid-19-china-hasn-t-learned-its-lesson-view

Penrod, J. (2010). Technological improvements in plasma collection. *The Source*, *4*(3), 26–27.

Penrod, J., & Gustafson, M. (2009). The evolution of safety in source plasma collection. *The Source*, *3*(2), 16–18.

Peterson, V. S. (ed.) (1992). *Gendered States: Feminist (Re)Visions of International Relations Theory*. Lynne Rienner Publishers.

Peterson, V. S. (1999). Political identities/nationalism as heterosexism. *International Feminist Journal of Politics*, *1*(1), 34–65. https://doi.org/10.1080/146167499360031

Peterson, V. S. (2014a). Family matters: how queering the intimate queers the international. *International Studies Review*, *16*(4), 604–608. https://doi.org/10.1111/misr.12185

Peterson, V. S. (2014b). Sex matters. *International Feminist Journal of Politics*, *16*(3), 389–409. https://doi.org/10.1080/14616742.2014.913384

Pin-Fat, V., & Stern, M. (2005). The scripting of Private Jessica Lynch: biopolitics, gender, and the 'feminization' of the US military. *Alternatives: Global, Local, Political*, *30*(1), 25–53. https://doi.org/10.1177/030437540503000102

Platt, R., & Warwick, L. (2020). Are some ethnic groups more vulnerable to COVID-19 than others? | Inequality: the IFS Deaton Review. *Institute for Fiscal Studies*. https://www.ifs.org.uk/inequality/chapter/are-some-ethnic-groups-more-vulnerable-to-covid-19-than-others/

Plumwood, V. (1993). *Feminism and the Mastery of Nature*. Routledge.

Polaris Market Research (2022). Blood plasma market share, size, trends, industry analysis report, by application (hemophilia, hypogammaglobulinemia, immunodeficiency diseases, Von Willebrand's disease, others); by type; by end-use; by region; segment forecast, 2022–2030. *polarismarketresearch.com*. https://www.polarismarketresearch.com/industry-analysis/global-blood-plasma-market

Pollack, A. (2009). Is money tainting the plasma supply? *New York Times*. www.nytimes.com/2009/12/06/business/06plasma.html

Pollock, A., & Subramaniam, B. (2016). Resisting power, retooling justice: promises of feminist postcolonial technosciences. *Science Technology and Human Values*, *41*(6), 951–966. https://doi.org/10.1177/0162243916657879

Potts, A. (2000). 'The essence of the hard on': hegemonic masculinity and the cultural construction of erectile dysfunction. *Men and Masculinities*, *3*(1), 85–103.

PPTA (n.d.). Videos. *www.pptaglobal.org*. Retrieved 4 April 2019, from https://www.pptaglobal.org/media-and-information/videos

PPTA (2010). PPTA stakeholder report. *The Source*, *4*(2), 22–23.

PPTA (2016). The facts about…plasma collection. *www.pptaglobal.org*. https://www.pptaglobal.org/images/Fact_Sheets/Redone/2016/Fact_Sheet_Plasma_Collection.pdf

Preston, R. (2014). *The Hot Zone: The Chilling True Story of an Ebola Outbreak*. Corgi.

Prime Minister's Office 10 Downing Street, & The Rt Hon Boris Johnson MP (2021). Prime Minister announces national lockdown. *gov.uk*. https://www.gov.uk/government/news/prime-minister-announces-national-lockdown

Puar, J. K. (2005). Queer times, queer assemblages. *Social Text*, *23*(3-4), 84–85, 121–139. https://doi.org/10.1215/01642472-23-3-4_84-85-121

Puar, J. K. (2006). Mapping US homonormativities. *Gender, Place and Culture*, *13*(1), 67–88. https://doi.org/10.1080/09663690500531014

Puar, J. K. (2009). Prognosis time: towards a geopolitics of affect, debility and capacity. *Women & Performance: A Journal of Feminist Theory*, *19*(2), 161–172. https://doi.org/10.1080/07407700903034147

Puar, J. K. (2012a). Coda: the cost of getting better: suicide, sensation, switchpoints. *GLQ: a Journal of Lesbian and Gay Studies*, *18*(1), 149–158. https://doi.org/10.1215/10642684-1422179

Puar, J. K. (2012b). 'I would rather be a cyborg than a goddess': becoming-intersectional in assemblage theory. *PhiloSOPHIA*, *2*(1), 49–66. https://doi.org/10.1353/phi.2012.0006

Puar, J. K. (2013). Rethinking homonationalism. *International Journal of Middle East Studies*, *45*(2), 336–339.

Puar, J. K. (2017a). *Terrorist Assemblages: Homonationalism in Queer Times*. Duke University Press.

Puar, J. K. (2017b). *The Right to Maim: Debility, Capacity, Disability*. Duke University Press.

Puar, J. K., & Rai, A. (2002). Monster, terrorist, fag: the war on terrorism and the production of docile patriots. *Social Text*, *20*(3), 117–148.

Public Health England (2020). Disparities in the risk and outcomes of COVID-19. PHE Publications. https://www.gov.uk/government/publications/covid-19-review-of-disparities-in-risks-and-outcomes

Public Health England (2021). Deaths in United Kingdom. *coronavirus.data.gov.uk*. https://coronavirus.data.gov.uk/details/deaths

Pulido, L. (2016). Flint, environmental racism, and racial capitalism. *Capitalism, Nature, Socialism*, *27*(3), 1–16. https://doi.org/10.1080/10455752.2016.1213013

Rainey, S. S. (2017). In sickness and in health: cripping and queering marriage equality. *Hypatia*, *32*(2), 230–246. https://doi.org/10.1111/hypa.12328

Rao, R. (2014). Queer questions. *International Feminist Journal of Politics*, *16*(2), 199–217. https://doi.org/10.1080/14616742.2014.901817

Razai, M. S., Kankam, H. K. N., Majeed, A., Esmail, A., & Williams, D. R. (2021). Mitigating ethnic disparities in covid-19 and beyond. *The BMJ*, *372*(m4921), 1–5. https://doi.org/10.1136/bmj.m4921

Recovering Warrior Task Force US Department of Defense (2013). Task force on the care, management and transition of recovering wounded, ill and injured members of the armed forces: business meeting, Tuesday April 2, 2013. *Rtwf.Defense.gov*. https://rwtf.defense.gov/Portals/22/Documents/Meetings/m14/m14040213transcript.pdf

Redden, S., & Terry, J. (2013). The end of the line: feminist understandings of resistance to full-body scanning technology. *International Feminist Journal of Politics*, *15*(2), 234–253.

Reed, A. M., Janak, J. C., Orman, J. A., & Hudak, S. J. (2018). Genitourinary injuries among female US Service Members during Operation Iraqi Freedom and Operation Enduring Freedom: findings from the Trauma Outcomes and Urogenital Health (TOUGH) project. *Military Medicine*, *183*(7–8), e304–e309. https://doi.org/10.1093/milmed/usx079

Reilly, J., & Graaf, M. de. (2014). Has Ebola hit Kansas? Medical officer being tested for deadly virus days after returning from commercial ship in west Africa … as Portland hospital quarantines a patient with similar symptoms. *MailOnline*. https://www.dailymail.co.uk/news/article-2790978/ebola-scare-dallas-passenger-removed-american-airlines-flight-nashville-airport-vomiting-board.html

Rhee, J. (2018). *The Robotic Imaginary: the Human and the Price of Dehumanized Labor*. University of Minnesota Press.

Richter-Montpetit, M. (2014). Beyond the erotics of Orientalism: lawfare, torture and the racial-sexual grammars of legitimate suffering. *Security Dialogue*, *45*(1), 43–62. https://doi.org/10.1177/0967010613515016

Richter-Montpetit, M. (2018). Everything you always wanted to know about sex (in IR) but were afraid to ask: the 'queer turn' in international relations. *Millennium: Journal of International Studies*, *46*(2), 220–240. https://doi.org/10.1177/0305829817733131

Rinkunas, S. (2018). This is how a wounded veteran got a penis transplant. *Vice*. https://www.vice.com/en_us/article/mbxnwp/penis-transplant-veteran

Riska, E. (2010). Gender and medicalization and biomedicalization theories. In A. Clarke, L. Mamo, J. Fosket, J. Fishman, & J. Shim (eds.), *Biomedicalization: Technoscience, Health, and Illness in the US* (pp. 147–171). Duke University Press.

Robert Koch Institut (n.d.). Questionnaires and fever scanners. *www.Rki.De*. Retrieved 14 February 2018, from https://www.rki.de/EN/Content/infections/epidemiology/outbreaks/Ebola_virus_disease/Investigative_work/Exit-Screening.html

Rossdale, C. (2015). Enclosing critique: the limits of ontological security. *International Political Sociology*, *9*(4), 369–386. https://doi.org/10.1111/ips.12103

Roston, A. (2009). Blood and treasure. *The National*. http://www.thenational.ae/news/world/blood-and-treasure#full

Rougeron, V., Feldmann, H., Grard, G., Becker, S., & Leroy, E. M. (2015). Ebola and Marburg haemorrhagic fever. *Journal of Clinical Virology*, *64*, 111–119. https://doi.org/10.1016/j.jcv.2015.01.014

Rushton, S. (2019). *Security and Public Health*. Polity Press.

Saldívar, J. D. (1997). *Border Matters: Remapping American Cultural Studies*. University of California Press.

Salian, V. S., Wright, J. A., Vedell, P. T., Nair, S., Li, C., Kandimalla, M., et al. (2021). COVID-19 transmission, current treatment, and future therapeutic strategies. *Molecular Pharmaceutics*, *18*(3), 754–771. https://doi.org/10.1021/acs.molpharmaceut.0c00608

Salter, M. B. (2007). Governmentalities of an airport: heterotopia and confession. *International Political Sociology*, *1*(1), 49–66. https://doi.org/10.1111/j.1749-5687.2007.00004.x

Schell, H. (1997). Outburst! A chilling true story about emerging-virus narratives and pandemic social change. *Configurations*, *5*(1), 93–133.

Scheper-Hughes, N. (2001). Bodies for sale – whole or in parts. *Body & Society*, *7*(2–3), 1–8.

Schiebinger, L. (2004). *Nature's Body: Gender in the Making of Modern Science*. Rutgers University Press.

Schreiber, G. (2014). Addressing the questions of residual risk. *The Source*, *8*(3), 18–20.

Sedgwick, E. K. (1993). *Tendencies*. Duke University Press.

Segal, M. (2016). The problem with the word 'queer.' *Advocate*, 11 February. http://www.advocate.com/commentary/2016/2/11/problem-word-queer

Serano, J. (2007). *Whipping Girl: a Transsexual Woman on Sexism and the Scapegoating of Femininity*. Seal Press.

Serlin, D. (2015). Constructing autonomy: smart homes for disabled veterans and the politics of normative citizenship. *Critical Military Studies*, *1*(1), 38–46. https://doi.org/10.1080/23337486.2015.1005392

Sharp, L. A. (2000). The commodification of the body and its parts. *Annual Review of Anthropology*, *29*, 287–328.

Shaw, M. (2002). Risk-transfer militarism, small massacres and the historic legitimacy of war. *International Relations*, *16*(3), 343–359.

Shears, P., & O'Dempsey, T. J. D. (2015). Ebola virus disease in Africa: epidemiology and nosocomial transmission. *Journal of Hospital Infection*, *90*(1), 1–9. https://doi.org/10.1016/j.jhin.2015.01.002

Sheller, M., & Urry, J. (2006). The new mobilities paradigm. *Environment and Planning A*, *38*(2), 207–226. https://doi.org/10.1068/a37268

Shepherd, L. J., & Sjoberg, L. (2012). Trans- bodies in/of war(s): cisprivilege and contemporary security strategy. *Feminist Review, 101*(1), 5–23. https://doi.org/10.1057/fr.2011.53

Shildrick, M. (1996). Posthumanism and the monstrous body. *Body & Society, 2*(1), 1–15.

Shildrick, M. (1997). *Leaky Bodies and Boundaries: Feminism, Postmodernism and (Bio)ethics*. Routledge.

Shildrick, M. (2015). 'Why should our bodies end at the skin?': embodiment, boundaries, and somatechnics. *Hypatia, 30*(1), 13–29. https://doi.org/10.1111/hypa.12114

Shultz, J. M., Espinel, Z., Espinola, M., & Rechkemmer, A. (2016). Distinguishing epidemiological features of the 2013–2016 West Africa Ebola virus disease outbreak. *Disaster Health, 3*(3), 78–88. https://doi.org/10.1080/21665044.2016.1228326

Sjoberg, L. (2012). Toward trans-gendering international relations? *International Political Sociology, 6*(4), 337–354. https://doi.org/10.1111/ips.12005

Sjoberg, L. (2014). Queering the 'territorial peace'? Queer theory conversing with mainstream international relations. *International Studies Review, 16*(4), 608–612. https://doi.org/10.1111/misr.12186

Sjoberg, L. (2015). Seeing sex, gender, and sexuality in international security. *International Journal, 70*(3), 434–453. https://doi.org/10.1177/0020702015584590

Slonim, R., Wang, C., & Garbarino, E. (2014). The market for blood. *The Journal of Economic Perspectives, 28*(2), 177–196.

Smith, G. (2019). A trans woman was told she couldn't donate plasma. Now she's suing. *Lgbtqnation.com*. https://www.lgbtqnation.com/2019/03/trans-woman-told-couldnt-donate-plasma-now-shes-suing/

Spade, D. (2003). Resisting medicine/remodeling gender. *Berkeley Women's Law Journal, 63*(1997), 15–37.

Sparke, M. (2006). A neoliberal nexus: economy, security and the biopolitics of citizenship on the border. *Political Geography, 25*(2), 151–180.

Spehr, M. (2003). Identification of a testicular odorant receptor mediating human sperm chemotaxis. *Science, 299*(5615), 2054–2058. https://doi.org/10.1126/science.1080376

Spillers, H. (1987). Mama's baby, papa's maybe: an American grammar book. *Diacritics, 17*(2), 64–81.

Squire, V. (2012). Attuning to mess. In M. B. Salter & C. E. Mutlu (eds.), *Research Methods in Critical Security Studies: an Introduction* (pp. 108–117). Routledge.

Squire, V. (2014). Desert 'trash': posthumanism, border struggles, and humanitarian politics. *Political Geography, 39*, 11–21. https://doi.org/10.1016/j.polgeo.2013.12.003

Starr, D. (1999). *Blood: an Epic History of Medicine and Commerce*. Alfred A. Knopf.

Stephens, E. (2007). The spectacularized penis: contemporary representations of the phallic male body. *Men and Masculinities*, *10*(1), 85–98.

Stephens, E. (2008). Pathologizing leaky male bodies: spermatorrhea in nineteenth-century British medicine and popular anatomical museums. *Journal of the History of Sexuality*, *17*(3), 421–438. https://doi.org/10.1353/sex.0.0023

Stern, A. M. (1999). Buildings, boundaries, and blood: medicalization and nation-building on the US–Mexico border, 1910–1930. *The Hispanic American Historical Review*, *79*(1), 41–81.

Stern, A. M. (2005). Sterilized in the name of public health: race, immigration, and reproductive control in modern California. *American Journal of Public Health*, *95*(7), 1128–1138. https://doi.org/10.2105/ajph.2004.041608

Sundberg, J. (2008). 'Trash-talk' and the production of quotidian geopolitical boundaries in the USA–Mexico borderlands. *Social & Cultural Geography*, *9*(8), 871–890. https://doi.org/10.1080/14649360802441424

Talecris plasma-En español (2022). ¡Bienvenidos! ¡Buenas noticias! Los donantes de visa con visas B1 o B2 pueden donar con nosotros a partir de hoy. No dude en ponerse en contacto con nuestro centro para obtener más información. Si no ha donado en más de 6 meses, se le considerará como un. *Facebook*. https://www.facebook.com/plasmagrifols/photos/a.850381209676332/850488702998916/

Tapper, M. (1995). Interrogating bodies: medico-racial knowledge, politics, and the study of a disease. *Comparative Studies in Society and History*, *37*(1), 76–93.

Terry, J. (2017). *Attachments to War: Biomedical Logics and Violence in Twenty-First-Century America*. Duke University Press.

Thomas, J. (2002). Arachaelogy's humanism and the materiality of the body. In Y. Hamilakis, M. Pluciennik, & S. Tarlow (eds.), *Thinking through the Body: Archaeologies of Corporeality* (pp. 29–46). Springer Science+Business Media, LLC.

Trudy (2013). Misogyny, in general vs. anti-black misogyny (misogynoir), specifically. *Gradientlair.com*. http://www.gradientlair.com/post/60973580823/general-misogyny-versus-misogynoir

Tuck, G. (2003). Mainstreaming the money shot: reflections on the representation of ejaculation in contemporary American cinema. *Paragraph*, *26*(1–2), 263–279. https://doi.org/10.3366/para.2003.26.1-2.263

Turner, S. (1999). Intersex identities: locating new intersections of sex and gender. *Gender & Society*, *13*(4), 457–479.

Ungar, S. (1998). Hot crises and media reassurance: a comparison of emerging diseases and Ebola Zaire. *British Journal of Sociology*, *49*(1), 36–56. https://doi.org/10.2307/591262

United States Census Bureau (n.d.). 2013–2017 ACS 5-year narrative profile El Paso County, Texas. *Census.gov*. Retrieved 8 October 2019, from https://www.census.gov/acs/www/data/data-tables-and-tools/narrative-profiles/2017/report.php?geotype=county&state=48&county=141

United States Census Bureau (2017). Selected characteristics of people at specified levels of poverty in the past 12 months. *American Community Survey*. https://data.census.gov/cedsci/table?q=S17&d=ACS 1-Year Estimates Subject Tables&table=S1703&tid=ACSST1Y2017.S1703&lastDisplayedRow=42&hidePreview=true&g=0500000US48141

United States Census Bureau (2018). QuickFacts El Paso County, Texas. *Census.gov*. https://www.census.gov/quickfacts/fact/table/elpasocountytexas/RHI125218#RHI125218

Uppendahl, M., & Murphy, N. (2019). *The Hot Zone*. 20th Television.

US Department of Veterans Affairs (n.d.). Infertility treatment. *www.va.gov*. Retrieved 30 October 2018, from https://www.va.gov/COMMUNITYCARE/programs/veterans/ivf.asp

US Food and Drug Administration (2023). FDA finalizes move to recommend individual risk assessment to determine eligibility for blood donations. *Content.govdelivery.com*. https://content.govdelivery.com/accounts/USFDA/bulletins/359eabd

Vandenberghe, F. (2008). Deleuzian capitalism. *Philosophy & Social Criticism*, *34*(8), 877–903. https://doi.org/10.1177/0191453708095696

Vetter, P., & Kaiser, L. (2020). Ebola: an uncontrolled outbreak despite vaccines and new treatments. *Revue Medicale Suisse*, *16*(690), 739–743.

Vila, P. (2000). *Crossing Borders, Reinforcing Borders: Social Categories, Metaphors, and Narrative Identities on the US–Mexico Frontier*. University of Texas Press.

Villagran, L., & Dodt, S. (2019). Luring donors from Mexico, El paso offers rich market for plasma collection. *El Paso Times*. https://eu.elpasotimes.com/story/news/2019/10/11/mexicans-donate-blood-plasma-border-immigration/3944750002/

Villareal, H., Al-Bayati, S., Wang, C. P., Pugh, M. J., & Liss, M. A. (2021). Transitional care of service members with genitourinary injury. *Military Medicine*, *186*(9), 969–974. https://doi.org/10.1093/milmed/usab086

Voelkner, N. (2011). Managing pathogenic circulation: human security and the migrant health assemblage in Thailand. *Security Dialogue*, *42*(3), 239–259. https://doi.org/10.1177/0967010611405393

Volkow, P., Perez-Padilla, R., Del-Rio, C., & Mohar, A. (1998). The role of commercial plasmapheresis banks on the AIDS epidemic in Mexico. *Revista de Investigación Clínica*, *50*(3), 221–226.

Wain, H. J., Young, L. C., & Santiago, P. N. (2017). Genital injury and the psychiatric consult liaison service. In E. C. Ritchie (ed.), *Intimacy Post-Injury: Combat Trauma and Sexual Health* (pp. 179–190). Oxford University Press.

Wajcman, J. (2000). Reflection on gender and technology studies: in what state is the art? *Social Studies of Science*, *30*(3), 447–464.

Wajcman, J. (2007). From women and technology to gendered technoscience. *Information Communication and Society*, *10*(3), 287–298. https://doi.org/10.1080/13691180701409770

Waldby, C. (1996). *AIDS and the Body Politic: Biomedicine and Sexual Difference*. Routledge.

Waldby, C. (2002a). Biomedicine, tissue transfer and intercorporeality. *Feminist Theory*, *3*(3), 239–254. https://doi.org/10.1177/146470002762491980

Waldby, C. (2002b). Stem cells, tissue cultures and the production of biovalue. *Health: an Interdisciplinary Journal for the Social Study of Health, Illness and Medicine*, *6*(3), 305–323.

Waldby, C., & Mitchell, R. (2006). *Tissue Economies: Blood, Organs, and Cell Lines in Late Capitalism*. Duke University Press.

Washington, H. A. (2008). *Medical Apartheid: the Dark History of Medical Experimentation on Black Americans from Colonial Times to the Present*. Anchor Books.

Waskul, D. D., & van der Riet, P. (2002). The abject embodiment of cancer patients: dignity, selfhood, and the grotesque body. *Symbolic Interaction*, *25*(4), 487–513. https://doi.org/10.1525/si.2002.25.4.487

Weaver, M., & Dodd, V. (2023). UK rail worker dies of coronavirus after being spat at while on duty. *The Guardian*. https://www.theguardian.com/uk-news/2020/may/12/uk-rail-worker-dies-coronavirus-spat-belly-mujinga

Weber, C. (1999). *Faking It: US Hegemony in a 'Post-Phallic' Era*. University of Minnesota Press.

Weber, C. (2015). Why is there no queer international theory? *European Journal of International Relations*, *21*(1), 27–51. https://doi.org/10.1177/1354066114524236

Weber, C. (2016). Queer intellectual curiosity as international relations method: developing queer international relations theoretical and methodological frameworks. *International Studies Quarterly*, *60*(1), 11–23. https://doi.org/10.1111/isqu.12212

Weheliye, A. (2014). *Habeas Viscus: Racializing Assemblages, Biopolitics, and Black Feminist Theories of the Human*. Duke University Press.

Weldon, R. A. (2001a). An 'urban legend' of global proportion: an analysis of nonfiction accounts of the ebola virus. *Journal of Health Communication*, *6*(3), 281–294. https://doi.org/10.1080/108107301752384451

Weldon, R. A. (2001b). An 'urban legend' of global proportion: an analysis of nonfiction accounts of the Ebola virus. *Journal of Health Communication*, *6*(3), 281–294. https://doi.org/10.1080/108107301752384451

Welland, J. (2013). Militarized violences, basic training, and the myths of asexuality and discipline. *Review of International Studies*, *39*(04), 881–902. https://doi.org/10.1017/S0260210512000605

Wellington, D. (2014). Blood money: the twisted business of donating plasma. *The Atlantic*. https://www.theatlantic.com/health/archive/2014/05/bloody-money-the-twisted-business-of-donating-plasma/362012/

Wenham, C. (2017). What we have learnt about the world health organization from the Ebola outbreak. *Philosophical Transactions of the Royal Society B: Biological Sciences*, *372*(1721). https://doi.org/10.1098/rstb.2016.0307

Wenham, C. (2021). *Feminist Global Health Security*. Oxford University Press.

Westbrook, L., & Schilt, K. (2013). Doing gender, determining gender: transgender people, gender panics, and the maintenance of the sex/gender/sexuality system. *Gender & Society*, *28*(1), 32–57. https://doi.org/10.1177/0891243213503203

White House Office of the Press Secretary (2014). FACT SHEET: the US response to the Ebola epidemic in West Africa. *Obamawhitehouse.Archives.gov*. https://obamawhitehouse.archives.gov/the-press-office/2014/1/06/fact-sheet-us-response-ebola-epidemic-west-africa

Whitworth, S. (2005). Militarized masculinity and the politics of peacekeeping: the Canadian case. In K. Booth (ed.), *Critical Security Studies in World Politics* (pp. 89–106). Boulder, CO: Lynne Rienner Publishers.

Wilcox, L. (2015). *Bodies of Violence: Theorizing Embodied Subjects in International Relations*. Oxford University Press.

Wilcox, L. (2017). Practising gender, queering theory. *Review of International Studies*, *43*(5), 789–808. https://doi.org/10.1017/S0260210517000183

Wilcox, S. L., Schuyler, A., & Hassan, A. M. (2015a). Genitourniary trauma in the military: impact, prevention, and recommendations. *www.Cir.Usc.Edu*. http://cir.usc.edu/wp-content/uploads/2015/03/CIR_Policy-Brief_GU-Trauma_March2015.pdf

Wilcox, S. L., Schuyler, A., & Hassan, A. M. (2015b). Genitourniary trauma in the military: impact, prevention, and recommendations. *www.Cir.Usc.Edu*.

Williams, C. L. (1994). Militarized masculinity. *Qualitative Sociology*, *17*(4), 415–422. https://doi.org/10.1007/BF02393339

Williams, M., & Jezior, J. (2013). Management of combat-related urological trauma in the modern era. *Nature Reviews Urology*, *10*(9), 504–512. https://doi.org/10.1038/nrurol.2013.148

Winters, J. L. (2006). Complications of donor apheresis. *Journal of Clinical Apheresis*, *21*(2), 132–141. https://doi.org/10.1002/jca.20039

Wood, D. (2012). Beyond the battlefield: Afghanistan's wounded struggle with genital injuries. *The Huffington Post*. https://www.huffingtonpost.co.uk/entry/beyond-the-battlefield-afghanistan-genital-injuries_n_1335356?ri18n=true

Woodhouse, M. (2015). Plasma center is economic lifeline for Ambos Nogales. *Nogales International*. http://www.nogalesinternational.com/news/plasma-center-is-economic-lifeline-for-ambos-nogales/article_2b540928-1611-11e5-8af3-e3c4929e2c4a.html

Woodward, R. (1998). 'It's a man's life!': soldiers, masculinity and the countryside. *Gender, Place & Culture*, 5(3), 277–300. https://doi.org/10.1080/09663699825214

Woodward, R. (2000). Warrior heroes and little green men: soldiers, military training, and the construction of rural masculinities. *Rural Sociology*, 65(4), 640–657.

World Health Organization (2014a). Guinea: screening for Ebola at Conakry International Airport. *www.who.int*. htttp://www.who.int/features/214/airport-exit-screening/en

World Health Organization (2014b). Statement on the 1st meeting of the IHR Emergency Committee on the 2014 Ebola outbreak in West Africa. *www.who.int*. https://www.who.int/mediacentre/news/statements/2014/ebola-20140808/en/

World Health Organization (2014c). Technical note for Ebola virus disease preparedness planning for entry screening at airports, ports and land crossings. *www.who.int*. http://apps.who.int/iris/bitstream/10665/144819/1/WHO_EVD_Guidance_PoE_14.3_eng.pdf?ua=1&ua=1

World Health Organization (2014d). Travel and transport risk assessment: interim guidance for public health authorities and the transport sector. *www.who.int*. https://apps.who.int/iris/bitstream/handle/10665/132168/WHO_EVD_Guidance_TravelTransportRisk_14.1_eng.pdf?ua=1

World Health Organization (2016). Situation report: Ebola virus disease 1 June 2016. *www.who.int*. http://apps.who.int/iris/bitstream/10665/208883/1/ebolasitrep_10Jun2016_eng.pdf?ua=1

World Health Organization (2017). WHO model list of essential medicines: 20th List (March 2017). *www.who.int*. http://www.who.int/medicines/publications/essentialmedicines/20th_EML2017.pdf?ua=1

World Health Organization (2022). *Therapeutics for Ebola Virus Disease*. World Health Organization.

Wynter, S. (2003). Unsettling the coloniality of being/power/truth/freedom: towards the human, after man, its overrepresentation – an argument. *CR: The New Centennial Review*, 3(3), 257–337. https://doi.org/10.1353/ncr.2004.0015

Young, I. M. (2005). *On Female Body Experience: 'Throwing Like a Girl' and Other Essays*. Oxford University Press.

Zaleski, A. (2019). Meet the wounded veteran who got a penis transplant: he nearly lost it all to an IED blast in Afghanistan. But a pioneering procedure changed everything. *MIT Technology Review*. https://www.technologyreview.com/2019/10/14/132305/meet-the-wounded-veteran-who-got-a-penis-transplant/

Zalewski, M. (2006). Distracted reflections on the production, narration, and refusal of feminist knowledge in international relations. In B. Ackerly, M. Stern, & J. True (eds.), *Feminist Methodologies for International Relations* (pp. 42–61). Cambridge University Press.

Index

References to endnotes show both the page number and the note number (231n3).

A

Afghanistan 87–91, 95, 114
Afghan National Disability Survey 88
Africa
  colonial Western imaginaries 60
  Ebola as 'natural' 61
  exporter of disease 70
  as the heart of darkness 58
  legitimizing deaths 70
  see also Ebola vomit
agency of fluids 107–108
Ahmed, Sara 101
AIDS virus 118
airport screening 55–56, 67–70
airport security 24, 58
air travel 64–66
American donors 45
'American' plasma 50
Ancient Greeks 26
anti-blackness discourses 60
anti-coagulants 48
anti-queerness 87
Anzaldúa, Gloria 33
Aradau, C. 106, 107, 108
Armed Forces Institute of Regenerative Medicine's second programme (AFIRM II). 73, 82
assemblages 18–22
  see also body-assemblages
  assemblages of violence 122
  assemblage theory 16–18, 21–22, 23, 113

B

B-1/B-2 visas 35
Baaz, M. E. 11
Bailey, Moya 7
Bananas, Beaches and Bases (Enloe) 7
Bass, J. D. 63
Baxter 32
becoming(s) 18, 21
Belling, C. 63

Bennett, Jane 107–108, 109
Benton, A. 69–70
Berlant, Lauren 30, 121
bioavailability (Cohen) 40–41
BioLife Plasma Services 32n1
'biological masculinity' (Johnson) 83
bio-medical technologies 25
biopolitical forms of power 79
biopolitical governance 2, 11, 30, 117
biopolitical military-medical assemblages 79
biopolitics 4, 29, 30–31, 117–118
biopower 29, 30
bios 23, 37, 48, 50, 117
black African bodies
  airport screening practices 24, 27, 63
  quarantining and mobility 70–71
  stigmatizing responses to Ebola 61
  white bodies as a lethal threat 67
bodily fluids
  absent in literature 101
  agential matter in international politics 108–109
  biological lives 29–30
  biopolitical governance 30
  controlling 105
  defining 28–29
  disgusting 99–100
  dis/re/connect bodies 111–112
  distinctions between bodies 104–105
  feminist technoscience 118
  forging connections and relationships 104
  and FTS 120
  as gendered/gendering 100
  infectious material 57
  international politics 27–31, 104, 105–106
  and international security 2
  and life–death 118–120
  as a method/ological 100, 101, 102
  political substances 105
  and queerfeminist thought 3
'bodily fragments' 25

the body 14
  becoming-Other 18
  continually changing 18–19
  gendered as feminized location 63
  microcosm of assemblages 25
  sex, gender and race 117
  Western philosophy 26
body assemblages 16–17, 18, 20–28, 113, 117
  see also assemblages
body boundaries 64–68, 103, 105
borderland communities 36
borderland donation practices 44
  see also Mexicana/o donors;
    US–Mexico border
borderlands 32–34
Braidotti, R. 19
Brantly, Kent 55
'bricolage' (Aradau) 106–107
Brinkema, E. 57
Burkle, Frederick, Jr 89
'bushmeat' 61
Butler, Judith 5

C

Cafferkey, Pauline 71
Calderón, Felipe 36
catalyst for diseases 43
Cayenne (dog) 109–110
Cetrulo, Curtis 81
Charles Monet (*The Hot Zone*) 59–60, 65–66
Chicana/o 41
cis bodies 80–84
cishetero male bodies 74, 95
Cohen, L. 40
colonial histories of representation 45–46
colonialism 39, 60–61, 68–70
colonial violence 33
colours of evil, purity and virtue 61
Comité Fronterizo de Obrer@s (CFO) 36
corporeal hierarchies of difference (Puar) 22
Costs of War project 88, 111
COVID-19 1–3, 121–123
Cox, Robert 5
Crenshaw, Kimberlé 6–7
CSL Plasma Inc 32, 35
CSL Plasma Inc v. US Customs and Border Protection 35
Cuidad Juárez, Mexico 35–36, 37

D

Daily Mail 41, 44
darkness/black as evil 61
death 30, 119–120
debility/capacity (Puar) 30–31
Deleuze, G. 14, 16, 17, 18–22
Dionne, K. Y 69, 70
disgust 103–104
distribution of life–death 4
  Afghanistan and Iraq 89–90, 91

African EVD deaths 70
airport screening 64
bodily fluids 113, 120
international security 104, 111
phallocentric genital hierarchies 83–84
and power 114
transplant and fertility treatments 74, 87
Dominican Republic 64
donating blood 46–47, 103
  see also plasma donors and donations
donor bodies 16–17, 39, 47–48
donor embodiment 41–42
donor testicles 79
  see also penis transplants
Douglas, Mary 103
Dumit, Joe 101
Duncan, Thomas 55
Duran, Araceli 36
dying 30, 119

E

'Ebola' chants 61
Ebola virus disease (EVD) 52–72
  airport security assemblages 24, 52, 55–56
  burial practices 69
  colonial Western imaginaries 60
  deaths 54, 70
  exit-screening practices 54–55
  fear of 53, 61
  geopolitical hierarchy of life–death 68
  haemorrhagic fever and symptoms 53, 60n7
  health interventions 69
  mechanisms of infection 65
  'natural' to African landscape 61
  as a predator 60
  questionnaire 56–57
  racializing/racialized discourses 58–59
  screening technologies 56
  transmission 10–11, 54, 69, 108
  unhygienic and diseased landscapes 69
  vaccines 54
  West Africa 2013–16 10–11, 12–13, 52, 113–114
  Western coverage 55, 61
Ebola vomit 10–11
  'black vomit' 60–61, 62
  'bleeding out' of Africa 66–67
  body boundaries 64–68
  controlled, channelled and restrained 64
  and international air travel 65
  property of black African bodies 68
  racializing 58–68
  threatening whiteness 67
  see also vomit
Edelman, L. 87
ejaculative penises 77–78, 79, 82, 83
El Paso, Texas 36
'emasculation' 75
Enloe, Cynthia 6, 7–8, 114

INDEX

F

Faking It (Weber) 94
Federal Trade Commission (FTC) 32
feeling and knowledge production 102
female bodies 19, 80
FemaleMan (Haraway) 118
feminism 101
feminist international relations theory 114
feminist technoscience studies (FTS) 10, 14–15
  assemblage theory 17–18
  biopolitics 48, 117–118
  bodily fluids 114, 120
  body-assemblages 21–27, 31, 113
  debility/capacity 30
  defining 15
  mundane matters 114–116
  queerfeminist curiosity 25, 27, 28
fertility treatments 84–87
fluid method/ology 98, 104–107, 109n1
  see also method/ology
fluids as and/or life–death 28–31
flu outbreaks 70
following fluids 107–110
following guts 101–102
'follow the object' methodological principle (Aradau) 108

G

gaze of health screening 62–63
gender-affirming surgeries 84
gendered subjectivity 19–20
gender identities 75
gender/race/sexuality/disability framework 6
gender, sex and genitalia 75, 80
'gender variables' 6
genital hierarchies 82
genitals, semen and masculinity 77
'genitourinary agents' 78
genitourinary injuries (GUIs) 11, 73–96, 111, 115
  ciscentric understandings of sex and gender 81
  fertility problems 84–87
  fertility treatments 80
  impact on lives 74
  instability of masculine embodiments 93
  Iraq and Afghanistan 88, 90–91
  limbo of signification 77
  loss of masculinity and castration 76
  masculinity and heterosexuality 94–95
  non-normative phalluses 82
  politics of militarism 92–95
  PTSD 75
  racialized distribution of injuries 87–91
  surgical treatments 79–84
  trauma and emasculation 75–77
  as the ultimate sacrifice 92
  see also semen
geopolitical hierarchy of life–death 68

GI bill 1944 86
global plasma market 34
global power dynamics 48–49
Going Viral (documentary) 59
good and bad queer bodies 24
governance of bodily fluids 104, 105, 114, 120
governance of life–death 118
governance of semen 74, 79, 86, 87
  see also semen
Grady, D. 76, 92
Grifols 32, 35
Grosz, Elizabeth 21, 22, 24, 118
Guattari, F. 14, 16, 17, 18–22
Guinea 54, 55, 69
guts and gut instinct 101–102

H

Halberstam, J. 112
Hall, K. 61
Halperin, David 9–10
Haraway, Donna 24, 50, 63, 107, 109, 113, 115, 117–118
Harcourt, W. 98
health screening 55–56, 57, 62–63
'hegemonic masculine ideal' (Johnson) 77
hegemonic masculinities 77
heteronormative ideals of marriage 85
hierarchy of living 68
Hispanic 36n4
HIV/AIDS epidemic 26, 46–47
The Hot Zone (Preston) 13, 59–60, 65
'the human' 19

I

ideal human 26
idealized bodies 65–66
identity and difference 22
improper bodily fluids 9
improvised explosive devices (IEDs) 73–74
infectious diseases
  donor bodies as risky potentialities 17
  and Mexicana/o donors 34, 42, 43, 51
  and mobility 53
  see also COVID-19; Ebola virus disease (EVD)
infertility health cover 85
'insecurity' and 'security' 5
International Monetary Fund (IMF) 70
international politics 27–31, 104, 105–106, 113
International Relations (IR) 5, 9, 14
international relations literatures 101
international security and bodily fluids 2
intersectional feminist approaches 7
'intersectionality' (Crenshaw) 6–7
in vitro fertilization (IVF) 84
Iraq 87–91, 95, 114
Israeli military 78

159

J

Johns Hopkins Medicine 79, 81, 82
Johnson, M. 77, 83

K

Kunduz Trauma Centre, Afghanistan 89–90, 91

L

language of the body and bodily fluids 6
Latina/o 36n4, 41
Latinx 33
Law, J. 110
Lee, Dr 82
LGB marriage rights 85
LGBTQAI community 8–9
Liberia 54, 55, 69
life–death 4
  airport screening 70
  and bodily fluids 118–120
  'degrees' of biopolitics 31
  geopolitical hierarchy 68
  international distribution 70
  phallocentric genital hierarchies 83
  unequal distribution 91
light/white of purity and virtue 61
Little Hans (Deleuze and Guattari) 20
looking-as-knowing 62
looking sick 56
Lungi airport, Sierra Leone 56, 71

M

'male' bodies 80–81
Marburg virus 60n6
marginalized ethnicities 122–123
marriage and married couples 85
Martin, L. 79
masculine body ideals 99
masculine power 76–77, 82
masculinity
  and FTS 26
  losing following GUIs 76
  non-normative genitalia 82
  and the penis 75
  restoring 82, 83
  and semen 77–78
masculinized screening gazes 62
Massachusetts General Hospital 81
Masters, Cristina 57
McCarran Airport, Las Vegas 64
Médecins Sans Frontières (MSF) 90
medical surveillance 90–91
men's sexuality 79
'method' 97
method/ology 98, 104, 106, 109
  see also fluid method/ology
Mexicana/o donors 16, 105, 119
  biovalue and racist history 39
  "blood smugglers" 41
  borderland spaces 41
  colonial histories of representation 44–45
  communicable diseases 43
  desubjectified 32, 34
  FTS approaches 27
  global plasma market 34
  governance 50
  health of plasma 47
  health precarity 49–50
  idealization of American body/plasma 45
  as infectious 44
  physical symptoms 48
  plasma as a dangerous entity 50
  racism 41–42, 46
  representations 47
  source of extractable life 42
  threat to plasma supply 43
  valuing 113
  see also plasma donors and donations
Mexicanas/os
  border sites 33–34
  as dirty and diseased 46
  not to be 'American' 41
  racial category 44
  'sterilizing' practices 46
micro-biological relationships 26
migrant labourers 47
militarism 92–95
militarized masculinity 78
military insurance schemes 81
military ultra-masculine heterosexual space 94
misogynoir (Bailey) 7
mobility of African people 70–71
Monson, Sarah 61
Moore, Lisa 79
Mujinga, Belly 121–122
mundane matters 114–116

N

Nash, Jennifer 23, 118
'natural' masculinity 80–84
New Jersey elementary schools 61
North American blackout (2003) 107–108
North American Free Trade Agreement (NAFTA) 36
novel pathogens 44, 45–47
novel viruses 121

O

Obergefell v. Hodges 85
objectifying plasma 37, 38
Octapharma 32, 35
OncoMouse (transgenic mouse) 118
Operation Enduring Freedom (OEF) 73–74, 81
Operation Iraqi Freedom (OIF) 73–74, 81
orgasms 79
the Other 21–22
Outbreak (film) 59

INDEX

P

Patton, Cindy 118
penetration of the gaze 63
penises
　able to ejaculate 77–78, 79, 82, 83
　erectile dysfunction medicines 78
　and masculinity 75, 76–77
　not ejaculating 86–87
penis transplants
　donors helping veterans 92
　and donor testicles 79
　gender, sex and genitalia 80
　and GUIs 75–76, 81–82
　seminal capacity 78–80
　technologically mediated phallus 84
　violent relationship of life–death 95
phallocentric discourses 82–84
phallocentric genital hierarchies 83
Pin-Fat, V. 93
Pink Flamingos (film) 102
plasma
　as a commodity 38
　essential medicine 34
　global market 34
　and health security 47
　as life/bios 39–40
　Mexicana/o donors 119
　objectification 37–38, 50
　racialized 45
　reactions to 108
　'therapeutic tool' 38
plasma-derived medicines 49
plasma donation assemblages 33
plasma donors and donations 32–51
　as an act of giving 40
　bioavailable 40–41
　compensation/income from 34, 35, 36–37, 49
　donation centres 35–36
　'obtain' and 'collect' 39
　physical symptoms 48
　politics of life–death 49
　racialization 37, 50
　'units' and 'extraction' 38
　see also donating blood; Mexicana/o donors
plasmapheresis 37–38, 48
Plasma Protein Therapeutics Association (PPTA) 12, 35, 40, 42–43
politics of life–death 49–50
politics of security 4, 5
Pollock, A. 48
power
　body-assemblages in international politics 20
　distribution of life–death functions 114
　Mexican donors with biovalue 39
　phallocentric curations of semen 83
　phalluses 82
　(re)producing body assemblages 24
power differences 21

PPE 122–123
Preston, Richard 13, 59–60, 61, 65
Puar, Jasbir 22, 24, 30–31, 78, 91
pure bodies 61, 66

Q

quarantine 2, 64–71
queer
　defining 8
　disgust and the grotesque 102
　donating blood 46–47, 103
　invisible 87
　sexuality and race 24
queer bodies and queer lives 86–87
queer communities 22
queer couples 85
queerfeminist curiosity 6–10, 25, 27, 28, 42, 63
queerfeminist guts 101–104
queerfeminist thought 3
queer international theorists 9
queer IR theory 8, 9
queer logics 10
queer logics of and/or 29, 106
queer logics of both/and 42
queerness 10, 87, 102–103
queer studies 8–9, 10
queer theory 9–10

R

racial capitalism 122
racialization of plasma 50
racializing Ebola vomit 58–64
racial mingling 43
'racial mixing' and 'pollution' 46
racism
　Mexicana/o plasma donors 41–42
　and misogyny 6–7
racist borderland assemblages 41
racist narratives 69
racist stereotypes 46
racist violence 33
radical potential 21
reading bodily appearance 56
relational groupings 23
(re)producing body assemblages 24
reproductive technologies 86–87
research processes 97
The Right to Maim (Puar) 30–31
romanticism of sacrifice 93
Rumsfeld, Donald 89
Rwanda 61

S

same-sex couples 85
SARS-CoV-2 121
screening assemblages 62, 68
screening gazes 62
screening practices
　disparity in procedures 70–71

and travel restrictions 55
visualized vomit 57
vomit and black African bodies 67–68
screening technologies 56, 58, 62–64
securing semen and heterosexuality 84–87
security assemblages
  mobility of African people 70
  'vision and knowledge' 57
security gazes 53, 58, 62–64
security practices 2–3
security sites 115
security studies 5
Sedgwick, E. K. 8
semen 13
  ejaculation and masculinities 77, 79
  fertility treatments 86–87
  and fertilization 109
  governance of service members 86
  guiding objects 111
  sex and ejaculation as mundane 115
  symbolic potential 78–79
  trails of 91
  see also genitourinary injuries (GUIs); governance of semen
seminal capacity 74, 77, 78, 79
Serlin, David 86
sex, gender and race 117
sexual hierarchies 19
'sexuality variables' 6
sexualized form of looking 63
Sharp, Lesley 40
Sierra Leone 54, 55, 69, 71
Sjoberg, L. 71
skin colour 67
smallpox outbreaks 70
social ontology 16
sodium citrate 48
soldiers (service members) 27
  ejaculative capacity 86
  fetishism of bodies 92–93
  penis transplant 79
  phalluses 93
  reproductive technologies 86–87
The Source (magazine) 12, 42–43
Spillers, Hortense 118
stable and fixed identities 18–19
State Department 89
Staying with the Trouble (Haraway) 109
'sterilizing' practices 46
Stern, M. 11, 93
string figures 107, 109
structural adjustment programmes (IMF) 70
Subramaniam, B. 48
surveillance of bodies 27, 52–53, 71

T

Talecris 32n1, 43
technological languages 37–38
technologically mediated phalluses 84
techno-security gaze of screening assemblages 57
temperature checks 56, 57, 71
Toumkara, Ibrahim 61
trans bodies 20, 80–84
trans people of colour 22
Trauma Outcomes and Urogenital Health project (TOUGH) 73
TRICARE 78, 85, 86
Trudy (Gradient Lair) 7

U

unhygienic and diseased landscapes/cultures 69
'unhygienic' diets 61n8
United Kingdom (UK) 103
United Nations Children's Fund (UNICEF) 89
urine and urinating 20, 109–110
US
  invasion of Iraq 89
  plasma donors 34
  responses to Ebola 61
US Agency for International Development (USAID) 89
US Army Medical Research and Materiel Command 73
US Centers for Disease Control and Prevention (CDC) 12, 53, 55, 56, 57, 111
US Customs and Border Protection Agency (CBP) 35
US Defense Health Agency 78
US Department of Defense (DoD) 73, 81–82, 111
US Department of State 89
US Food and Drug Administration (FDA) 47n10
US–Mexico border 10, 33, 34–35
US military
  biological reproduction of hetero-masculinity 87
  fertility treatments 84–85
  'fixing' GUIs 77–80
  governing semen 74
  heterosexual families 86
  militarized masculinity 78
  phallic power 93–94
  racialized distribution of injuries 87–91
  trauma and emasculation 75–77
  unequal distribution of life–death 91
  see also genitourinary injuries (GUIs)
US military imperialism 91

V

VA 82, 84–85, 86
vaginas and ovaries 80
Veterans Health Agency 78
Viagra 78
Victoria station, London 121–122

viral marker rates 43
vomit 10–11, 12, 55–58, 63, 111
  see also Ebola vomit
'vomit negro' (Preston) 59–60, 63, 65, 66

W

Waldby, Catherine 26, 68, 118
Walter Reed National Military Medical Center 83
Wannik, Lee 61
Waters, John 102
Weber, Cynthia 94
Weheliye, Alexander 117
West Africa
  Ebola deaths 54
  histories of mistrust 69
  temperature checks 56
Western philosophies
  bodily materialization and gender 80–81
  body as territory of the self 26
  semen and masculinity 77

White American plasma donors 41
white bodies
  pure bodies 61, 66
  threats to black bodies 67
  threats to racial purity 105
white colonialism 58, 61
white feminists 6
white masculine technoscientific colonization 39
'whiteness' as orderly and hygienic 46
white supremacists 30, 33, 46
white Western rational men 19
women of colour 6–7
Womme, Guinea 69
World Health Organization (WHO) 12, 34, 53, 54, 89, 111
World War I 70
Wynter, Sylvia 19

Z

Zambia 61

www.ingramcontent.com/pod-product-compliance
Lightning Source LLC
Chambersburg PA
CBHW071710020426
42333CB00017B/2209